PATERNOSTER BIBLICAL MONOGRAPHS

Joy in Luke-Acts: The Intersection of Rhetoric, Narrative, and Emotion

Series Editors

I. Howard Marshall, Honorary Research Professor of New Testament, University of Aberdeen, Scotland, UK

Richard J. Bauckham, Professor of New Testament Studies and Bishop Wardlaw Professor, University of St Andrews, Scotland, UK

Craig Blomberg, Distinguished Professor of New Testament, Denver Seminary, Colorado, USA

Robert P. Gordon, Regius Professor of Hebrew, University of Cambridge, UK

Tremper Longman III, Robert H. Gundry Professor and Chair of the Department of Biblical Studies, Westmont College, Santa Barbara, California, USA

Stanley E. Porter, President and Professor of New Testament, McMaster Divinity College, Hamilton, Ontario, Canada

PATERNOSTER BIBLICAL MONOGRAPHS

Joy in Luke-Acts

David H. Wenkel

Foreword by Graham A. Cole

First published 2015 by Paternoster

Paternoster is an imprint of Authentic Media
52 Presley Way, Crownhill, Milton Keynes, Bucks, MK8 0ES, UK

www.authenticmedia.co.uk
Authentic Media is a division of Koorong UK, a company limited by guarantee

09 08 07 06 05 04 03   8 7 6 5 4 3 2 1

British Library Cataloguing in Publication Data
A catalogue record for this book is available from the British Library

ISBN 978–1–84227–819–2

Typeset by David H. Wenkel
Printed and bound in Great Britain
for Paternoster
by www.printondemand-worldwide.com

Series Preface

One of the major objectives of Paternoster is to serve biblical scholarship by providing a channel for the publication of theses and other monographs of high quality at affordable prices. Paternoster stands within the broad evangelical tradition of Christianity. Our authors would describe themselves as Christians who recognise the authority of the Bible, maintain the centrality of the gospel message and assent to the classical credal statements of Christian belief. There is diversity within this constituency; advances in scholarship are possible only if there is freedom for frank debate on controversial issues and for the publication of new and sometimes provocative proposals. What is offered in this series is the best of writing by committed Christians who are concerned to develop well-founded biblical scholarship in a spirit of loyalty to the historic faith.

To my wife Kara

Contents

FOREWORD

Seeing a former student of mine publish is a great pleasure. The pleasure is compounded when his revised doctoral thesis adds to scholarship in such an able fashion. Dr Wenkel's work fills a lacuna in Lucan studies. The joy motif and its importance in Luke-Acts (especially Luke) is widely acknowledged but has been somewhat neglected in scholarship until now. His literature review establishes this point as he critically examines previous scholarship from Gulin to Inselmann. He persuasively shows not only the importance of the joy theme but its rhetorical power. He also shows that the emotion of joy is the appropriate response to the mighty saving acts of God whether those acts are on view in an Old Testament text such as that of the prophet Isaiah or a New Testament one like Luke-Acts.

Wenkel astutely explores the theme of the great reversals that generate joy when God so acts: a barren woman gives birth as in Luke 1 (e.g. Elizabeth) and a new convert rejoices as in Acts 8 (e.g. the Ethiopian eunuch). Indeed joy is a phenomenon in evidence when the gospel enters new territory as programmatically set out in Acts 1:8. With sensitivity to the role of rhetoric in the ancient world with its employment of ethos, logos and pathos Wenkel points out that the reader is invited into the narrative of the great reversals through the door of joy. This is the door offered narratively to Theophilus.

Wenkel writes in his conclusion: 'As the reader engages the narrative world. The emotion of joy presents them with an attractive world of beliefs and facts that one must accept or reject.' Moreover accepting that world is not merely a matter of assent to certain propositions although that is involved. Rather '[t]*hose who embrace the risen Lord by faith must: listen learn, do, and feel.*' (Original emphasis.) In other words, Luke-Acts argues for what an earlier generation called 'the felt Christ' (e.g. J. C. Ryle) and does so with rhetorical power. As does Wenkel himself come to think of it.

Graham A. Cole
Birmingham, Alabama
February 2013

Acknowledgements

There are many people to whom I owe thanks for bringing this project to fruition. My supervisors, Mike Bird and I.H. Marshall provided excellent guidance and direction. The staff and librarians at Highland Theological College were very helpful and welcoming during my stay in Dingwall. Particular thanks are due to Jamie Grant, Martin Cameron, Jason Maston, and Hector Morrison.

My wife Kara has been a wonderful blessing and source of joy during this project. I am forever grateful to my uncle Dr. Jim Davia for his support and benefaction. My parents, Howard and Jean Wenkel, also sacrificed in order to support me during the many years of study, travel, and writing. Jamie Grant was also helpful in applying for the Scottish Overseas Research Award.

The following brothers provided encouragement, prayers, fellowship, and wise counsel at various points along the way: Lee Wilson, Adam Short, Peter Kanetis, Daniel Noonan, Scott Carlson, Charles Moore, Jr., Raj Rao, Mark Ward, Jr., Jonathan Krueger, David Kirk, Angus Budge, and Chris Medina. I have also been blessed by brothers and sisters in various churches, including: God's People Church, Winnetka Bible Church, First Southern Baptist Church of Waukegan, Dingwall Baptist Church, and the Dingwall Castle Street Church of Scotland. In addition, numerous friends, students, and teachers at Trinity Evangelical Divinity School provided a stimulating environment during part of my doctoral studies. Above all, my deepest thanks are due to the Lord.

David H. Wenkel
2013

Acknowledgements

Abbreviations

AB	Anchor Bible
BECNT	Baker Exegetical Commentary on the New Testament
BibSac	*Bibliotheca Sacra*
BTB	*Biblical Theology Bulletin*
BZNW	Beihefte zur Zeitschrift für die neutestamentliche Wissenschaft
CBCOT	Collegeville Biblical Commentary on the Old Testament
CNTUOT	*Commentary on the New Testament Use of the Old Testament*
EKK	Evangelish-Katholisher Kommentar [Evangelical Catholic Commentary]
ISBL	Indiana Studies in Biblical Literature
IVPNTC	InterVarsity Press New Testament Commentary
JETS	*Journal of the Evangelical Theological Society*
JPTSup	*Journal of Pentecostal Theology*, Supplement Series
JSJSup	*Journal for the Study of Judaism*, Supplement Series
JSNT	*Journal for the Study of the New Testament*
JSNTSup	*Journal for the Study of the New Testament*, Supplement Series
JSOT	*Journal for the Study of the Old Testament*
JSOTSup	*Journal for the Study of the Old Testament*, Supplement Series
LNTS	Library of New Testament Studies
LXX	Septuagint
MT	Masoretic Text
NAC	New American Commentary
NETS	*New English Translation of the Septuagint*
NICNT	New International Commentary on the New Testament
NIGTC	The New International Greek Testament Commentary
NovT	*Novum Testamentum*
NSBT	New Studies in Biblical Theology
NTS	*New Testament Studies*
SBLMS	SBL Monograph Series
SNTSMS	Society for the New Testament Studies Monograph Series
STI	Studies in Theological Interpretation
VT	*Vetus Testamentum*
WBC	Word Biblical Commentary
WUNT	Wissenschaftliche Untersuchungen zum Neun Testament

CHAPTER 1

Introduction

This chapter will introduce the Lukan joy theme as it relates to the rhetoric of reversal. The God of Israel has visited his people and the fulfillments of his promises are cause for celebration. This visitation will turn the world upside-down.

Statement of Thesis

'What a trumpet-note of joy, courage, and triumph sounds through the whole Lukan history, from the first to the last pages! *Vexilla regis prodeunt!*'[1] This quotation is a short but accurate portrayal of the emotion latent in the biblical text of Luke-Acts. The sentiment that Luke's Gospel contains a strong emphasis on joy is shared by many.[2] Several scholars refer to Luke's Gospel as the 'gospel of joy'.[3] Scholars who have examined Luke and Acts together have arrived at a similar conclusion.[4] It is relatively undisputed that 'joy' is one of the major themes that runs through the narrative of Luke-Acts. The theme of

---

[1] A. Harnack, *Luke the Physician* (trans. W.D. Morrison; London: Williams & Norgate, 1907), 163-64 as quoted in W. Morrice, *Joy in the New Testament* (Grand Rapids: Eerdmans, 1984), 91. The Latin (Abroad the regal banners fly) is a quotation from the Latin hymn 'Vexilla Regis' by Venantius Fortunatus, Bishop of Poitiers (c. 509-c.600/609).

[2] J. Painter, 'Joy', in *Dictionary of Jesus and the Gospels* (eds. J. Green and S. McKnight; Leicester: InterVarsity, 1992), 394; E. Lohse, *Freude des Glaubens: Die Freude im Neuen Testament* (Göttingen: Vandenhoeck & Ruprecht, 2007), 8; M.A. Powell, *What Are They Saying About Luke?* (Mahwah: Paulist, 1989), 116.

[3] W. Morrice, *We Joy in God* (London: SPCK, 1977), 36; Elliott, *Faithful Feelings*, 167; Painter, 'Joy', *Dictionary of Jesus and the Gospels*, 394.

[4] P. Borgman, *The Way According to Luke: Hearing the Whole Story of Luke-Acts* (Grand Rapids: Eerdmans, 2006), 374. Similarly, W.S. Kurz, *Reading Luke-Acts: Dynamics of Biblical Narrative* (Louisville: WJKP, 1993), 79; C.J. Martin, 'A Chamberlain's Journey and the Challenge of Interpretation for Liberation', *Semeia* 47 (1989): 106; R.F. O'Toole, *The Unity of Luke's Theology: An Analysis of Luke-Acts* (Wilmington: Michael Glazier, 1984), 167.

joy in the Lukan corpus is vast and stretches across both Luke and Acts.[5]

Many studies of Luke have catalogued the joy theme but the joy theme is rarely examined as an important tool for appealing to the emotions (*pathos*) in the context of a Greco-Roman world that often made appeals to the emotions as well as logic (*logos*) and credibility (*ethos*).[6] The widespread recognition of the theme alongside the absence of rhetorical studies of joy provides the justification for this study. It raises the question: how does the joy theme function rhetorically across both Luke's Gospel and Acts? This study seeks to establish the following answer: *joy is used to empower the rhetoric of reversal in both Luke and Acts.*[7]

Our study of joy in Luke-Acts will argue that the rhetoric of reversal is empowered by an appeal to the emotion of joy. The most significant monograph that addresses reversal is John O. York's study on bi-polar or double reversal in Luke. Double reversal entails the movement wherein x becomes y and y becomes x. In this formula, the x and y can be pairs of sociological or historical categories such as poor / rich or sad / joyful. In this view, faith in the resurrected Christ radically changes one's identity. From a broad perspective, the corpus of Luke-Acts seeks to depict a world turned upside down so that God's people can understand their identity.[8]

Simeon's prophetic words about Jesus summarize the clarity and significance of reversal, for Jesus 'is appointed for the fall and rising of many' (Lk 2:34).[9] In similar manner, the Thessalonians charged Christians with

---

[5] A.B. du Toit, *Der Aspekt der Freude im urchristlichen Abendmahl* (Winterthur: P.G. Keller, 1965), 122.

[6] *Pathos* can be understood as 'force' or 'energy'. See B. Witherington III, *What's in the Word: Rethinking the Socio Rhetorical Character of the New Testament* (Waco: Baylor University Press, 2009), 75, also 13. This tri-partite classification of *logos, ethos,* and *pathos* originates in Aristotle. G.A. Kennedy defines '*pathos*' as a 'universal factor in any rhetorical or persuasive situation' that is composed of 'emotional reactions the hearers undergo as the orator "plays upon their feelings"' in *New Testament Interpretation Through Rhetorical-Criticism* (Chapel Hill: North Carolina Press, 1984), 15. Kuhn suggests that pathos in Luke-Acts *guides* the audience's response to the text. K.A. Kuhn, *Luke: The Elite Evangelist* (Collegeville: Liturgical, 2010), 71.

[7] This statement is similar to K.A. Kuhn's thesis that 'Affective appeal in varying forms is the means by which narratives, including biblical narratives, compel us to enter their storied world and entertain the version of reality they present', with three qualifications. First, this study focuses primarily on the emotion of joy whereas Kuhn examines emotions in general. Second, Kuhn's study is not meant to examine the entirety of Luke's gospel or even an entire theme. Third, Kuhn does not develop what 'storied world' Luke is working from and how this might be related to intertextuality. Kuhn, *Heart of Biblical Narrative*, 56.

[8] D.L. Bock notes: 'Luke-Acts explains the identity and place of the new community in the world' in *A Theology of Luke-Acts* (Grand Rapids: Zondervan, 2012), 42.

[9] English Bible quotes are from the English Standard Version unless otherwise noted. *The Holy Bible: English Standard Version* (Wheaton: Crossway, 2001). The English

turning 'the world upside down' (Acts 17:6). Even though the reversal motif has a relatively strong base of scholarship, the relationship between reversal and joy is underdeveloped.[10] The emotion of joy provides the *pathos* or emotional power that helps the reader to embrace this upside down world.[11]

Significance of the Study

While the joy theme has been identified in many Lukan studies, it has not received the attention of other themes such as 'banqueting' or 'travelling'. Although joy has been recognized as a large motif in the Lukan corpus, only a handful of studies have addressed it in the last fifty years.

One possible explanation for this is that the dichotomy between theology and history has played a long and extensive role in Lukan studies. Another possible explanation for this lacuna is the atomistic nature of many historical critical studies. Luke Timothy Johnson comments that the neglect of 'religious experience and power' in New Testament scholarship has complex causes, including a 'bias in favor of theology against religion, and the lack of an epistemology specifically calibrated to the religious dimensions of human existence'.[12] It is also likely that the widely held division between emotion and rationality in the scientific community has led many to de-emphasize the role of specific emotions (such as joy) in biblical theology and exegesis.[13]

On the other hand, socio-rhetorical analysis has become much more popular in the last twenty-five years.[14] In spite of this, the Lukan joy theme remains largely untouched. This study seeks to advance Lukan scholarship by acknowledging the legitimacy of joy as a genuine emotion on the one hand,

---

translations of the LXX Esaias (Isaiah = Esaias) are from M. Silva, trans. Esaias. *A New English Translation of the Septuagint* (eds. A. Pietersma and B.G. Wright; Oxford: Oxford University Press, 2007).

[10] J. Painter's article is significant for the study of the Lukan joy theme because he explicitly supports the thesis that joy in Luke's Gospel is connected to reversals. However, Painter does not explain *how* emotions such as joy may be used rhetorically to influence and persuade the reader. Painter, 'Joy', *Dictionary of Jesus and the Gospels*, 394-95. For sources on Luke's use of reversal see K.P. De Long, *Surprised by God: Praise Responses in the Narrative of Luke-Acts* (BZNW 166; Berlin: Walter de Gruyter, 2009), 129; D. Pao, *Acts and the Isaianic New Exodus* (WUNT 2; Grand Rapids: Baker, 2002), 105; P. Mallen, *The Reading and Transformation of Isaiah in Luke-Acts* (LNTS 367; London, T&T Clark, 2008), 107, passim.

[11] I understand that the 'reader' in the first century was most likely an 'auditor'.

[12] L.T. Johnson, *Religious Experience in Earliest Christianity* (Minneapolis: Fortress, 1998), 4.

[13] A suggestion posed by M. Elliott, *Faithful Feelings: Rethinking Emotion in the New Testament* (Grand Rapids: Kregel, 2006), 54.

[14] Amador concurs that rhetorical-critical studies have increased exponentially in the last 15 to 20 years in *Academic Constraints in Rhetorical Criticism of the New Testament*, 16.

while acknowledging that it plays a significant rhetorical role on the other hand. In order to achieve this, the study will employ a socio-rhetorical method.

Method and Procedure

Methodology

This study seeks to examine the 'joy' theme as it appears across the narratives of Luke-Acts by using rhetorical criticism that is sensitive to sociological aspects as well as literary or narrative aspects. Socio-rhetorical criticism has been applied to the Lukan corpus by scholars such as Ben Witherington and literary-rhetorical criticism has been applied by Robert Tannehill.[15] These two designations are best understood as a matter of emphasis rather than two separate methodologies. Although idiosyncratic, perhaps the best label for the method used here would be literary-socio-rhetorical criticism (but I retain 'socio-rhetorical' for the sake of simplicity).

Edith Humphrey's study of vision-reports across Luke-Acts and other New Testament literature also recognizes the problem of methodological nomenclature. She chooses the designation 'literary-rhetorical' over 'socio-rhetorical' but still appropriates the socio-rhetorical method from Vernon K. Robbins as I do.[16]

Karl Allen Kuhn presents an interdisciplinary methodology that includes rhetorical and narrative considerations but focuses on the use of emotions. Kuhn calls this approach 'affective-rhetorical' but does not intend it to be a 'stand-alone method'.[17]

Regardless of which nomenclature one uses, there is little conceptual deviation between them. Ultimately, one must ask how a text is being used to persuade the audience.[18] The socio-rhetorical method is particularly suitable for the Lukan corpus because of its use of quotations, allusions, and echoes from a wide range of texts.[19] Rhetorical criticism and intertextuality are often woven

---

[15] B. Witherington III, *The Acts of the Apostles: A Socio-Rhetorical Commentary* (Carlisle, Cumbria: Eerdmans/Paternoster, 1998); 39-50; Witherington, *What's in the Word*, 139; R.C. Tannehill, *The Shape of Luke's Story: Essays on Luke-Acts* (Eugene: Wipf and Stock, 2005), xii.

[16] E. Humphrey, *And I Turned to See the Voice: The Rhetoric of Vision in the New Testament* (STI; Grand Rapids: Baker, 2007), 26-27.

[17] Kuhn, *The Heart of Biblical Narrative*, 57.

[18] B. Witherington III, *New Testament Rhetoric: An Introductory Guide to the Art of Persuasion in and of the New Testament* (Eugene: Cascade, 2009), 166.

[19] For a discussion on the difficulty of defining the terms 'echo' and 'allusion' and the unlikely prospect that scholars will agree see D.L. Stamps, 'The Use of the Old Testament in the New Testament as a Rhetorical Device: A Methodological Proposal' in *Hearing the Old Testament in the New Testament* (ed. S. Porter; Grand Rapids:

together because of the importance of the 'relationships among texts'.[20] In some sense, the socio-rhetorical method is not technically a 'method' at all. Vernon K. Robbins prefers to called it an 'interpretive analytic' because it does not require precise rules and steps to follow.[21]

An interdisciplinary socio-rhetorical methodology is challenging because it seeks to 'bring practices of interpretation together that are often separated from one another'.[22] This will allow the stu dy to be interdisciplinary while narrow in scope. In addition, the concept of 'texture,' allows us to see the text as an 'intricately woven tapestry'.[23] The socio-rhetorical approach employed here will incorporate four diagnostic questions.

The first question will ask: how does joy function as *inner texture* (this is concerned with the text itself) within the pericope or unit? Often, inner texture is concerned with communication vis-à-vis the narrator and the characters.[24] Corollary questions will include: does joy function in a way that reverses particular feelings, responses, arguments, or judgment?[25] This question will also explore how the joy theme and related vocabulary are used as repeated keywords or concepts for the purpose of amplification.[26] The use of repeated keywords provides what Witherington calls *micro-rhetoric* that works within

---

Eerdmans, 2006), 12-14. I focus on 'foregrounding' versus 'backgrounding' of intertextual references to establish a spectrum of relationships.

[20] P. Tull, 'Rhetorical Criticism and Intertextuality' in *To Each Its Own Meaning: An Introduction to Biblical Criticisms and Their Application* (eds. S. McKenzie and S. Haynes; Louisville: WJKP, 1999), 156.

[21] Thanks to V.K. Robbins for pointing this out in personal correspondence. See the discussion in V.K. Robbins, 'Socio-Rhetorical Interpretation', in *The Blackwell Companion to the New Testament* (ed. D.E. Aune; Chicester: Wiley-Blackwell, 2010), 192.

[22] V.K. Robbins, *Exploring the Texture of Texts: A Guide to Socio-Rhetorical Interpretation* (Harrisburg: Trinity Press International, 1996), 2.

[23] Robbins identifies the term 'texture' as a 'metaphor' that is useful for engaging the rhetorical nature of texts in V.K. Robbins, 'The Present and Future of Rhetorical Analysis' in *The Rhetorical Analysis of Scripture: Essays from the 1995 London Conference* (eds. S.E. Porter and T.H. Olbricht; JSNTSup 146; Sheffield: Sheffield Academic Press, 1997), 30. For an analysis of V.K. Robbins' concept of 'texture' and the interpretation of texts, see V.G. Shillington, *Reading the Sacred Text: An Introduction to Biblical Studies* (London: T&T Clark, 2002), 277.

[24] V.K. Robbins, *The Tapestry of Early Christian Discourse: Rhetoric, Society and Ideology* (London: Routledge, 1996), 27-28.

[25] V.G. Shillington, *An Introduction to the Study of Luke-Acts* (London: T&T Clark, 2007), 53.

[26] 'The repetitive texture of a span of text regularly exhibits initial glimpses into the overall rhetorical movements in the discourse'. Robbins, *Exploring the Texture of Texts*, 8.

the text (as opposed to a macro-rhetoric that operates on the structural level).[27]

The second question will ask: how does joy function as related to *intertexture* (this is concerned with the rewriting of other texts)?[28] The rhetorical study of the use of the Old Testament in the New Testament is based on the concept that the very act of quoting or alluding to the Old Testament is a rhetorical act.[29] This question will inquire about the presence of quotations and echoes of texts that are woven into the text. Special attention will be given to quotations, allusions, and echoes of Isaiah.[30] When repetition is connected to the recitation or re-contextualization of outside texts the result is rhetorical narrative amplification.[31]

The third question will ask: how does joy function as part of the *sacred texture* (this is concerned with the implications of the intersection of human life and the divine)?[32] Stated broadly, this question will examine the vertical dimension between the human and the divine.[33] As part of a social-scientific approach, the question can be posed to both scripture and non-scriptural texts. The question is an attempt to explore the connection between the textures of the texts as they are related to the divine. Whereas some approaches focus entirely on the imminent or empirical, this question does not presuppose a closed system but is open to describing how the text portrays the divine in the text. This helpful question reflects the fact 'what we think about God will determine what we think about everything else'.[34] As of Luke-Acts follows in the narrative tradition of Samuel-Kings and 1-2 Maccabees, this question allows the exegesis to consider the text as a historical source and as scripture.[35]

The fourth question will ask: how does joy function with respect to the *ideological texture* (this is concerned with speech as action in light of structures and institutions of power)?[36] As the text takes a position and places itself in opposition to the values of the society and culture, how does the joy theme

---

[27] Witherington, *What's in the Word*, 13. The conceptual categories of forensic rhetoric, deliberative rhetoric and epideictic rhetoric belong to the macro-level; I discuss this further in the procedure section of this chapter.

[28] Robbins, *The Tapestry of Early Christian Discourse*, 30.

[29] Stamps, 'The Use of the Old Testament in the New Testament as a Rhetorical Device', 35. For an introduction to the rhetorical use of the Old Testament see G.K. Beale, *Handbook on the New Testament Use of the Old Testament* (Grand Rapids: Baker, 2012), 78-81.

[30] Shillington, *Introduction to the Study of Luke-Acts*, 53-54.

[31] Robbins, *Exploring the Texture of Texts*, 51.

[32] Humphrey, *And I Turned to See the Voice*, 115.

[33] Shillington, *An Introduction to the Study of Luke-Acts*, 54.

[34] C.K. Rowe, *World Upside Down: Reading Acts in the Graeco-Roman Age* (Oxford: Oxford University Press, 2002), 17.

[35] Kurz, *Reading Luke-Acts*, 4, 11; Bock, *A Theology of Luke-Acts*, 48.

[36] Robbins, *Tapestry of Early Christian Discourse*, 36. I do not intend to use the word 'ideology' in a strictly negative or pejorative sense.

establish an ethic or challenge its readers to act?[37] I combine Robbin's fourth texture (social and cultural texture) with the ideological texture because both deal with the concept of the text in the world.[38] By placing the text in the world we may ask: what is the text trying to persuade the reader to do or think?[39] This question is related to the concept of the implied reader and seeks to understand how the text calls for a new value system or reversal of values within a given locale.[40] Where possible, a socio-rhetorical analysis should move beyond asking *what* is the text trying to persuade the reader to do or think to *how* is the text trying to persuade the reader to do or think? Here we will focus on the role of emotion (*pathos*) as it is integral to the whole persuasive task.

In order to facilitate this connection between joy and ideological concerns we will borrow from the interdisciplinary study by Sidney Callahan whose work developed connections between reason and emotion. Callahan's work answers part of the *how* question by stating:

> Stories created by the imagination and actual historical events move and shape our moral lives. Every culture has known the power of stories to pass on the traditional wisdom and morally educate the young. There is "a power of enchantment" and empathetic emotional engagement in parable and story. Mind and heart, reason and emotion are simultaneously stimulated to respond to a narrative. The moral images in a narrative are more emotionally compelling, more real, more vivid, more concrete and contextual than a set of abstracted principles and rules. Stories don't simply impart information; they demonstrate and recreate experience through imagery and form.[41]

This interdisciplinary model connects emotion and the narrative (Luke-Acts) to explain how the reader is moved through 'empathetic emotional engagement in the parable and story'.[42] Callahan continues, 'Moral emotions make morality appear 'real'.[43] Again, we must be careful not to distinguish some emotions as

---

[37] Because Luke-Acts was not written for a 'monolithic community' it reflects 'various ideological systems'. This means that identifying ideological concerns will be dependent upon the textual unit under consideration. P.E. Spencer, *Rhetorical Texture and Narrative Trajectories of the Lukan Galilean Ministry Speeches: Hermeneutical Appropriation by Authorial Readers of Luke-Acts* (LNTS 341; London: T&T Clark, 2007), 35.

[38] Humphrey, *And I Turned to See the Voice*, 115.

[39] For a discussion on rhetoric as persuasion see Tull, 'Rhetorical Criticism and Intertextuality', 160-61.

[40] Shillington, *Introduction to the Study of Luke-Acts*, 54.

[41] S. Callahan, *In Good Conscience: Reason and Emotion in Moral Decision Making* (NY: HarperCollins, 1991), 206-7. For a similar concept see K.J. Vanhoozer, *The Drama of Doctrine: A Canonical-Linguistic Approach to Christian Theology* (Louisville: WJKP, 2005), 282.

[42] Callahan, *In Good Conscience*, 206-207.

[43] Callahan, *In Good Conscience*, 208.

moral and others as non-moral. That is simply not how emotions work. If the goal is 'conformity' as Callahan asserts, this connects ideology and rhetoric with its goal: conformity and identity.[44] Although we have qualifications in terms of methodology, Callahan's point stands: emotions have potential to make something happen; they have a certain force that impacts the reader.

This model may raise several criticisms. First, it is not always clear how this model relates to historical questions. This is likely due to the integration of literary criticism that has tended to view the text as an isolated world. This study seeks to address this by interacting with the dominant model of honour and shame and the importance of social values in the hierarchy of power around the temple, and cultural reciprocity.

Second, interest in rhetoric has been dominated by Greco-Roman influence and technical classical models. It is lamentable that the 'Jewish literary and rhetorical conventions that shaped Acts'[45] are relatively unexplored. This study seeks to address this problem by urging caution about classifying rhetoric and by taking intertextuality seriously.

Third, this model has been critiqued for destroying intellectual egalitarianism by elevating practitioners of the field to the place of experts.[46] Some scholars desire a thorough-going reader-response method in which all readers are placed on the same level. On the contrary, this study takes the position that some exegesis is more historically accurate (and truthful!) than others.[47] An interest in the historical will always be *exclusive* and *hegemonic* in some sense because it is staking a claim about what actually occurred. By locating Luke-Acts in the first-century we are also distancing ourselves from the radical postmodern readings and other reader response methods.[48]

Fourth, the socio-rhetorical method can often be unwieldy.[49] I believe that there are often too many threads to practically manage when trying to examine

---

[44] 'If one concentrates only on teaching words, one gets only words in return, with only an outward verbal *conformity* to moral standards'. Callahan, *In Good Conscience*, 208. Emphasis mine. Our interest is not conformity to moral standards per se but conformity to belief.

[45] E.J. Schnabel, 'Fads and Common Sense: Reading Acts in the First Century and Reading Acts Today', *JETS* 54:2 (2011), 263. Also Spencer, *Rhetorical Texture and Narrative Trajectories*, 48-50.

[46] J.D. Hestor Amador, *Academic Constraints in Rhetorical Criticism of the New Testament: An Introduction to a Rhetoric of Power* (JSNTSup 174; Sheffield: Sheffield Academic Press, 1999), 181-207.

[47] G. Carey wonders if Amador views 'historically-grounded inquiry' that characterizes socio-rhetorical criticism as 'worthwhile, hopelessly compromised, or the enemy' in 'Review of *Academic Constraints in Rhetorical Criticism of the New Testament* by J.D. H. Amador,' in *RBL* [http://www.bookreviews.org] (2000).

[48] For a helpful discussion see Kurz, *Reading Luke-Acts*, 174-76.

[49] For a summary list of Robbins' methodology see Shillington, *Introduction to the Study of Luke-Acts*, 53-54.

exegetical issues that cover large textual units. This is why I have included social aspects within the ideological texture section in this study. In general, Robbins' own methodology is flexible and skeletal enough to be appropriated and modified by those who want maintain a historical-grammatical or historical-theological hermeneutic.[50]

In sum, this modification of Robbins' socio-rhetorical method allows this study to commence in a manner comparable to other social-sciences. It incorporates the integration of several dimensions while uniting them in four specific questions. Answering these questions will keep the study objective as I prove the thesis that the joy theme provides emotional power to the rhetoric of reversal.

Procedure and Outline

Procedurally, I will apply these four diagnostic questions to a selection of texts from Luke-Acts where the joy theme appears.[51] I will be privileging Old Testament (Septuagint) literature as background because of the *quantity* of references to Isaiah and the *quality* or significance of references to Isaiah.

However, Luke-Acts is still an inter-connected corpus that acts as a foundational document for the early Christian community. As an identity creating narrative it shares elements with the Jewish literature of the first century that used the Passover ritual and Exodus story to establish identity, as well as with Greek literature that used ritual games such as the Olympics and Homeric stories for similar ends.

My procedure in selecting primary and secondary texts will evidence that I privilege Old Testament literature while acknowledging the importance of the Greco-Roman context. This reflects the concern of the text of Luke-Acts and the quantity and quality of intertextual allusions and quotations from Isaiah and other Old Testament references.

There is a critical distinction that must be noted in the way this study proceeds with respect to its evaluation of rhetoric. I draw a distinction between individual speeches and the narrative as a whole. A majority of the studies of

---

[50] V.K. Robbins acknowledges this flexibility in his unpublished paper 'Beginnings and Developments in Socio-Rhetorical Interpretation' (Emory University, 2004), 21-22. Spencer, *Rhetorical Texture and Narrative Trajectories*, 46, 49, 65, 76, 103, 194, 201.

[51] I work with Luke-Acts as a two-volume unified corpus that shares (1) authorial unity, (2) theological unity, and (3) narratival unity. The scholarship on the matter is well-known and voluminous. For recent work in this area see Bock, *A Theology of Luke-Acts*, 55-61; M. Bird, 'The Unity of Luke-Acts in Recent Discussion', *JSNT* 29:4 (2007): 425-47. For a recent dissenting view on the unity of Luke-Acts see P. Walters, *The Assumed Authorial Unity of Luke and Acts: A Reassessment of the Evidence* (JSNTSup 145; Cambridge: Cambridge University Press, 2009). For a helpful but somewhat dated bibliographic discussion on the unity of Luke-Acts see M.A. Powell, *What Are They Saying About Acts?* (Mahwah: Paulist, 1991), 6-7.

rhetoric in Luke-Acts focus on speeches to the exclusion of the whole.[52] The individual speeches represent an important dimension but attention must also be given to the persuasive task of the whole (while also considering the unity of Luke-Acts). The failure to pay attention to the differences between the rhetoric in the speeches and the whole corpus may account for the lack of clarity and occasional debate about the nature of Lukan rhetoric.[53] A failure to draw this distinction is likely the source of putting too much emphasis on technical categories of Greco-Roman rhetoric such as forensic, deliberative, and epideictic. Often these studies do not acknowledge any Jewish influence through texts, persons, or theology. Amador concurs that the Greco-Roman context is often misleading. He points out that 'the sayings attributed to Jesus were composed during a period where civil ceremony, law courts and civic assemblies were no longer the dominant social settings'.[54] While Luke-Acts was written in a Hellenistic milieu, we must be careful to nuance the Jewish and Greco-Roman influences of this time and place.[55]

Furthermore, it is not clear how this matrix of Greco-Roman categories (forensic, deliberative, and epideictic) could accommodate the quantity and quality of influence from the Septuagint.[56] There are obviously a variety of speeches in Acts and a variety of potential and historical audiences. And it is widely acknowledged that both Luke and Acts contain a variety of genres. This study does not use technical Greco-Roman rhetorical categories due to the on-going debate about Lukan rhetoric and also because such categories cannot account for the integration of the LXX and Jewish argumentation.[57] This does

---

[52] Likewise, Robbins notes that 'A major problem in New Testament studies is the separation between rhetorical interpreters of epistolary and narrative discourse' ('The Present and Future of Rhetorical Analysis', 32). For a recent study of Lukan speeches see O. Padilla, *The Speeches of Outsiders in Acts: Poetics, Theology and Historiography* (SNTSMS 144; Cambridge: Cambridge University Press, 2008), passim.

[53] K. Maxwell concludes: 'we see that most scholars disagree on Luke's level of education and rhetorical skill' in *Hearing Between the Lines: The Audience as Fellow-Worker in Luke-Acts and its Literary Milieu* (LNTS 425; London: T&T Clark, 2010), 124. However, I think that Maxwell's study (and others) could benefit from the distinction between the rhetoric of the narrative as a whole and the rhetoric of individual speeches.

[54] Amador, *Academic Constraints in Rhetorical Criticism*, 197.

[55] Amador, *Academic Constraints in Rhetorical Criticism*, 170 n141.

[56] According to Robbins, New Testament discourse 'grounds its images of authority in biblical and Jewish traditions rather than Greco-Roman traditions' ('The Present and Future of Rhetorical Analysis', 38).

[57] For a contrasting position with W. Braun's approach see Meynet who states, 'Rhetorical analysis asserts that these compositions [the Gospels] do not obey the rules of Greco-Roman rhetoric, but the specific laws of Hebraic rhetoric, of which the authors of the New Testament are the direct inheritors'. R. Meynet, *Rhetorical Analysis: An Introduction to Biblical Rhetoric* (JSOTSup 256; Sheffield: Academic Press, 1998), 21-22; W. Braun, *Feasting and Social Rhetoric in Luke 14* (SNTSMS 85; Cambridge:

not deny the presence of technical Greco-Roman rhetoric in individual Lukan speeches. As this study pursues a socio-rhetorical examination of joy I will focus on the persuasive nature of the whole narrative. This pursuit begins by examining how the Lukan corpus itself provides clues and frames that guide the reader in their journey.

After a brief historical comparison of joy in Greco-Roman and Old Testament literature, I will seek to prove that the joy theme provides emotional force to the rhetoric of reversal. This is not to state that joy is *itself* the inauguration of the new age but that joy is *associated* with the inauguration of the new age. The third chapter will begin by examining Luke's agenda according to Luke 1:1-4. This chapter will continue by examining the joyous reversal of Zechariah and Elizabeth in Luke 1:5-25. The third chapter works together with chapter four to analyze the joy theme in narratives that frame the whole discourse and establish expectations for the readers. The fourth chapter examines the infancy narratives of Jesus and John in Luke 1:26-66 as well as the reversal of the shepherds and the birth narrative of Jesus in Luke 2:1-21.

The fifth chapter will focus on joy in the Galilean ministry of Jesus. The Galilean ministry of Jesus covers Luke 3:23-9:50 but I will be focusing on the Sermon on the Plain in Luke 6, the messengers from John the Baptist in Luke 7 and the joy of belief in Luke 8. The sixth chapter will focus on joy in the journey of Jesus to Jerusalem. This will examine joy in the story of the return of the seventy in Luke 10 and the lost-then-found stories in Luke 15. The seventh chapter will conclude the study of Luke by looking at joy in the persecution and vindication of Jesus. This chapter will examine Jesus' entry into Jerusalem in Luke 19 and the Ascension of Jesus in Luke 24. The eighth chapter will examine joy in the journey of the Word (*logos*) from Jerusalem. As a whole, the journey of the *logos* from Jerusalem covers Acts 8:1-19:38. This chapter will follow joy as it functions in conjunction with the spread of the 'word of the Lord' through Acts 8, 13, and 16.

The socio-rhetorical method employed will examine uses of the joy theme as it is employed through a rather large semantic range.[58] The author Luke uses a plethora of words for the emotion of joy. John Painter's article on 'joy' in the *Dictionary of Jesus and the Gospels* begins by affirming that the joy theme encompasses no less than seven Greek words (ἀγαλλιάω, ἀγαλλίασις, εὐφραίνω, σκιρτάω, χαίρω, συγχαίρω, and χαρά).[59] Of particular importance is the note that εὐφραίνω and σκιρτάω are 'strongly attested in the LXX' and used

---

Cambridge University Press, 1995), passim. Also see Elliott, *Faithful Feelings*, 169; Spencer, *Rhetorical Texture and Narrative Trajectories*, 113, 199.

[58] This is very similar to Anke Inselmann's methodology in *Die Freude im Lukasevangelium: Ein Beitrag zur Psychologischen Exegese* (WUNT 322; Tübingen: Mohr Siebeck, 2012), 16.

[59] Painter, 'Joy', *Dictionary of Jesus and the Gospels*, 394.

only by Luke in all four Gospels.[60] The very reason why Painter asserts that Luke merits the title 'the Gospel of joy' is because the *whole range* of possible vocabulary is used.[61] This is in contrast to the Gospel of Mark where 'Joy is not a significant focus'.[62]

Intertextuality and the Isaianic New Exodus

Because intertextuality will play an important role in this work, it will be helpful to clarify several points. As a matter of definition, I follow the definition of intertextuality: contextual meaning of an earlier text used in a later text is carried over into the later text.[63]

This study interacts with David Pao's exploration of the Isaianic New Exodus structure of Luke and Acts.[64] I will not be arguing that the New Exodus is a controlling motif.[65] Rather, it is a motif that plays a major role in influencing Luke's use of joy. The New Exodus is simply an Isaianic motif that works alongside others. Luke uses the Septuagint form of Isaiah as a *whole* and he draws from the entire text. Throughout this study I interact with Pao's undeveloped thesis that the 'Isaianic New Exodus functions as a hermeneutical key to *both* Luke and Acts'.[66] Whereas Pao focuses on Acts, I seek to understand its role in the whole Lukan corpus.

This study will further develop Peter Mallen's conclusion that intertextual use 'of Scripture cannot be separated from his [Luke's] overall rhetorical purpose'.[67] Above all, this study seeks to understand the intersection of emotion, rhetoric, and intertextuality (with specific reference to Isaiah).

Luke's world was both Jewish and Greco-Roman. He primarily used the Septuagint form of the Hebrew Scriptures (the Old Testament, and Isaiah in particular) to support his writings.[68] I will seek to understand the rhetorical

---

[60] Painter, 'Joy', *Dictionary of Jesus and the Gospels*, 394.

[61] Painter, 'Joy', *Dictionary of Jesus and the Gospels*, 394.

[62] Painter, 'Joy', *Dictionary of Jesus and the Gospels*, 394.

[63] G.K. Beale, *We Become What We Worship: A Biblical Theology of Idolatry* (Downers Grove: IVP, 2008), 27.

[64] For critical comments on Pao's thesis see Mallen, *The Reading and Transformation of Isaiah*, 16-17, 72.

[65] Mallen warns against viewing the New Exodus as a controlling motif. He also concludes that the New Exodus 'supports key themes in Luke's narrative' in *The Reading and Transformation of Isaiah*, 19, similarly 15, 207.

[66] Pao, *Acts and the Isaianic New Exodus*, 80.

[67] Mallen, *The Reading and Transformation of Isaiah*, 208.

[68] I use 'Old Testament' and 'Hebrew Scriptures' interchangeably throughout this study because they are the least problematic. However, this terminology presupposes a Christian canon and is somewhat anachronistic. The problem of how to refer to the biblical texts has not been resolved. I seek to provide further specificity by my discussions about the use of the LXX.

power of joy in light of Luke's use of the Septuagint.[69] I seek to understand how intertextuality intersects with affective persuasion (*pathos*) in Luke-Acts. Intertextuality in Luke-Acts provides a source for promise-fulfillment as well as coherence and meaning.

There is an unnecessary debate about the use of the Old Testament in Luke-Acts.[70] One group views Old Testament intertextuality as serving a promise-fulfillment/prediction-fulfillment motif. The second group has challenged this conclusion and has offered other suggestions such as 'coherence' in its place, albeit unsuccessfully. There is no good reason why we cannot affirm both groups and include the notion of the Old Testament providing a source for prophetic fulfillment *and* the use of the Old Testament as providing coherence and a narrative framework. In other words, Luke's use of the Old Testament is not monolithic. The Old Testament provides both prophetic promises and coherence/meaning.

One of the pillars upon which the Lukan narrative rests is its use of scripture. The intertextuality of the Lukan writings is used to illuminate and provide a hermeneutical framework. The foundational story for this framework is the Exodus narrative as 'developed and transformed' through Isaiah.[71] The Gospel of Luke presents the New Exodus programme primarily in terms of the Isaianic theme of 'the arrival of the salvation of God in Jerusalem'.[72]

In addition to the aforementioned theme, David Pao introduces four recurring themes surrounding the New Exodus and the Isaianic prologue of Isaiah 40:1-11: (1) the restoration of Israel, (2) the power of the word of God, (3) anti-idol polemic, and (4) a universal concern for the nations.[73] Pao's study focuses explicitly on Acts and leaves the question of Isaiah's role in Luke out of his main focus. Thus, one of the questions of my study is: does the joy theme in Luke and Acts reflect a development of the Isaianic New Exodus structure? Some implications of Pao's study have yet to be explored, including how themes such as joy fit into this framework.

We cannot engage in studying intertextuality without defining our terms and setting up criteria. Richard Hays' seminal work *Echoes of Scripture in the Letters of Paul* (1989) revolutionized New Testament studies by drawing attention to the need for criteria when discussing indirect 'echoes' versus direct

---

[69] Spencer argues that in Luke, a 'repertoire of LXX concepts is assumed by the implied author as *topoi* for rhetorical argument in *Rhetorical Texture and Narrative Trajectories*, 113; also 33, 199.

[70] S. Porter, 'Scripture Justifies Mission', in *Hearing the Old Testament in the New Testament* (ed. S. Porter; Grand Rapids: Eerdmans, 2006), 107.

[71] Pao, *Acts and the Isaianic New Exodus*, 5.

[72] Pao, *Acts and the Isaianic New Exodus*, 13; M. Strauss, *The Davidic Messiah in Luke-Acts: The Promise and Its Fulfillment in Lukan Christology* (JSNTSup 110; Sheffield: Sheffield Academic Press, 1995).

[73] Pao, *Acts and the Isaianic New Exodus*, 13.

citations or quotations.[74] This work has now permeated most areas of New Testament studies.[75] The following criteria are used for establishing Scriptural echoes: (1) 'volume, that is repetition in wording, plot, setting or genre, (2) availability in the cultural repertoire, and (3) thematic development'.[76] Given these criteria, my approach to intertextuality will be based on four related steps.

The first step in understanding intertextuality in Luke-Acts is to allow the text itself to provide introductory texts that frame the narrative or discourse by establishing relationships.[77] What differentiates this step from the next step is that it exclusively focuses on the introduction or introductory textual units. The introductory narratives of Luke provide information that creates expectations based on Isaiah. Both John the Baptist and Jesus are to be understood through the lens of Isaiah. The introduction (Acts 1:8) provides a broad narrative structure: the word of the Lord will be carried by witnesses from Jerusalem to Judea-Samaria to the Ends of the Earth. This path will turn the world upside-down with dramatic reversals. In both instances, the introductory texts are key sources for understanding intertextuality. The information needed to understand Isaiah's important role in Luke-Acts is provided in these introductory texts. This step accounts for the fact that intertextuality must be guided by the clues given by the author in the text.

The second step to understanding intertextuality in Luke-Acts is to find direct/explicit quotations and indirect echoes. Some imprecision is 'unavoidable' when dealing with the lines between different intertextual relationships.[78] We find that Luke begins his second volume with a clear reference to his own first book (the Gospel of Luke) in Acts 1:1. Most importantly we find Luke sets up some measure of expectation because of the way that Isaiah 40:3-5 is cited in Luke 3:4-6 and Isaiah 61:1-2 is cited in Luke 4:18-19. Having found Isaiah on the lips of Jesus sets up the reader to find continuity in Acts, which is the narrative of the resurrected Jesus that is ever-present in the church. In both Luke and Acts, we find that the introductory texts that frame the narrative clearly rely on Isaiah to provide the reader with relationships that provide anticipation and a hermeneutical lens for the whole.

---

[74] R. Hays, *Echoes of Scripture in the Letters of Paul* (New Haven: Yale University Press, 1989), passim, esp. 29-32. Hays provides a more fully developed set of criteria and responses to critiques in *The Conversion of the Imagination: Paul as the Interpreter of Israel's Scripture* (Grand Rapids: Eerdmans 2005), passim, esp. 47-49 and 163-170.

[75] K. Litwak, *Echoes of Scripture in Luke-Acts: Telling the History of God's People Intertextually* (JSNTSup 282; London: T&T Clark, 2005), 30-31; R. Brawley, *Text to Text Pours Forth Speech: Voices of Scripture in Luke-Acts* (ISBL; Bloomington/Indianapolis: Indiana University Press, 1995), 88.

[76] Brawley, *Text to Text Pours Forth Speech*, 88.

[77] Here I follow Pao's use of introductory texts that frame the narrative by providing hermeneutical keys or hermeneutically significant relationship that establish expectations for what follows.

[78] Litwak, *Echoes of Scripture in Luke-Acts*, 52.

We may then move forward from the clarity of direct quotations to explore the indirect relationships between echoes.

The third step to understanding intertextuality in Luke-Acts is to find literary themes through identifying repetition to establish thematic relationships. Intertextual studies are often atomistic and do not interact with narrative and literary concerns. This may involve identifying themes and relationships in the text under consideration (Luke-Acts) as well as external source texts (such as Isaiah). We cannot separate intertextuality from the genre of the narrative. As a writer, Luke utilizes literary themes. These themes should be treated as a unit or related thread. The importance of relating echoes in the narrative back to the framework as a unit. This is where inner texture (repetition) intersects with intertexture. Literary themes that function as a unit are important for intertextuality if keywords or word-choice creates relationships with co-texts or external sources such as the Septuagint.[79] Intertextual and thematic relationships create literary relationships that endure throughout the narrative.

The fourth step to understanding intertextuality in Luke-Acts is to attempt to establish proximity of various sources when they are grouped together. By 'proximity', I am using a spatial metaphor to setup the language of 'foregrounding' and 'backgrounding'.[80] Establishing proximity means that some sources or relationships are stronger than others are. Those that are stronger are foregrounded as opposed to weaker relationships that are in the background. Luke's use of the Hebrew Scriptures often conjoins various texts into a new transformed text.

This four-step process allows us to clearly establish the thesis question of this study: how does the joy theme function within the New Exodus programme across Luke-Acts? Others have recognized that Luke uses Isaiah rhetorically but they have not examined Isaiah as a source that creates intricate relationships between emotion and the mighty acts of YHWH.[81] Luke the writer utilizes Hebrew Scriptures such as Psalms, Isaiah, and Joel for a wide variety of purposes such as persuasion, promise-fulfillment, narrative sub-structure. But we deny that Luke set out to write his two-volume corpus as exegetical documents. Following the distinction between *exegesis* and *interpretation*, we

---

[79] As noted earlier, I use several terms for the LXX interchangeably because of the difficulty with nomenclature. Even the term 'Septuagint' is anachronistic as there is no use of this term prior to the second century. See the discussion in K.H. Jobes and M. Silva, *Invitation to the Septuagint* (Grand Rapids: Baker, 2000), 32.

[80] This language reflects the same usage of the spatial metaphor in the verbal aspect approach to Koine Greek. This metaphor allows us to speak about an order or priority of relationships when one text uses another text. For an explanation of this metaphorical language for verbal aspect see C.R. Campbell, *Basics of Verbal Aspect in Biblical Greek* (Grand Rapids: Zondervan, 2008), 130.

[81] Mallen, *The Reading and Transformation of Isaiah*, 21.

want to identify Luke-Acts as interpreting Isaiah without exegeting Isaiah.[82] There is no evidence in the text that Luke set out to exegete, in the sense of analyze or clarify, the Septuagint. Rather, Luke sets out to transform or appropriate the Septuagint (such as Isaiah) for 'literary or rhetorical re-envisioning'.[83]

This re-envisioning is not so much a response to a crisis as it is a response to a crisis-and-victory. The crisis of the cross and the triumph of the resurrection of Jesus became a critical historical event that provoked the textual-exegetical imagination of the followers of the Way.[84] Theological and persuasive aims cannot be separated.[85] Luke-Acts is not, therefore, about inner-biblical exegesis as much as it is about inner-biblical interpretation. As far as interpretation goes, Luke the writer respects the context of the Scriptures that he quotes or echoes. Ultimately, we must allow the text itself to guide our analysis of it. This is related to our analysis of the introductory text of Luke's Gospel in the next chapter.

This study intends to demonstrate that the use of joy provides emotional force (*pathos*) to Luke's rhetorical agenda and draws from the persuasive power of using the authoritative text of the Old Testament. The presence of the emotion of joy is persuasive because it is a 'signal' that God's promises have begun to be fulfilled and this provides an interpretive and holistic framework for understanding the mighty works of God.[86]

Joy as an Emotion

Recent scholarship has helped to open new paths of interdisciplinary study

---

[82] A. Berlin, 'Interpreting Torah Traditions in Psalm 105' in *Jewish Biblical Interpretation and Cultural Exchange: Comparative Exegesis in Context* (eds. N.B. Dohrmann and D. Stern; Philadelphia: University of Pennsylvania Press, 2008), 22.

[83] Berlin, 'Interpreting Torah Traditions in Psalm 105', 23.

[84] V.K. Robbins sets his model of intertextuality in relation to the trajectory set by the inner biblical exegesis of M. Fishbane in *The Tapestry of Early Christian Discourse*, 98. Robbins follows Fishbane but seeks to open up the boundaries of influence to the Hebrew Bible and the Grecro-Roman world of the first-century. Most studies in inner-biblical exegesis are not interested in rhetoric or ideology but in using intertextuality as an avenue to explore source criticism and compositional history. For a helpful discussion see L. Eslinger, 'Inner-Biblical Exegesis and Inner-Biblical Allusion: The Question of Category', *VT* 42 (1992): 47-58. M. Fishbane's work remains influential because of the way in which it examines intertextuality according to midrashic methods of argumentation: *Biblical Interpretation in Ancient Israel*. Oxford: Oxford University Press, 1988.

[85] Mallen, *The Reading and Transformation of Isaiah*, 8.

[86] This concept of a 'signal' is similar to R.E. Watts' sub-thesis where he seeks to establish correlations between components of the New Exodus schema such as healing of the blind, forgiveness of sins and feeding of the multitudes as 'signals' of the inauguration of the Isaianic New Exodus. R.E. Watts, *Isaiah's New Exodus in Mark* (Tübingen: J.C.B. Mohr [Paul Siebeck], 1997), 137.

between psychology and New Testament studies. Worthy of note is Matthew Elliott's study of emotion in the New Testament. Elliott directly interacts with 'joy' in Luke and concludes that it is worthy of the title 'gospel of joy'.[87] He laments that New Testament scholarship has not paid sufficient attention to the emotional dimension of emotive language such as joy. He states: 'In New Testament studies, the emotion of joy in the New Testament is often not seen as significant'.[88]

The interdisciplinary nature of Elliott's study begins by situating the thesis in the context of psychology then in the context of the New Testament. He first establishes two contrasting views of emotion: cognitive and non-cognitive. The non-cognitive view understands emotion as independent of cognition. In contrast, a cognitive view of emotion places 'thought, appraisal and belief' at the centre.[89] This does not mean every emotion is reasonable or that emotions do not affect cognition. As Elliott states in these two summary sentences, 'Emotion is always about something; it has an object. Emotion tells us about our values and beliefs'.[90] This is particularly important for the present study because it establishes a scientific basis for asking questions such as: how did the beliefs of the writer of Luke-Acts impact his use of emotive language? Or, how did the appraisal of Old Testament prophecy create the emotion of joy as promises were being fulfilled? In the non-cognitive approach, such questions are unsound because of the independent nature of emotions.

Elliott moves from the discipline of psychology to biblical studies by surveying background and context from the Greco-Roman world and the Jewish world. He finds that the Greco-Roman world had elements of both cognitive and non-cognitive approaches to emotions. His findings conclude that, 'Emotions were considered a major topic of philosophical inquiry at the time of the New Testament. The emotions also had an important place in literature and society. The philosopher's rhetoric about emotion was in large measure an attempt to correct the abuses of their society'.[91] In sum, the world of the New Testament had a range of views of emotion that spanned the range of philosophical traditions and the reactions each received.

Following the Greco-Roman background Elliott has devoted a chapter to emotion in Jewish culture and writings. He surveys the emotions of the righteous and the emotions of the wicked by examining important concepts and vocabulary. For the righteous, joy in the present can have theological causes. He explains, 'Present joy can come out of the assurance or expectation of future deliverance and Israel is to wait with confidence for a future filled with great

---

[87] Elliott, *Faithful Feelings*, 167.
[88] Elliott, *Faithful Feelings*, 165.
[89] Elliott, *Faithful Feelings*, 31.
[90] Elliott, *Faithful Feelings*, 42.
[91] Elliott, *Faithful Feelings*, 78.

joy (Ps 14:7; Isa 9:2-3, 12:6, 61:9-11, 66:14; Zech 8:19, 9:9; Zeph 3:14-17)'.[92] The strong connection between joy and divine revelation establishes that celebration and festival were based on facts or cognitive realities. Thus, 'Joyful celebration was to be based on good theology'.[93] Elliott goes as far as saying, 'In summary, joy in God is at the centre of Judaism'.[94]

Having established this cognitive-based position about emotion, his study covers the entire New Testament but he focuses part of a chapter specifically on 'joy' as it is found in the Gospels and devotes particular interest in Luke. He defines 'joy' as being an 'emotion plain and simple'.[95] This definition is significant because it differs from authors, such as Morrice, who deny that joy is essentially an emotion.[96] Thus, Elliott provides an important correction by arguing that it is not necessary to posit a dichotomy between emotion and theology.[97] He states,

> Many scholars emphasize the eschatological content of joy in the New Testament. The age of salvation has come with Christ and he is coming again. But in emphasizing eschatology, they often blatantly dismiss the possibility that Christian joy is a present emotional experience.[98]

While granting that much of the joy language is indeed identifying a 'spontaneous' cognitive event, this does not exhaust how emotion is used in various contexts.[99] Elliott himself states, 'First, there is a clear emphasis on joy being firmly based in eschatology and the coming kingdom'.[100] What is left unresolved is how or why or when joy is used in conjunction with eschatology, rhetoric, and other theological interests. Having agreed that joy is emotive and related to cognition, it is not clear how Elliott's thesis went far enough to explain his own observations about 'eschatology' – a matter addressed in my study. Elliott provides a strong link to this study of joy because his correction leaves the question open: given that joy is a genuine emotion driven by cognition, how is it integrated into Luke's historical-theological corpus?

Literature Review

Many studies on Luke-Acts have recognized that 'joy' is a major theme. Several studies have engaged in short or narrowly focused literary-critical

---

[92] Elliott, *Faithful Feelings*, 90.
[93] Elliott, *Faithful Feelings*, 91.
[94] Elliott, *Faithful Feelings*, 91.
[95] Elliott, *Faithful Feelings*, 166.
[96] Morrice, *We Joy in God*, 80.
[97] Elliott, *Faithful Feelings*, 179.
[98] Elliott, *Faithful Feelings*, 179.
[99] Elliott, *Faithful Feelings*, 180.
[100] Elliott, *Faithful Feelings*, 176,

studies. Few have evaluated how joy is used rhetorically. A review of the scholarship on the Lukan joy theme will reveal that there remains a need to examine how the joy theme functions from a socio-rhetorical vantage point. The review is structured chronologically. I conclude the review by summarizing and evaluating shorter studies that are also relevant.

E.G. Gulin

E.G. Gulin (1893-1975) was a Lutheran bishop in Finland and an important figure in the ecumenical movement. *Die Freude im Neuen Testament* (*Joy in the New Testament*) examines joy in Jesus, the early Christian community, and Paul. This volume is one of the earliest studies of the joy theme in the Lukan corpus. Several of his conclusions are important for the current study. The first important conclusion is that the topic of joy in Luke is worthy of a 'special heading'.[101]

The second important conclusion is that Luke's joy theme can be demonstrated to be part of his unique contribution by means of a redaction study. According to Gulin, the joy theme is part of the way that Luke enriched the tradition.[102] Gulin explains that the emphasis on joy is not the product of incorporating the work of others involving other gospels or documents. This can be proven by a comparative study with Matthew and Mark because when they know nothing about the people having joy, Luke does.[103]

The third important conclusion Gulin arrives at is the primary way that joy is defined. He argues that joy is related to the 'redemptive joy' of God.[104] Because of this connection, joy is both redemptive and soteriological. Gulin explains that because Luke ties joy to Jesus.[105] This focus on 'soteriologische Freude' is helpful does not take into account the ecclesiological interests of Luke-Acts that define the People of God or the rhetorical means to achieve that goal. Gulin's conclusions simply require more nuance.

J. Navone

Themes of St. Luke by John Navone covers twenty different themes including 'joy'. He notes that the content of Luke's Gospel makes it more suitable for an analytic study rather than a synthetic.[106] Nevertheless, these twenty themes are ultimately 'variations on the overriding Lucan theme of salvation in Christ'.[107]

---

[101] E.G. Gulin, *Die Freude im Neuen Testament: I* (Helsinki: Druckerei-A.G. der Finnischen Literatur-Gesellschaft, 1932-1936), 95.

[102] Gulin, *Die Freude im Neuen Testament*, 100.

[103] Gulin, *Die Freude im Neuen Testament*, 99.

[104] J. Jeremias picks up the importance of Gulin's comment regarding Luke's use of joy in *The Parables of Jesus* (NY: Charles Scribner's Sons, 1963), 136.

[105] Gulin, *Die Freude im Neuen Testament*, 97.

[106] J. Navone, *Themes of St Luke* (Rome: Gregorian University, 1970), 9.

[107] Navone, *Themes of St Luke*, 9.

His survey of themes in Luke is a 'sketch' and 'does not aim at an exhaustive treatment'.[108] While giving the joy theme a cursory examination, he provides several insights that can lead to further exploration.

Navone's approach begins with a wide semantic range that includes vocabulary for joy (e.g. χαρά, χαίρειν, σκιρτάω, etc.) as well as vocabulary for glorification (δόξα and δοξάζειν) and magnification (μεγαλύνω).[109] After noting the distinctiveness of the wide range of vocabulary connected to the joy theme, he examines joy in the ten pericopes of the travel narrative. Navone concludes that Luke's particular use of joy includes an 'eschatological' dimension that is related to the inaugurated eschatology present in Luke's banquet theology.[110]

Navone's study focuses on the travel narrative in Luke's Gospel which provides a detailed window into the joy theme that other thematic and narrative studies do not achieve. He views the joy theme as integral to the expression of the 'ultimate realization' of 'prophecies'.[111] He draws attention to the intertextual backdrop of Isaiah 55 for joy in the eschatological banquet. In addition, he makes several notes about the unity of Luke's Gospel and how redaction will demonstrate that the joy theme is unique against Matthew.

Furthermore, he catalogues ten actions associated with joy: (1) being willing, (2) belonging, (3) being eschatological, (4) saving, (5) being connected to the Holy Spirit, (6) hearing and keeping, (7) enduring, (8) working, (9) preparing, and (10) renouncing.[112] This catalogue is helpful but it is simplistic to a fault. It misses out on some of the narrative aspects that provide nuances to Luke's use of emotional rhetoric.

Where Navone does consider the story line, he is only able to devote attention to the travel narrative in the Gospel of Luke (Lk 9:51-19:44). This simply begs the question: how is joy used across the whole narrative of Luke-Acts?

P. Bernadicou

Paul Bernadicou's *Joy in the Gospel of Luke* is based on his doctoral dissertation and his acknowledgment indicates that the impetus for the study began with lectures under John Navone who published *Themes of St. Luke* in the same year. The scope of his study is limited to the Gospel of Luke although he concludes with possible implications for the joy theme in Acts.[113] His central thesis question focuses on Lukan travel narrative (9:51-19:27) and investigates

---

[108] Navone, *Themes of St Luke*, 9.

[109] Navone, *Themes of St Luke*, 71-73.

[110] Navone, *Themes of St Luke*, 80.

[111] Navone, *Themes of St Luke*, 78.

[112] Navone, *Themes of St Luke*, 74-75.

[113] P. Bernadicou, *Joy in the Gospel of Luke* (Rome: Gregorian Pontifical University, 1970), 34.

how joy functions with respect to its 'communitarian dimension'.[114] He devotes a large amount of space to Luke's broad vocabulary of joy.[115]

Bernadicou's stated method anticipates present concerns. He attempts to avoid methodological myopia by intentionally employing the following methods: linguistic analysis, redactional analysis, and an interest in 'applied meaning' that is akin to an interest in the implied reader.[116] He summarizes his integrationist approach as a type of *Redaktionsgeschichte* that allows for theological and textual inquiry.[117] While Bernadicou's work supports the present study by recognizing the need for an interdisciplinary study of joy, he does not substantially engage in a discussion of rhetoric.

Furthermore, the lack of discussion about the LXX is conspicuous. He states that the vocabulary of joy shows a 'marked preference for the language and thought patterns of the Old Testament, in its LXX version'.[118] He does not explore how or why these texts were chosen or what role they play in the Lukan narrative. The question of intertextuality remains.

Another point of intersection with the present study is the short but significant comment that Bernadicou makes about the reversal motif. He notes: 'Luke's reversal theme insists repeatedly that the selfish rich of this world will be humbled, for salvation comes to the poor and outcast'.[119] Beyond a reference to Isaiah 55:1-3, there is no discussion of how joy and reversal work together as Old Testament echoes. At the time of this dissertation (1970), Bernadicou states that there was no study on the theme of joy in the Gospel of Luke.[120] Bernadicou's work remains one of the few studies entirely focused on the joy theme in the Lukan corpus.

R.F. O'Toole

O'Toole's study, *The Unity of Luke's Theology: An Analysis of Luke-Acts* made its contribution to Lukan scholarship by examining how themes, figures, and events create parallels and synergy between both Luke and Acts.[121]

O'Toole uses redaction criticism or what he calls 'composition criticism' to synthesize various themes including the joy theme.[122] He presents Luke-Acts as

---

[114] Bernadicou, *Joy in the Gospel of Luke*, 10.

[115] Bernadicou, *Joy in the Gospel of Luke*, 11.

[116] Bernadicou, *Joy in the Gospel of Luke*, 10.

[117] Bernadicou, *Joy in the Gospel of Luke*, 11.

[118] Bernadicou, *Joy in the Gospel of Luke*, 14.

[119] Bernadicou, *Joy in the Gospel of Luke*, 27.

[120] F. Bovon notes that as of 2005 this was also the case in *Luke the Theologian: Fifty-Five Years of Research (1950-2005)* (Waco: Baylor University Press, 2006), 459 n118.

[121] A point also made by J.P. Meier in his footnotes, *Companions and Competitors: A Marginal Jew: Rethinking the Historical Jesus, Volume 3* (NY: Random House, 2001), 84 n4.

[122] O'Toole, *Unity of Luke's Theology*, 11, 77, 79-80, 112, 116.

a two volume entity that presents the continuation of salvation history.[123] He argues that the main theme of Luke-Acts is that Israel's God continues to bring salvation to his people through Jesus Christ.[124]

What is significant about O'Toole's study is that he explicitly parts company with his colleague John Navone over the range of words related to these reactions. O'Toole wants to remove χαρίζομαι (to grant or bestow) from the range of joy vocabulary and to add other words including: γελάω (to laugh) and συγχαίρω (to rejoice with).[125] What advances the conversation is not his individual word studies but his argument that Luke uses word groupings or clusters.

The first significant reference to the joy theme is in reference to the content of what Jesus and his followers were preaching. O'Toole asserts that there is a parallelism between the preaching of Jesus and the preaching of his disciples. The parables of Luke 15 are used as examples of the message of joy.[126] Paul's message of repentance in Acts 17 parallels the joyful message of Jesus. However, it is not clear how joy plays a role in preaching.

The second significant analysis of the joy theme is his assertion that a parallelism can be drawn from the way that Luke describes Jesus and his followers – namely, both are full of 'joy'.[127] He lists several passages in Luke and Acts where 'to rejoice' (χαίρω) parallels the use of 'joy' (χαρά).

In sum, a large amount of proof-texts and data are covered but he does not provide socio-rhetorical or narrative-critical analysis. While providing a compendium of data and redactional analysis, it provides little in the way of intertextual, narrative, or socio-rhetorical analysis.[128]

W. Morrice

Joy in the New Testament by William Morrice is a revised dissertation from the University of Aberdeen. As a religious phenomenon, the New Testament in its entirety is described as a 'most joyful book'.[129] He initially locates joy in the New Testament within the historical context of Greco-Roman religion and philosophy; particularly Stoicism, Epicureanism, and the mystery religions. Morrice argues that joy was absent from both Stoicism and Epicureanism but

---

[123] O'Toole, *Unity of Luke's Theology*, 12.

[124] O'Toole, *Unity of Luke's Theology*, 17.

[125] O'Toole, *Unity of Luke's Theology*, 225.

[126] O'Toole, *Unity of Luke's Theology*, 77.

[127] O'Toole, *Unity of Luke's Theology*, 79-80.

[128] A similar criticism notes that he 'explicitly excludes any analysis of these themes [e.g. 'joy'] in the wider context'. J.T. Squires, *The Plan of God in Luke-Acts* (SNTSMS 76; Cambridge: Cambridge University Press, 1993), 5.

[129] Morrice, *Joy in the New Testament*, 15. Morrice also has a short popular treatise on joy in the New Testament that is thematically arranged around the Christian narrative of redemption in *We Joy in God*, passim.

possibly present in the ecstasy and enthusiasm of the mystery religions. Thus he locates the 'Eastern' religion of Christianity in contrast with the 'Western' (Greco-Roman) religions.[130]

Morrice devotes an entire chapter to Luke-Acts in his survey of joy in various New Testament documents. By making use of his word groups, he states that 24% of the New Testament vocabulary for joy is found in the Lukan writings.[131] Because Morrice's study is based on a wide semantic range he finds the joy theme throughout Luke's Gospel.

The Book of Acts is described by Morrice as 'The Sequel to the Gospel of Joy'.[132] While mentioning intertextual issues that intersect with the joy theme, a significant focus is given to the impact of joy upon the implied reader. The bulk of Morrice's analysis of the joy theme in Acts mirrors his analysis of Luke; he moves through the narrative of the text and describes how the joy theme is present. His summary of the joy theme in Acts asserts that (1) the presence of a joy theme is undeniable, and (2) it is connected to the 'good tidings brought by Jesus Christ'.[133]

In his conclusion, Morrice avers 'While Luke in his gospel shows the joy of Jesus, in the Acts of the Apostles he describes the ever-widening circle of joy in the early Church'.[134] For Morrice, the source of this joy theme is rooted in both theology and history. The source of joy amongst the early Christian documents flows from the distinctive nature of their faith and from events such as the incarnation and resurrection.[135] This conclusion does not directly address his initial question about the distinctive nature of Christian joy amidst the Greco-Roman and Hellenistic background.

Morrice's helpful survey of joy helps the reader to see how important and central the matter is to both Luke and Acts.

C.C. Conver

Christopher C. Conver's doctoral dissertation from The Southern Baptist Theological Seminary is entitled: *The Portrayal of Joy in the Gospel of Luke.* Conver finds that the joy theme is prominent in the Gospel of Luke although the treatments present at the time (1985) were too brief.[136] This dissertation is significant because of its narrow focus on the joy theme in Luke's Gospel.

Conver states, 'The portrayal of joy in the Gospel of Luke, then, was Luke's effort to communicate to his readers how to respond to sorrow'.[137] In Conver's

---

[130] Morrice, *Joy in the New Testament*, 14.
[131] Morrice, *Joy in the New Testament*, 91.
[132] Morrice, *Joy in the New Testament*, 96.
[133] Morrice, *Joy in the New Testament*, 99.
[134] Morrice, *Joy in the New Testament*, 152.
[135] Morrice, *Joy in the New Testament*, 153.
[136] Conver, *Portrayal of Joy in the Gospel of Luke*, 9.
[137] Conver, *Portrayal of Joy in the Gospel of Luke*, xv.

'summation' he states that 'Luke used joy as a literary device to exhort those believers to remain faithful' in the face of suffering.[138] Conver understands joy to be an emotion that reverses fear, suffering, and sorrow. For example, his study finds that Luke only uses the joy theme to overturn fear on four occasions (Lk 1:12-14, 29-47; 2:9-10; 24:37-41). By understanding joy as simply overturning an opposite negative emotion, Conver is not able to see how other reversals are taking place. A broader and nuanced view of reversal is required to understand how Luke uses emotion to reverse positions of honour and shame as well as power and weakness, among others.

The most helpful aspect of Conver's study is his redaction analysis between Mark and Luke and Matthew and Luke. His redaction analysis examines the synoptics through the categories of alteration, omission, and addition. He proceeds to demonstrate that Luke's presentations included a 'more extensive' use of joy (and sorrow).[139] He finds that when compared to Mark, Luke favours contexts for joy such as meals, miracles, teachings, and the temple.[140] Likewise, when compared to Matthew, the Lukan presentation 'portrays more of an emphasis on joy'.[141] Then, Conver examines the unique Lukan material and finds that it also accentuates the joy theme.[142]

This study is largely redactional. Thus any interest in narrative dynamics or persuasion is secondary and undeveloped. Conver's study also lacks interaction with the joy theme in Acts.[143]

This present study addresses two key lacunae in Conver's study. Whereas Conver only examines Luke's Gospel, this study will examine both Luke and Acts. And whereas Conver concludes from his redaction study that Luke has a demonstrable focus on joy, it is not clear how joy functions with respect to his rhetorical goals.

K.P. De Long

Kindalee P. De Long's published dissertation from Notre Dame is entitled: *Surprised by God: Praise Responses in the Narrative of Luke-Acts*. This study examines the motif of praise which she carefully distinguishes from the closely related theme of joy.[144] De Long concludes that joy is more ambiguous whereas praise is more positive.[145] Her approach is interdisciplinary and narratologically

---

[138] Conver, *Portrayal of Joy in the Gospel of Luke*, 224.

[139] Conver, *Portrayal of Joy in the Gospel of Luke*, 29.

[140] Conver, *Portrayal of Joy in the Gospel of Luke*, 67.

[141] Conver, *Portrayal of Joy in the Gospel of Luke*, 85.

[142] Conver, *Portrayal of Joy in the Gospel of Luke*, 131.

[143] This criticism of Conver's lack of comparative study with Acts is noted by De Long, *Surprised by God*, 7.

[144] De Long, *Surprised by God*, 8.

[145] De Long, *Surprised by God*, 135 n3.

sensitive.[146] She argues that the praise theme follows the unfolding plot of divine visitation throughout the Lukan corpus. Specifically, praise is a response to the presence of Jesus as revealed by God. She finds that Isaiah is the primary source for Luke's language of praise.[147] Then, she concludes that praise 'fulfills early Jewish expectations' through 'joyous praise' in response to God's restorative acts for both Jews and Gentiles.[148] While she favours the term 'transformation', she finds the use of reversal to be significant for praise. God's intervention must overturn or reverse difficulties before praise can occur.[149] De Long concludes that even though there is some overlap, her study of praise covers different ground than the theme of joy.

A study of the theme of joy is also justified and required because De Long does not examine crucial texts that include joy but not praise. These crucial texts provide certain nuances to the joy theme. For example, her study lacks an in-depth exegesis of the joy theme or praise when the gospel reaches Judea/Samaria in Acts 8:4-40.

The strength of this study lies in her thematic approach.[150] This approach is also a weakness because it does not account for certain narrative developments in Acts that follow the Isaianic New Exodus framework. It also is not clear how emotion plays a role in Luke's rhetorical strategy. De Long recognizes the significance of the joy theme in texts such as the angel's joyful greeting of Mary (Lk 1:28) but it does not fit directly within the narrow scope of praise toward God.[151]

In contrast to De Long, my study casts a wider net in order to accommodate the breadth of the joy theme. In sum, De Long's study provides conclusions that parallel and strengthen the conclusion of this study. Her study also anticipates certain lacunae that this study seeks to fill.

A. Inselmann

The most robust and up-to-date (2012) study of the joy theme in the Gospel of Luke is Anke Inselmann's German-language *Joy in the Gospel of Luke: A Study in Psychological Exegesis* (*Die Freude im Lukasevangelium: Ein Beitrag zur Psychologischen Exegese*). Unfortunately, this volume was published after my dissertation was written. The benefit of this is that Inselmann's work may provide an independent source for comparison with my own study.

Inselmann supports our contention that Luke's interest in the emotion of joy is unique and worthy of specific attention. She notes that a comparison of Luke with Mark (or Q) will demonstrate that linguistic expressions of joy are more

---

[146] De Long, *Surprised by God*, 14.
[147] De Long, *Surprised by God*, 15.
[148] De Long, *Surprised by God*, 16.
[149] De Long, *Surprised by God*, 54.
[150] De Long, *Surprised by God*, 15.
[151] De Long, *Surprised by God*, 139-41.

prominent in Luke.[152] Inselmann also seeks to understand joy in Luke as a feeling or *emotion*.[153] This welcome conclusion bolsters the case made here. The major difference is that Inselmann is only able to investigate Luke's Gospel rather than the whole Lukan corpus of Luke-Acts as I do.

In order to study this difficult phenomenon, Inselmann seeks to address both ancient and modern theories of emotional experience.[154] Inselmann attempts an 'interdisciplinary perspective' that applies 'new methodological approaches'.[155] Inselmann calls her approach 'psychological exegesis', as indicated by the title of the book. Her method is definitely not a simplistic reader-response methodology. She seeks historical and exegetical conclusions that engage literary aspects, intertextuality, and early Christian cultural contexts. She begins with repetition of vocabulary or lexical data and then seeks to investigate three central questions related to (1) redaction or conscious use of the leitmotif, (2) literary relationships, and (3) the role of joy as a response to the Gospel of Luke and its impact upon early Christian communities. A minor of point disagreement is her narrow focus on the lexeme χαρά. She concludes that the leitmotif of joy has been 'expanded quantitatively and qualitatively'.[156] Joy is an emotion that was intended to strengthen the faith of the early Christian communities and would have made early Christianity attractive for missionary activity.

When we place Inselmann's 'psychological exegesis' next to this study we find many similar conclusions. Inselmann is surely on the right track. I agree that joy was an important part of the 'behavior and experience of the first Christians'.[157] But how did this happen? In this volume I will argue that this joy empowered Luke's rhetoric of reversal – the emotion of joy added pathos or emotional power to Luke's portrayal of a world turned upside-down by the cross of Christ.

Summary

A survey of literature on the Lukan corpus regarding joy reveals two remarkable things. First, there is widespread acknowledgement that joy is a prominent leitmotif or theme in both Luke and Acts. Second, it has received little attention beyond redaction studies.[158] As a result, this survey of literature

---

[152] Inselmann, *Die Freude im Lukasevangelium*, 2.

[153] Inselmann, *Die Freude im Lukasevangelium*, 15.

[154] Inselmann, *Die Freude im Lukasevangelium*, 9.

[155] Inselmann, *Die Freude im Lukasevangelium*, 9.

[156] Inselmann, *Die Freude im Lukasevangelium*, 9-10.

[157] Inselmann, *Die Freude im Lukasevangelium*, 21.

[158] As recently as 2009, Kuhn noted that commentators often 'fail to consider how pathos may be employed by the biblical author in the shaping of narrative' (*Heart of Biblical Narrative*, 28).

on the topic resembles a patchwork of scholarship. Only two works of scholarship by two authors stand out: (1) K.P. De Long, and (2) Anke Inselmann. But De Long's study is focused on 'praise' rather than 'joy' and Inselmann's study of joy is focused on Luke rather than Luke-Acts. It is clear that further work remains.

One further insight that can be derived from this survey is that joy is often connected to soteriology with little consideration given to ecclesiology or concern for identity. Although Mark Allen Powell correctly observed that Lukan studies were moving toward the study of ecclesiology in Luke-Acts, the study of joy does not reflect this concern.[159] The only monograph dedicated to the topic of joy in the Lukan corpus by Bernadicou appeared in 1970 and is limited to the Lukan travel narrative. Conver's study is the only recent unpublished dissertation on the joy theme and it is solely focused on redaction. Out of all of these studies a broad question remains: what is the significance of the plethora of quotations and echoes from the Old Testament? Furthermore, while recognizing soteriological concerns, what role does Luke-Acts play in establishing the identity of the people of God or the inauguration of the new age and the reconstitution of Israel?

It is also widely acknowledged that Luke-Acts utilizes a 'rhetoric of reversal'. This rhetoric of reversal is often bi-polar: *up* becomes *down* and *down* becomes *up*. The world has been flipped upside-down by the dawning of the new age that has been inaugurated with the visitation of YHWH. The resurrection of the Lord Jesus confirms that nothing will ever be the same. These conclusions are rather uncontroversial. But one must ask how the reader is persuaded to move from the literary upside-down world of the narrative into the real world. One must ask how the rhetoric of reversal works in the context of the logos, ethos, and pathos. And more importantly, how can we integrate the joy theme into Luke's stated agendas for Luke-Acts. Out of these questions comes the focus of this study: *the joy theme provides emotional energy to the rhetoric of reversal.*

---

[159] M.A. Powell, *What Are They Saying About Luke?* (Mahwah: Paulist, 1989), 58.

CHAPTER 2

Joy in Barrenness Turning to Birth: Luke 1

This chapter begins our exegetical study of joy in Luke-Acts. This chapter will examine joy at the inauguration of the new age in the opening passages of the Gospel of Luke. In Luke 1, the emotion of joy adds emotional force to the rhetoric of reversal as Luke frames the inauguration of the new age.

Introduction

Our first task is to understand Luke's prologue. In this section I will offer a very simple argument: the opening passages of Luke 1:1-4 communicate that Luke is seeking to persuade his readers. How we understand this act of 'persuasion' must be nuanced according to the genre and agenda established by the text. The Gospel of Luke as well as the other synoptic gospels are best understood as being of the genre of *bios* or Greco-Roman biography.[1] However, the Gospel of Luke is unique because the opening passage of Luke 1:1-4 draws upon patterns from both (1) Greco-Roman rhetorical history and (2) Hellenistic Jewish history. This section seeks to develop a balanced and nuanced approach to understanding the sub-genre of Luke 1:1-4.

Luke's Rhetoric According to the Lukan Prologue: Luke 1:1-4

The opening of Luke's Gospel draws upon elements of Greco-Roman rhetorical history. Ben Witherington III argues that Luke 1:1-4 represents a Greco-Roman *exordium* of which Quintilian would have been proud.[2] This places at least part of Luke's writing in the category of rhetorical discourse that follows a general pattern of *exordium, narratio, propositio, probatio,* and *peroratio.*[3] Witherington states, 'the preface sets up the expectation that rhetorical history writing with rhetorical patterns will follow, and indeed they do'.[4] The centrality of rhetorical training in classical education encourages us to understand Luke's preface in the tradition of rhetoricians such as Quintilian.[5] Joel Green states that

---

[1] Bock, *Theology of Luke-Acts*, 45.
[2] Witherington, *New Testament Rhetoric*, 39.
[3] Witherington, *New Testament Rhetoric*, 16.
[4] Witherington, *New Testament Rhetoric*, 39.
[5] J.B. Green, *The Gospel of Luke* (Grand Rapids: Eerdmans, 1997), 33.

Luke 1:1-4 is simply a 'Greek-style preface'.[6] Green's approach is not without nuance. He also refers to Luke's 'narrative rhetoric'.[7] This language of 'narrative rhetoric' may be Green's attempt to balance the notion of classical rhetoric with the whole nature of Luke's Gospel.

Instead of finding a formal *propositio* following the *exordium,* we find a poetic and historical narrative or διήγησις. Luke's narrative simply does not fit tidily within the pattern of *exordium, narratio, propositio, probatio,* and *peroration,* even if the preface does make a persuasive appeal to provide a historical narrative based on eyewitnesses (Lk 1:2).[8] Our caution here is against reading Luke as a *purely* technical work, even if it bears some resemblances to the work of professional Greco-Roman historians or scientific works.[9] The use of the word *exordium* to describe Luke 1:1-4 is sound if one key qualification is in place – it does not follow from the preface that a formal pattern of rhetoric follows throughout the whole.

The ancient narrative theory is an integration of the horizons of the author, narrative, and audience into one unit that we cannot easily tear apart.[10] This model is helpful but it seems to tilt the scale of genre just slightly too far toward the Greco-Roman side. The original readers would have likely understood the epistemology and social function of the historical genre that is set forth in Luke 1:1-4.[11] If this is true, Luke may be tied to the ancient narrative theory to Aristotle, Polybius, and other Greco-Roman historians. Luke's rhetorical historiography is in some respects, 'not unlike Polybius and Diodorus'.[12] But the best model for understanding Luke's rhetoric will engage the fact that Luke's διήγησις is about the distinctly Jewish 'plan of God'.[13]

---

[6] Green, *Gospel of Luke,* 34.

[7] Green, *Gospel of Luke,* 312, 450, 626, 646 n110, 782.

[8] Dibelius' proposed model of rhetoric in Luke-Acts followed a four part schema of *exordium, narratio, argumentatio,* and *peroratio.* V.K. Robbins' criticism of this model is similar to our criticism of Witherington's model: 'the stories transmit the authority and role of Jesus on their own terms'. B.L. Mack and V.K. Robbins, *Patterns of Persuasion in the Gospels* (Santa Rosa: Polebridge Press, 1989), 5, 17.

[9] F.G. Downing, 'Theophilus's First Reading of Luke-Acts', in *Luke's Literary Achievement: Collected Essays* (ed. C.M. Tuckett; JSNTSup 116; Sheffield: Sheffield Academic Press, 1995), 97; L. Alexander, *The Preface to Luke's Gospel: Literary Convention and Social Context in Luke 1.1-4 and Acts 1.1* (SNTSMS 78; Cambridge: Cambridge University Press, 1993).

[10] D.P. Moessner, 'Reading Luke's Gospel as Ancient Hellenistic Narrative', in *Reading Luke: Interpretation, Reflection, Formation* (eds. C.G. Bartholomew, J.B. Green and A.C. Thiselton; Carlisle: Paternoster, 2006; Grand Rapids: Zondervan, 2005), 126.

[11] Moessner, 'Reading Luke's Gospel as Ancient Hellenistic Narrative', 126.

[12] Moessner, 'Reading Luke's Gospel as Ancient Hellenistic Narrative', 126; Squires, *The Plan of God in Luke-Acts,* 15-52.

[13] Moessner, 'Reading Luke's Gospel as Ancient Hellenistic Narrative', 126.

The opening of Luke's Gospel draws upon elements of Hellenistic Jewish History. The sub-genre of Luke 1:1-4 represents Hellenistic-Jewish history that is intentionally following the pattern of Old Testament biblical history. The problem with this position is that there is both continuity and discontinuity between the Lukan corpus and Greco-Roman writings. Whereas the Lukan corpus shares continuity with Greco-Roman rhetorical historiography in that divine providence guides history, Luke 1:1 is concerned about 'the things that have been fulfilled' (τῶν πεπληροφορημένων) as they relate to the Scriptural promises and fulfillment of the God of Israel.[14]

Specifically, the textual unit of Luke 24:13-27 relates the plot of Jesus' life and death to Moses, the Prophets and 'all the Scriptures'.[15] The formulation of divine providence and control over history by Luke has discontinuity with Greco-Roman divine providence and 'necessity' because what has been accomplished in history has eternal significance that is explained by God's own personal interaction and intervention in history through Jesus. Even where we see promise-and-fulfillment concepts appearing in Greco-Roman history, such as Herodotus viewing earthquakes as the fulfillment of omens, this is based on a 'reasonable deduction' rather than divine-personal explanation.[16] For Herodotus, divine control of the world by the gods is at times indistinguishable from the natural realm, both being inscrutable.[17] The rhetorical appeal of Luke's claim to provide a narrative of what has been fulfilled reflects a Hellenistic milieu that was influenced not only by Greco-Roman dimensions of Hellenism but also by the Jewish dimensions of Hellenism.

Returning to our discussion of the identity of Luke's rhetorical historiography, it is best to conclude that Luke 1:1-4 represents Hellenistic-Jewish history that is intentionally following the pattern of Old Testament biblical history.[18] Osvaldo Padilla's distinction between Jewish historiography and Hellenistic *topoi* in Acts suggests that a similar distinction could be made about Luke's first volume.[19] Even the prologue quickly moves from a Greek style into a Semitic style abundant in clues such as typological parallels of barrenness and birth that point the reader to the 'world of the Old Testament'.[20]

---

[14] Lk 1:1

[15] Lk 24:27

[16] T. Harrison, *Divinity and History: The Religion of Herodotus* (Oxford: Oxford University Press, 2000), 96.

[17] J. Romm, 'Herodotus and The Natural World' in *The Cambridge Companion to Herodotus* (eds. C. Dewald and J. Marincola; Cambridge: Cambridge University Press, 2006), 183-84.

[18] This does not preclude the use and intentional inclusion of speeches that use classical rhetorical structures.

[19] Padilla, *Speeches of Outsiders in Acts*, 3 n5.

[20] M.L. Strauss, *The Davidic Messiah in Luke-Acts: The Promise and its Fulfillment in Lukan Christology* (JSNTSup 110; Sheffield: Sheffield Academic, 1995), 86. Bovon also finds that the Gospel of Luke follows 'in the footsteps of the writers of the Hebrew

Exegetically, the prologue of Luke's gospel (Lk 1:1-4) must establish lines of continuity and discontinuity with the Greco-Roman and Jewish sides of his Hellenistic milieu.[21]

Luke establishes two important pillars for understanding the rhetorical thrust of his whole narrative (Luke-Acts). The significance of these will become more evident as we examine how the emotion of joy adds rhetorical power to his rhetoric of reversal.

First, Luke 1:1 makes it clear that his narrative (διήγησις) *was based on delivery by eyewitnesses.* The key-phrase in the sentence in Luke 1:2 is: 'who were eyewitnesses'. This phrase about witnesses is connected via καθώς to the clause regarding the whole διήγησις and provides an argument for its 'reliability'.[22] Luke's concept of eyewitness testimony can be developed by comparisons with what he says throughout the corpus. For example, Acts 26:16 is a parallel passage that establishes eyewitness experience as the basis for being witness (μάρτυς).[23] The vocabulary for eyewitness (αὐτόπτης) reflects the inner texture of the prologue that uses key words (also πρᾶγμα; Lk 1:1) to reflect his intention to write historically and accurately. The emphasis of this sentence structure is such that it is clear that Luke's narrative is not propaganda.[24] This conclusion can be enhanced slightly by explicitly noting the rhetorical nature of Luke's διήγησις: Luke is *persuading* the reader of his veracity.

Second, the goal of this narrative that is based on eyewitnesses and evidence is certainty. The key-phrase in Luke 1:4 is: 'that you may have certainty' (ἐπιγνῷς τὴν ἀσφάλειαν). The noun ἀσφάλεια remains at the end of the sentence and is due an amount of emphasis based on this separation.[25] Based on ἵνα plus the subjunctive, Luke 1:4 is best understood as a purpose clause.[26] The lack of criticism about other accounts has led some to conclude that Luke may

---

Bible'. Bovon also find that Luke is essentially 'persuasive' or rhetorical but is it not clear why he sets persuasion against 'instruction'. F. Bovon, *Luke 1: A Commentary on the Gospel of Luke 1:1-9:50* (Trans. C.M. Thomas; Hermeneia; Minneapolis: Fortress Press, 2002), 5.

[21] This conclusion is similar to that of Marguerat who finds Luke's prologue 'heavily indebted to the cultural standard in the Roman Empire' but essentially a biblical 'confessional history'. Marguerat, *First Christian Historian*, 25.

[22] For a fuller discussion of handing down oral or written testimony and similar examples see Marshall, *Gospel of Luke*, 41.

[23] Nolland, *Luke 1:1–9:20*, 7.

[24] Marshall, *Gospel of Luke*, 41.

[25] Nolland, *Luke 1:1 – 9:20*, 10. For a contextual discussion of the noun ἀσφάλεια see D.P. Moessner, 'The Appeal and Power of Poetics: Luke 1:1-4' in *Jesus and the Heritage of Israel: Luke's Narrative Claim upon Israel's Legacy* (ed. D.P. Moessner; Harrisburg: Trinity Press International, 1999), 84-123.

[26] I.S.C. Kwong, *The Word Order of the Gospel of Luke: Its Foregrounded Messages* (JSNTSup 298; London: T&T Clark, 2005), 35.

have regarded them as erroneous or incomplete.[27] It is not clear whether Luke viewed other sources as erroneous.[28] Whatever the case may be, Luke is determined that his will succeed.

Luke's use of ἀσφάλεια and similar language is that of a historian.[29] Luke's history is a persuasive history.[30] What we are seeking to further is the connection between history and persuasion as articulated by Witherington in light of a socio-rhetorical method.[31] This expands upon Howard Marshall's suggestion that the prologue of Luke's gospel may contain a 'polemical reference to heretics who disputed the truth of the message, as it had been told to them'.[32] It is the observation by Marshall that Luke's writing may have a polemical nature that is important at this point. Conceptually, Marshall's observation is similar to what I am suggesting here: *Luke is writing a persuasive history.*

The critique has been raised that categories such as 'intertexture' or 'inner texture' would be foreign to Luke. [33] This critique essentially states that discussing the various textures of the text in terms of such categories is anachronistic and amounts to a failure to understand Luke on his own terms. But we must politely disagree on this matter. We cannot confuse terminology with concepts. When examining the texture and rhetoric of Luke's corpus we are not supposing that he neatly breaks his text down into such categories. We are simply saying that there are different textures or threads within the tapestry of the Lukan corpus.

Before proceeding, we must also address Loveday Alexander's claim that calling the preface 'rhetorical' would be 'misleading, or at least unhelpful'.[34] At first glance, this sounds like a strong disagreement with our position that Luke's Gospel (and his prologue) is best understood as rhetorical. We may alleviate the concern that Alexander's critique affects our study because she is focusing on a very narrow rhetorical tradition rooted in the Classical Greek rhetoricians. On the one hand Alexander states, 'the rules devised for prefaces in rhetoric were devised for a very specific situation and are of limited

---

[27] F. Craddock, *Luke* (Louisville: John Knox, 1990), 17.

[28] V.K. Robbins argues that Luke views previous accounts as reliable in 'The Claims of the Prologues and Greco-Roman Rhetoric' in *Jesus and the Heritage of Israel: Luke's Narrative Claim upon Israel's Legacy* (ed. D.P. Moessner; Harrisburg: Trinity Press International, 1999), 76.

[29] Nolland, *Luke 1:1 – 9:20*, 10.

[30] R. Strelhan argues that word ἀσφάλεια conveys rhetorical argumentation that reflects literary patterns for defending against contradiction in 'A Note on ἀσφάλεια (Luke 1.4)', *JSNT* 30:2 (2007), 163-71.

[31] Witherington, *New Testament Rhetoric*, 37.

[32] Marshall, *Gospel of Luke*, 43.

[33] Witherington, *New Testament Rhetoric*, 6.

[34] Alexander, *Preface to Luke's Gospel*, 65.

usefulness outside that situation'.[35] On the other hand, Loveday Alexander acknowledges that 'the influence of rhetoric was widely extended in time, both through its application to other branches of literature and through its controlling interest in education.'[36] It is this last quotation that is crucial for our contention that Luke's Gospel is persuasive in nature. It is not Luke's persuasive goals that are in question. Ultimately, once we understand Alexander's argumentation, her conclusions do not stand in contrast with ours.

We must seek to understand Luke's own rhetorical goals on his own terms. The preface of Luke's Gospel indicates that he intends to persuade. This affects the study of joy in the Lukan corpus as we seek to show how this emotion strengthens the rhetoric of reversal. The rhetoric of reversal is to be understood as a device that seeks to persuade the implied reader of a new system of values based on the Kingdom that Jesus inaugurated.[37] Luke's rhetoric of reversal is unique in that it uses bi-polar reversals. In many of these reversals, both of the poles are reversed: *up* becomes *down* and *down* becomes *up*.[38] By using such contraries Luke creates tension through expanding the meaning of relationships between poles and then reversing them. This impacts the social dimension in that participation in the Kingdom requires a change in values.

Luke wants to persuade the reader that the God of Israel has indeed fulfilled what he promised. With respect to the reversal in the Magnificat, 'The eschatological reversal and the fulfillment of the promise are not simple realities apparent to all'.[39] The reality of YHWH's visitation in the person and work of Christ is a reality-jarring message that requires an element of persuasion.

In the preface of Luke 1:1-4, we find that this Gospel is a narration of words and deeds that have been 'fulfilled' (πληροφορέω) among us.[40] What God has 'fulfilled' through the inauguration of Jesus' kingdom necessitates a reversal of values. In sum, we will seek to fill the lacuna about the role of joy and develop how it strengthens the rhetoric of reversal. This is particularly clear in chapters one and two of the Gospel of Luke where he provides a framework for his narrative.

---

[35] Alexander, *Preface to Luke's Gospel*, 17.

[36] Alexander, *Preface to Luke's Gospel*, 17.

[37] I understand reversal as a micro-rhetorical device according to Witherintgon's terminology. Micro-rhetorical devices can be contrasted with macro-rhetorical devices used by forensic, deliberative, and epideictic rhetoric. Witherington, *New Testament Rhetoric*, 7.

[38] York, *The Last Shall Be First*, 42.

[39] Tannehill helps establish a relationship between reversal and fulfillment; for a critique of the 'eschatological reversal' terminology see the first chapter of my study (Tannehill, *Shape of Luke's Story*, 47).

[40] Witherington, *New Testament Rhetoric*, 37. In the wider co-text, the perfect participle refers to fulfilling the promises that YHWH made to Israel.

The Reversal of Zechariah and Elizabeth: Joy in Luke 1:5-25

The next step in our study of joy begins by examining the reversal of Zechariah and Elizabeth (Lk 1:5-25) in the infancy narratives. The fact that these infancy or birth accounts are unique to Luke's Gospel accentuates their role in framing the narratives.[41] In the narrative of Zechariah and Elizabeth, the emotion of joy strengthens the rhetoric of reversal in order to persuade the reader that the God of Israel has initiated a new age.

The hermeneutical key to the reversal motif of this pericope is present in the slightly repetitive description of Elizabeth. After stating that they had no child, Luke explains the obvious: 'because Elizabeth was barren' (Lk 1:7). This detail establishes Elizabeth's barren womb as a problem that will undergo reversal. The angel's speech to Zechariah in the temple confirms this: 'and your wife Elizabeth will bear you a son (Lk 1:13). The announcement of the birth of the child John is followed by the implication that this reversal of fortune from barrenness to birth for Zechariah and Elizabeth has implications beyond them. This birth is proclaimed in the future tense as the basis for Zechariah's (and Elizabeth's) joy (Lk 1:14a): 'and you will have joy and gladness, and many will rejoice at this birth'. Equally as important are the 'many' who will rejoice (in third person plural future tense): 'and many will rejoice at his birth'.

The text does seem to encourage a reading of the 'many' (πολλοὶ) as a reference to Israel (Lk 1:16a): 'many of the sons of Israel'.[42] The joy and emotion of rejoicing creates a rhetorical force that encourages the reader to understand that God has begun a new age for the blessing of *Israel*. The reversal of fortune for Elizabeth and Zechariah is a reversal of fortune for Israel and for the Gentiles. Elizabeth's pregnancy with John will be the occasion for joy for them as well as Israel.

Joy and Inner Texture

The inner texture of the reversal of Zechariah and Elizabeth in Luke 1:5-25 reveals that Luke is truly the 'Gospel of Joy'. The thematic repetition of joy is more than an aesthetic dressing. In Luke 1:5-25, joy is noticeable as a distinctive and repeated *Leitwort*.[43] One way to define a *Leitwort* is:

> Through abundant repetition, the semantic range of the word-root is explored, different forms of the root are deployed, branching off at times into phonetic

---

[41] Conver, *Portrayal of Joy in the Gospel of Luke*, 131.

[42] For a cautionary comment see Marshall, *Gospel of Luke*, 56. The singular (collective) λαός regularly refers to Israel (York, T*he Last Shall Be First*, 112 n6).

[43] D. Marguerat provides a helpful taxonomy of rhetorical devices in Acts, including amplification as a form of rhetoric in biblical narration in *The First Christian Historian: Writing the 'Acts of the Apostles'* (SNTSMS 121; Cambridge: Cambridge University Press, 2002), 183-84.

relatives (that is, word-play), synonymity, and antonymity; by virtue of its verbal status, the *Leitwort* refers immediately to meaning and thus to theme as well.[44]

Repetition is a distinct feature of the inner texture of Luke 1:5-25. In Luke 1:13-14 an angel appears before Zechariah in the temple, assures him of his peaceful intentions and articulates a prophetic description of what will come about by the ministry of John the Baptist. The repetition of the joy theme in Luke 1:14 is apparent in the following sentence: 'and you will have *joy* and *gladness*, and many will *rejoice* at his birth'.[45]. The use of repetition here is described as: 'The note of joy sounds throughout Luke-Acts'.[46] Furthermore, one finds joy spread across a moderately wide semantic range as Alter's model reflects. Three words 'express' the 'note of joy' in Luke 1:14 (χαρά, χαίρω, ἀγαλλίασις).

The function of this repetition of emotion is best understood as 'amplification'. The narrative of Luke-Acts is framed with joy because it is a theme that will be repeated in the wider text(ure). Joy is repeated in order to establish a *Leitwort* that will play a role in creating an emotional force to his argumentation throughout Luke and Acts. This repetition and amplification also frames the discourse. Ben Witherington III explains how this works:

> By this I mean that after Acts 2 sometimes Luke will repeat themes in speeches, but only allusively, because he has already established the theme in an earlier speech. These speeches, as we find them now in Acts, are meant to have a cumulative effect on the audience and should not be seen as isolated phenomena, however they functioned in the original historical setting. ...The rhetorical technique of 'amplification' or 'accumulation' is in play, and we will need to attend to it shortly, to see the full rhetorical force of what Luke is doing there.[47]

Whereas the quote above is primarily referring to Acts, the same technique of amplification is at work at the beginning of the Gospel of Luke. The joy theme in Luke 1-2 evokes joyful feelings to persuade through amplification and by appealing to the emotion of the reader. Although we are separating them for the purpose of analysis, the texture of Luke 1:5-25 is composed of inner textures and ideological textures that we cannot pull apart. In other words, our text is like a tapestry with threads that are distinct but interwoven.

Joy is the only emotion linked with the reversal and the promise of future joy and rejoicing for Zechariah and Israel is a direct result of the future birth of John the Baptist. First, the angel indicates that his presence and the reversal from barrenness to pregnancy are due to the prayer of Zechariah. This

---

[44] York, *The Last Shall Be First*, 43.
[45] The Greek of Luke 1:14 reads: καὶ ἔσται χαρά σοι καὶ ἀγαλλίασις καὶ πολλοὶ ἐπὶ τῇ γενέσει αὐτοῦ χαρήσονται.
[46] Marshall, *Gospel of Luke*, 56.
[47] Witherington, *New Testament Rhetoric*, 52.

relationship is established by the causal διότι in Luke 1:13. Second, there is the promise that Zechariah and Elizabeth will bear a son (in the future tense γεννήσει, καλέσεις). Throughout, the use of καὶ to connect the phrases in the pericope creates a very Semitic sounding parataxis. The result of this parataxis is two-fold. On the one hand, the repetition or amplification of joy brings it to the forefront of the innertexture. The second result is that joy is related to both fulfillment (to prayer) and to promise (as something future). With respect to the future and the birth of John, the entire angelic discourse from Luke 1:13-17, the emphasis is on the emotion of joy.

As the first narrative and first reversal in the Lukan corpus, Luke 1:5-25 presents a framework and anticipates further development. The relationship between joy and reversal in this first poetic narrative establishes a framework or precedent for the entire corpus of Luke-Acts. Luke and Acts have a 'narrative unity' and this 'one continuous streak of temporal events' begins with the birth announcement to Zechariah.[48] There are 'causal' connections between many situations in Luke-Acts: 'One event or situation prepares for or gives rise to another'.[49] What the inner texture of Luke 1:5-25 reveals is that the joy theme is based on such causal relationships. The movement from barrenness to birth is cause for joy. With an initial relationship between joy and reversal established in the first narrative. The narrative appeals to the reader by promising joy – even as Zechariah was promised joy.

In sum, Luke 1:5-25 finds that Luke chose and repeated vocabulary to create a pronounced emphasis on joy and rejoicing. This can be described as amplification through repetition.

Joy and Intertexture

Our interest in the intertexture (intertextuality) of Luke 1:5-25 will focus primarily on David Pao's argument that the hermeneutical key for understanding the new age or New Exodus in the whole Lukan corpus lies in the use of Isaiah 40 in Luke 3:4-6:

> As it is written in the book of the words of Isaiah the prophet, "The voice of one crying in the wilderness: 'Prepare the way of the Lord, make his paths straight. Every valley shall be filled, and every mountain and hill shall be made low, and the crooked shall become straight, and the rough places shall become level ways, and all flesh shall see the salvation of God'". (ESV)

If this quotation from the LXX is the 'hermeneutical key' for the 'Lukan program' as David Pao argues, it would follow that the earlier birth narratives

---

[48] Litwak, *Echoes of Scripture in Luke-Acts*, 41.
[49] Litwak, *Echoes of Scripture in Luke-Acts*, 41.

have some relationship to this.[50] This transformation of the LXX quotation from Isaiah 40:3-5 'signifies the unity of the Lukan writings on the basis of the scriptural tradition that Luke evokes'.[51] Luke transforms the Septuagint quotation with changes that are best understood as a redaction aimed at shifting the focus to Jesus.[52] This is the foundation for the idea that 'the rest of the Lukan narrative should not be read apart from the wider context of Isaiah 40-55'.[53] However, Pao does not look backward in the Gospel of Luke to examine Simeon's utterance in Luke 2:30 or the birth narratives.[54] Our goal in this section is to test this hypothesis against the presence of the joy theme in the birth narrative and in the reversal of Zechariah and Elizabeth in Luke 1:5-25.

The first connection between the reversal of Zechariah and Elizabeth in Luke 1:5-25 is the presence of the fulfillment of God's divine plan. Zechariah's lack of faith in his response is the occasion for a rebuke and the disciplinary action of the angel that prevents him from speaking (Lk 1:20). This disciplinary action functions as a contrast to Mary's response but also highlights God's sovereign plan. The angel's communication to Zechariah is itself the subject of fulfillment as it will be fulfilled (πληρωθήσονται) in God's plan. Luke understands God to have a sovereignly orchestrated plan that encompasses even the timing of Zechariah's renewed ability to speak. The emotion of joy is integral to God's plan within the Lukan corpus. Such language of fulfillment and divine control over providence provides a broad and indirect foundation for Luke's intertextual framework.

The question we will now answer is: *how does the reversal theme in Luke 1:5-25 relate to the Isaianic hermeneutical key in Luke 3:4-6?* York states that with regard to 'God's classical action of raising the low and bringing down the lofty'...'Only the Magnificat expresses such a reversal pattern'.[55] But if the reversal pattern begins with the Magnificat (Lk 1:46-55), then Luke 1:5-25 remains isolated and totally detached from the larger rhetorical framework. Contrary to York's position, we have found that the inner texture of Luke 1:5-

---

[50] Pao, *Acts and the Isaianic New Exodus*, 39. Other studies confirm that the LXX is the ultimate source for quotations and allusions in the infancy narratives. See the conclusions of C.W. Jung, *The Original Language of the Lukan Infancy Narrative* (JSNTSup 267; London: T&T Clark, 2004), 210.

[51] Pao, *Acts and the Isaianic New Exodus*, 39.

[52] For Pao, a focus on the differences between Luke and his Markan source 'fails to appreciate the dynamic role the Isaianic text plays in providing meaning and coherence for the Lukan narrative'. Pao, *Acts and the Isaianic New Exodus*, 39.

[53] Pao, *Acts and the Isaianic New Exodus*, 40.

[54] Pao, *Acts and the Isaianic New Exodus*, 40. Loveday Alexander suggests that Luke's use of the word πληροφορέω in Lk 1:1 encourages 'rereading [the text] backwards' in 'Formal Elements and Genre' in *Jesus and the Heritage of Israel: Luke's Narrative Claim upon Israel's Legacy* (ed. D. Moessner; Harrisburg: Trinity Press International, 1999), 26.

[55] York, *The Last Shall Be First*, 44.

25 also reveals a reversal pattern wherein the barren becomes fruitful. Arguably, this is even a double or bi-polar reversal pattern wherein the fruitful become barren by means of the lofty (unbelieving) speech of Zechariah becoming silence. Ultimately, Zechariah joins Elizabeth and so becomes part of a reversal from lowliness and barrenness to fruitfulness. Zechariah is pivotal for this double reversal pattern.[56]

There are three competing interpretations of the intertextual threads running through the reversal of Zechariah and Elizabeth. First, the primary intertextual source for Luke 1:5-25 is Elkanah and Hannah's pregnancy narrative from 1 Samuel 1.[57] However, this relationship between Luke and 1 Samuel is unlikely due to the fact that the term 'barren' is not present at all in 1 Samuel, even if the pious motif is.[58]

The second position argues that the thematic and textual parallels in Luke's text correspond to the story of Jacob in Genesis. This position is highly speculative and requires that Luke's gospel originated as a series of homilies that parallel the Palestinian triennial lectionary.[59]

The third position argues that Luke is using the long Scriptural tradition of reversal from barrenness to birth. For example, there may be a connection between John the Baptist's parents and Isaac's parents (Abraham and Sarah) in Genesis. John the Baptist's parents may also reflect Samson's parents in Judges 13.[60] This view could encompass those who highlight specific Old Testament birth narratives such as Jacob and Esau. [61] Kenneth Litwak summarizes thus: 'Luke is building his account with multiple annunciation stories in mind, though the annunciation to Zechariah probably owes more to the annunciation to Abraham than any other text'.[62] In this view, both Lukan annunciations are based upon the model of the great annunciations in Genesis 15-18, 1 Samuel 1,

---

[56] The case for a reversal pattern derived from Isaiah is strengthened by De Long's argument that Zechariah's 'transformation' (reversal) was a healing of his dumbness and his deafness that reflects Israel's restoration in Isa 35:5-6 (*Surprised by God*, 176-77). The argument that Zechariah was deaf is rather weak (see Kuhn, *Heart of Biblical Narrative*, 100). However, if De Long's argument about the intertextual relationship between Zechariah's healing and Isaiah 35 stands, it serves to strengthen the argument that Luke is using intertextual relationships with Isaiah to provide a lens for interpretation as well as promise-fulfillment.

[57] Brown, *Birth of the Messiah*, 268-69.

[58] Perhaps Litwak could be criticized for equating the word 'barren' with the concept so that the concept is only present where that word is (*Echoes of Scripture in Luke-Acts*, 76 n34).

[59] C.T. Ruddick, Jr. 'Birth Narratives in Genesis and Luke' in *The Composition of Luke's Gospel: Selected Studies from Novum Testamentum* (ed. D.E. Orton; Leiden: Brill, 1999), 14.

[60] Litwak, *Echoes of Scripture in Luke-Acts*, 76.

[61] De Long, *Surprised by God*, 145.

[62] Litwak, *Echoes of Scripture in Luke-Acts*, 76.

and Judges 13.[63] We may summarize thus: because Luke often draws from multiple intertextual sources, the question becomes which source is dominant or strongest.

Most commentators do not take the explicit reference to Isaiah 40:3-5 in Luke 3:4-6 as providing any clue to the intertextual dynamics at work. The benefit of Pao's approach is that he is relying upon a direct and explicit quotation (from Isaiah). Furthermore, the presence of the joy theme in both Isaiah 40-55 and Luke 1:5-25 bolsters the idea that Luke began his Gospel with Isaianic themes and only clearly articulated his hermeneutical key passage in Luke 3:4-6.

Returning to the New Exodus intertextual framework established by the appropriation of Isaiah 40:3-5 in Luke 3:4-6, I will demonstrate that the prologue establishes the theme of reversal from barrenness to birth based on Isaiah 40-55.[64] While there is a plethora of Old Testament texts that could serve as the basis for the echoes of joy resulting from the reversal of barrenness, Isaiah provides the best. Isaiah 40-55 provides us with a foregrounded source of intertextual allusions for the Lukan birth narratives because birth is connected to each of the four themes of the New Exodus.[65] The argumentation is similar to that of Litwak who does not argue that a specific text is in view in the intertexture of Luke 1:5-25. Rather there is an accumulation of allusions and echoes that have a series of texts in the foreground and background.[66]

The first relationship is between the concept of birth and the restoration of Israel. The restoration of Israel in Isaiah 49:14-16 (LXX) is described in terms of birth. Isaiah's role here is a statement on YHWH's behalf as a response to the charge that the Lord has forgotten Israel as represented by Zion.

> But Sion said, "The Lord has forsaken me; the Lord has forgotten me." Will a mother forget her child so as not to have mercy on the descendants of her womb? But even if a woman should forget these, yet I will not forget you, said the Lord. See, I have painted your walls on my hands, and you are continually before me. (LXX Isaiah 49:14-16).[67]

The restoration of Israel is nothing less than a total reversal of her

---

[63] J.A. Sanders, 'Isaiah in Luke' in *Luke and Scripture: The Function of Sacred Tradition in Luke-Acts* (Minneapolis: Fortress Press, 1993), 17.

[64] Pao, *Acts and the Isaianic New Exodus*, 13.

[65] Mallen finds large areas of similarity between the plots of Isaiah 40-55 and Luke's Gospel outside of the infancy narratives (*Reading and Transformation of Isaiah*, 124).

[66] The references to the LXX do not entail an argument for one LXX text. Following Moyise and Menken, we may note that 'Luke normally quotes a text in its Greek form more or less according to what we have in our printed editions of the LXX'. See S. Moyise and M.J.J. Menken, *Isaiah in the New Testament* (London: T&T Clark, 2005), 82 n12.

[67] *NETS*, Book of Esaias, 862-63.

circumstances. Prisoners will be free (Isa 49:9). Those who are in darkness will come into the light (Isa 49:9). Bare and desolate lands will be pastures (Isa 49:10). The way or path will be established as God will make 'all my mountains a road' (Isa 49:11). The appropriate response to God's reversal of Israel's fortune should be joy and singing (Isa 49:13).[68] Instead, Israel rejects God's restoration and claims: 'But Sion said, "The Lord has forsaken me, and the Lord has forgotten me' (Isa 49:14 LXX).

The response by YHWH to this charge against him by the people of Israel is to re-phrase his restoration programme in terms of a mother and her new-born. Thus, YHWH becomes like a mother and Israel like his (her) child. By way of metaphor, YHWH is established as Israel's progenitor or parent and wayward Israel is established as the child. In order to establish that God's love is greater than a mother's love, there is a sense in which God's actions are like those of a mother.[69] Such a background becomes important for a clearer picture of the restoration of Israel and the reversal from barrenness to birth in the new age in LXX Isaiah 54:1:

> Rejoice, O barren one who does not bear; break forth, and shout, you who are not in labor! Because more are the children of the desolate woman than of her that has a husband, for the Lord has spoken.[70]

In this passage, YHWH is both creator and husband (Isa 54:5). YHWH calls Israel to himself and reverses her fortunes as he moves in mercy and love after deserting her for a 'brief moment' (Isa 54:7). The combination of the song of joy and the reversal from barrenness to birth makes this a stronger possibility for the source of intertextual echo than Litwak's suggestion of Judges 13.

The second connection of note is between birth and anti-idol polemic. Birth is connected to anti-idol polemic in Isaiah 46:3-5 as YHWH establishes himself as the progenitor of the faithful remnant of Israel. The fact that YHWH carried Israel along from the womb and even before your birth is the reason why they should recognize that their idols are meaningless.

> Hear me, O house of Iakob and everyone who is left of Israel, you who are being carried from the womb and trained from the time you were a child. Until you old age, I am, and until you grow old, I am; I bear with you; I have made, and I will

---

[68] In the LXX and MT the Lord is the speaker in Isa 49:8-12 whereas the speaker inviting rejoicing in Isa 49:13 is unidentified. E.R. Ekblad, *Isaiah's Servant Poems According to the Septuagint: An Exegetical and Theological Study* (Louvain: Peeters, 1999), 127.

[69] *Contra* Oswalt, *The Book of Isaiah: Chapters 40-66*, 305 n71.

[70] *NETS*, Book of Esaias, 866. For a note on the vocabulary for joy in Isa 54:1and corresponding passages in the MT see H.G.M. Williamson, *The Book Called Isaiah: Deutero-Isaiah's Role in Composition and Redaction* (Oxford: Oxford University Press, 1994), 73.

set free; I will take up and save you. To who have you likened me? See, act with cunning, you who are going astray![71] (LXX Isaiah 46:3-5)

For Isaiah, YHWH is the one who makes and bears, carries and saves (Isa 46:4). This stands in contrast with idols that cannot move, carry, stand, or save. This statement brings together his creative power and his function as the progenitor (mother-figure) who gives birth to Israel. The end of this is salvation that excludes all idols or competitors for God's likeness.

The third relationship of note is between birth and the power of the word of God. In the same pericope as above in Isaiah 46 we find a connection between birth and the power of the word of God. The effectual power of the word of God is clear in LXX Isaiah 46:10-11 after God announces that 'I am God...'

...declaring the last things first, before they happen, and at once they came to pass, and I said, "My whole plan shall stand, and I will do all the things I have planned," calling a bird from the east and from a far country those concerning whom I have planned. I have spoken and brought it; I have created and made it.[72]

The word of God is present throughout as God 'declares', 'says', gives 'counsel', 'calls', and 'speaks'. The power of the word of God is integral and inseparable from YHWH's anti-idol polemic. Israel who has been borne by God must remember that God has 'spoken' (Isa 46:11) and this speech is entirely effectual to accomplish his purpose. The key idea presented here is that YHWH has carried the faithful remnant in his own womb (similar imagery appears in Isa 42:14). He has accomplished this and all of his other mighty deeds through his own word.

The fourth relationship of note is between birth and the universal concern for the nations. Birth is connected to a universal concern for the nations in Isaiah 49:19-23. This universal concern for the nations is integral to the vision of the restoration of Israel. The nations play a role in the reversal from the barrenness of Israel (Isa 49:21) to her status as one who finds children all around her. This imagery is prominent in LXX Isaiah 49:22-23:

Thus says the Lord: Look, I am lifting up my hand to the nations, and I will lift my signal to the islands, and they shall bring your sons in their bosom, and your daughters shall they lift on their shoulders. And kings shall be your foster fathers, and the women who rule, your nurses.[73]

This imagery of the nations is one of subjection to Israel (Isa 49:23b). The 'peoples' pay homage and admit subservience as well as act as foster parents for the people of God. The role of the nations or peoples is not entirely

---

[71] *NETS*, Book of Esaias, 860.
[72] *NETS*, Book of Esaias, 860.
[73] *NETS*, Book of Esaias, 863.

negative. The children are genuinely borne by Israel but they are raised by the peoples. God will cause the peoples to release or bring the children of Israel back from exile. The imagery of raising children (infants) provides for the humiliation and honour of the 'peoples'. The positive dimension of this text is stated by Rikki Watts: 'Jerusalem's restoration is not an end in itself. It will serve to spread the knowledge of YHWH'.[74]

There is continuity between the way Luke and Isaiah present their rhetoric of bi-polar reversal. In Isaiah, YHWH is the progenitor of Israel who establishes life in the womb. Whereas the Chaldeans who said 'I shall not sit as a widow or know the loss of children' (Isa 47:8): 'These two things shall come to you in a moment, in one day; the loss of children and widowhood shall come upon you in full measure, in spite of your many sorceries and the great power of your enchantments' (Isa 47:9). A bi-polar reversal is created: Israel who was barren becomes fruitful and the Chaldeans who were fruitful become barren. In sum, Isaiah 40-55 provides us with the best primary source that Luke used to evoke the intertextual allusion to birth and reversal from barrenness.

In sum, we can conclude that birth or the 'mother-son' theme is associated with each aspect of the New Exodus and YHWH is repeatedly portrayed as the cause of Israel's own birth or ability to give birth.[75] Most acknowledge that some Old Testament texts lie behind the reversal of Zechariah and Elizabeth but it is not clear which ones. This is due to the indirect and informal nature of echoes behind it. As an 'echo' the intertextual relationship between Luke 1:5-25 and the barrenness to birth theme in Isaiah 40-55 is complex and is best understood by the multi-dimensional socio-rhetorical method.[76] The force of the argument rests on two points. First, we can argue that Isaiah's New Exodus provides the foregrounded intertextual relationship without denying that other texts also lie in the background. Second, the presence of joy and the reversal of barrenness to birth in conjunction with the Isaianic New Exodus is strong evidence for intertextual echoes.

Joy and Sacred Texture

The sacred texture of the text of Luke 1:5-25 consists of the vertical dimensions that connect human life and the divine. In particular, we find that joy is related to the nature of God who brings about the reversals of the New Age. In the reversal of Zechariah and Elizabeth, the emotion of joy is built upon the intimate presence of God. The birth narrative establishes a reversal of fortune for Elizabeth and Zechariah as well as Israel. The movement from barrenness to pregnancy creates a sense of expectation. This reversal will bring about

---

[74] Watts, *Isaiah 34-66*, 748.

[75] For comments on the 'mother-sons' theme see Motyer, *Prophecy of Isaiah*, 396.

[76] D.L. Stamps, 'The Use of the Old Testament in the New Testament as a Rhetorical Device: A Methodological Proposal', in *Hearing the Old Testament in the New Testament* (ed. S. Porter; Grand Rapids: Eerdmans, 2006), 19.

rejoicing for both. What is significant about this poetic 'mini-drama' about the priest Zechariah is that the scene is filled with joy as well as the tension of discipline and the austere trappings of temple sacrifice. The narrative of the reversal of Zechariah communicates two things about the nature of the God of Israel. First, the God who can and will bring about joyful reversal is holy. Second, God cannot be forced into the constraints of traditional assumptions.

Luke wants to persuade the reader of what the God of Israel has done in Jesus. The nature of this God is challenging and the proper response may not be automatic. The narrative of Luke 1:5-25 portrays a God who is intimately associated with rejoicing as well as holiness. This close association of joy and God persists in spite of the use of angelic intermediaries. God never speaks directly in Luke 1:5-25, and yet the text indicates that the speech of his angelic intermediaries should be heard and responded to as though it were from God himself. The messages that the angel Gabriel delivers to Zechariah and Mary have strong elements of continuity.[77] Among the elements of continuity is the command not to fear, the promise of a child, the name the child is to be given and an explanation of what God will do with the child.

Gabriel to Zechariah		Gabriel to Mary	
μὴ φοβοῦ …	(Lk 1:13)	μὴ φοβοῦ …	(Lk 1:30)
γεννήσει υἱόν σοι …	(Lk 1:13)	τέξῃ υἱὸν …	(Lk 1:31)
καὶ καλέσεις …	(Lk 1:13)	καὶ καλέσεις …	(Lk 1:31)
ἔσται γὰρ …	(Lk 1:15)	οὗτος ἔσται …	(Lk 1:32)

The continuity between the two interactions is substantial but their 'rhetorical effect' lies in their discontinuity:[78]

> And Zechariah said to the angel, "How shall I know this? For I am an old man, and my wife is advanced in years". (Luke 1:18)

> And Mary said to the angel, "How will this be, since I am a virgin?" (Luke 1:34)

As the angel approaches Zechariah in the temple, the theme of piety and holiness has already been established. Both Zechariah and Elizabeth are described thus (Lk 1:6): 'And they were both righteous before God, walking blamelessly in all the commandments and statutes of the Lord'. Like the joy theme, the clustering of vocabulary establishes a theme of piety and

---

[77] Borgman, *The Way According to Luke*, 20.
[78] Borgman, *The Way According to Luke*, 21.

righteousness. The message does not come in the midst of a festival or celebration. Rather, the angel comes to Zechariah in the temple at an unexpected time that appears to be rather normal. Once Zechariah moves into the temple, the change of space creates a new realm of 'politics' and his unity with Elizabeth falls to the background.[79] Although Zechariah is 'righteous', his answer lacks the faith that God expects.

The reversal lies in the fact that the priest speaks in unbelief while the commoner speaks in faith. The pious priest Zechariah speaks in a way that reflects doubt and seeks a sign or proof (how will I know?) whereas Mary the commoner speaks in a way that reflects faith and seeks explanation (how can this be?).[80] The disciplining of Zechariah by shutting his mouth (Lk 1:20) reaffirms the piety motif.

The rhetorical power of the parallelism, with its continuity and discontinuity brings the reader into the drama but also persuades the reader about the nature of God: God's actions must not be forced into traditional cultic categories. Joy will be established in the home of Zechariah as well as in Israel, in spite of his moment of impiety. The emotion of joy stands in contrast to the austerity of the temple and the shame of the discipline that Zechariah receives.

By promising joy and rejoicing for his home and Israel, the faithfulness of YHWH comes to the forefront of Luke's persuasive purposes. The faithlessness of people will not impact the faithfulness of God. What God can do for his people and for Israel is beyond their expectations. A proper response to God's actions of reversal will not automatically be righteous and the narrative hints at the fact that a righteous response will be difficult for those officials surrounding the cult of the temple. God is establishing his own new way.

Joy and Ideological Texture

The joy in the reversal scene of Zechariah and Elizabeth adds an illocutionary force or emotional energy to the persuasiveness of the text. Joy is ideological because Luke is seeking to change (reverse) the values of the reader according to his point of view.

The reader must come to view the lowly maiden Mary as more pious and honourable than the priest Zechariah.[81] This does not mean we can go behind the text and achieve a psychological portrait of Luke as a writer. Rather it means Luke's intentions as located in the text are the basis for our analysis of his ideology. If ideology in the text is Luke's conscious 'enactment' of 'presuppositions, dispositions, and values held in common with other people', it

---

[79] V.K. Robbins, 'Bodies and Politics in Luke 1-2 and Sirach 44-50: Men, Women, and Boys', *Scriptura* 90 (2005), 829.

[80] Borgman, *The Way According to Luke*, 22.

[81] This is another instance of a bi-polar reversal in which A becomes B and B becomes A. In the case of Mary and Zechariah, the higher becomes lower and the lower becomes higher.

is possible to understand this enactment as persuasion.[82] As Luke seeks to persuade the reader that God has inaugurated a new age, his rhetoric is emotional or based on *pathos*. In the reversal narrative of Luke 1:5-25, joy is used to establish the reversal as God inaugurates the new age through the pregnancy of Elizabeth in anticipation of John the Baptist.

To speak of the pathos or emotional texture of the reversal narrative of Luke 1:5-25 allows us to locate the emotion of joy on the personal and corporate level. Returning to our inner textual analysis above, this joy is for the individual: birth is proclaimed in the third person singular future tense as the basis for Zechariah's (and Elizabeth's) joy (Lk 1:14a): 'and you will have joy and gladness'. Corporately, joy is for the 'many' who will rejoice in the future tense in Luke 1:14b: 'and many will rejoice at his birth'. To speak of ideology simply places rhetoric in the context of a community. The persuasiveness of the text is not a matter for psychology that focuses on the individual alone.

The characters in the narrative take on ideological qualities because of their portrayal as pious, yet lowly.[83] The households of 'ordinary' people become the instruments for YHWH's renewal of Israel.[84] The characters become models to imitate. Elizabeth is a model for all of Israel. The question for Israel in the narrative of Elizabeth is: 'How will 'the People' respond to the divine initiative to redeem God's people, to remove their shame in the face of the nations?'[85] Now we can connect Elizabeth's role with her emotion. The text itself demands an exegetical methodology that allows the text to address the values of the individual and the corporate whole of God's people. An ideological analysis of joy in the rhetoric of reversal must begin with the text.

Ideological texture can be manifest in different ways. Our concern in Luke 1:5-25 is to develop an exegetical and ideological analysis that is driven by the text itself. In this particular pericope, it is the juxtaposition of the young maiden (Mary) and the priest (Zechariah) and the reversal of expectation that is dominant. This is best described as a reversal that operates by challenging an ideology of power. Luke challenges the values of the reader by challenging the assumptions of the community of Israel. This communal assumption is supported textually by the way that Luke connects piety with the Temple service in Luke 1:5-6.[86] Specifically, the power and piety assumed to be present in the priest in the temple is lost. Zechariah is not even able to speak so as to perform any benediction or blessing.[87] It is through the lips of the weak and

---

[82] Robbins, *Exploring the Texture of Texts*, 95.

[83] De Long takes notice of these qualities (pious and lowly) in the infancy narratives but does not pursue how the experiences of divine visitation resulting in reversal would have sociological implications (*Surprised by God*, 178).

[84] Robbins, 'Bodies and Politics in Luke 1-2 and Sirach 44-50', 831.

[85] J.B. Green, *The Gospel of Luke* (Grand Rapids: Eerdmans, 1997), 81.

[86] Nolland, *Luke 1:1-9:20*, 23.

[87] Borgman, *The Way According to Luke*, 23.

lowly that the message of fulfillment comes. YHWH's plan for the new age is characterized by fruitfulness in the form of children (and a specific Son). The narrative of reversal plays on the level of the assumption of the reader about who is powerful and pious. These assumptions are then overturned with new values.

Central to understanding the role of the emotion of joy in the reversal of Zechariah and Elizabeth in Luke 1:5-25 is the fact that the reversal from barrenness to child-bearing intertwines both the individual and Israel. The intertexture of the pericope evokes the mother-sons theme from Isaiah 40-55 as noted above. We must also understand how the ideological texture is related to the inner texture of Luke 1:5-25. Elizabeth's barrenness is identical to Israel's barrenness and her pregnancy is identical to Israel's anticipation of children. This reversal inaugurates the new age and Luke wants to persuade the reader by means of emotion, specifically joy and rejoicing.

Conclusion

The narrative of the reversal of Zechariah and Elizabeth is framed by the rhetorical amplification of joy for the purpose of persuasion. The joyful messages of angelic intermediaries contain joyful messages from YHWH himself. God's emotions frame how humans should respond to the New Exodus that provides a redemption more miraculous than the first exodus. Joy is the appropriate emotional response to the call of 'salvation'.[88] But why is Luke so interested in including this in his narrative? The answer is that joy provides an emotional force to Luke's goal of persuading the reader about the salvation that YHWH has provided in visiting his people in Jesus.

Our examination of the texture of Luke 1:5-25 found that a co-textual reading supports Isaiah as a foregrounded (but not exclusive) source of Old Testament echoes. This conclusion locates Luke 1:5-25 within the larger Lukan framework of Isaiah 40-55. For those familiar with the Old Testament, the language of joy evokes God's promises for a new age that reverses the condition of the barren, the exiled, and the lowly – all for the benefit of Israel and even the Gentiles. The presence of joy works together with God's acts. It provides objective evidence that God's plan to save and re-establish Israel has begun.

In a Hellenistic milieu, this language of emotion or pathos would have served to persuade. This resonates with the pattern of using pathos or emotion in rhetoric as reflected by Cicero's student Quintilian: I am therefore all the more surprised at those who hold that there should be no appeal to the emotions in the narration. But why, when I am instructing the judge, should I refuse to move him as well?[89] The language of joy is persuasive as it promotes Luke's

---

[88] Navone, *Themes of St. Luke*, 73.

[89] Quintilian, *Institutes* 4.2.111, cited in Kuhn, *Heart of Biblical Narrative*, 6-7.

agenda to convince the reader that the new age has arrived. The emotion of joy operates on the level of the individual as well as on the corporate or national level for Israel. What once was barren is now fruitful.

CHAPTER 3

Joy at the Inauguration of the New Age: Luke 1-2

This is the second chapter that examines the introductory framing narratives of Luke 1-2. It examines three textual units where joy and reversal intersect: (1) the infancy narratives in Luke 1:26-56, (2) the birth of John the Baptist in Luke 1:57-66, and (3) the joyful shepherds in Luke 2:1-21.

Introduction

To recap the exegesis of the last chapter: we observed how the emotion of joy integrates into the task of persuasion. Objectively, joy is an important signal of YHWH's actions that also appeals to the emotion of reader. The reversal theme is so tightly interwoven into the worldview of the text that it is almost impossible to isolate particular reversals apart from the whole. Both Israel and the Gentiles are the recipients of the joyous new age that has turned the world upside down.

This chapter continues the examination of joy and reversal at the inauguration of the new age. YHWH has visited his people and this has inaugurated a new stage in the history of redemption. In these three textual units, the joy theme is used to empower the reversals that take place in accordance with the fulfillment of YHWH's promises. We will examine four different threads in the tapestry of Luke's Gospel: the inner texture, the intertexture, the sacred texture, and the ideological texture. All four threads lead to the conclusion that the emotion of joy is integral to Luke's rhetoric of reversal.

The Reversal of Mary and Birth of John: Joy in Luke 1:26-66

In the series of vignettes in Luke 1:26-66, the emotion of joy strengthens the rhetoric of reversal in order to persuade the reader that a new era is dawning. Although the pregnancy narratives fall after the preface, they frame the narrative(s) that follow by establishing connections and expectations. Joy persuasively reinforces Luke's implicit argument that the fulfillment of promises to Israel provides evidence of a reversal for Israel.[1] Although there is

---

[1] In the Magnificat, 'Mary rejoices in God her Saviour because of his mercy both to herself personally and to the nation of Israel'. Morrice, *We Joy in God*, 16.

an evident change in style between the prologue of Luke 1:1-4 and the rest of the gospel, this shift should not result in the conclusion that Luke has left rhetoric behind.[2] The shift between the prologue and the following birth narratives pulls the reader into the story.[3] These initial narratives frame the whole and provide the basis for a narratival rhetoric that seeks to persuade the reader about the joyful nature of the dawning new age.

The series of vignettes in Luke 1:26-66 portray a reversal of fortunes that correspond with the nature of the new age. John York states, 'The Magnificat creates an expectation that divine action reverses opposite human conditions, and the beatitudes and woes, the Rich Man and Lazarus, the Pharisee and the Publican, and other antithetic aphorisms echo the expectation'.[4] A new age has dawned in which Elizabeth and Mary's 'reversal of fortune' reflects a high point.[5] Following York's comments on reversal, I will demonstrate that this reversal from barrenness to pregnancy and lowliness to exaltation is empowered by the emotion of joy.

Joy and Inner Texture

In this section we will demonstrate that the inner texture of Luke 1:26-66 uses contrast and repetition to draw attention to the emotion of joy. The textual unit of Luke 1:26-66 is admittedly artificial. Nevertheless, this textual unit will be helpful for the pragmatic needs of exegesis. Specifically, there are two reasons for focusing here. First, the birth or pregnancy narratives of Mary and Elizabeth are woven together and constitute major reversals from barrenness to pregnancy.[6] Second, the reversal scene of Elizabeth and Zechariah in Luke 1:5-25 builds on the preface and frames the narratives that follow by establishing anticipation. The early narratives of Luke's Gospel are 'preparatory' and 'function to announce the interrelated themes of the story to follow'.[7]

Inner texture deals with the dimensions of the text that relate to linguistic patterns such as repetition, amplification, structural elements, and keywords (*Leitwörter*). An analysis of the inner texture of Luke 1:26-66 provides evidence that joy functions rhetorically: persuading the reader of the presence of the dawning New Age.

A cursory examination of Luke 1:26-38 will demonstrate that the joy theme is absent. The absence of joy in the reversal of Mary is striking because joy was so conspicuous in the pregnancy narrative of Elizabeth. When the angel's

---

[2] Dawsey, *Lukan Voice*, 19.

[3] Dawsey, *Lukan Voice*, 20.

[4] York, *The Last Shall Be First*, 93.

[5] C.T. Ruddick, Jr. 'Birth Narratives in Genesis and Luke' in *The Composition of Luke's Gospel: Selected Studies from Novum Testamentum* (ed. D.E. Orton; Leiden: Brill, 1999), 18.

[6] 'The one account recalls and interprets the other'. Green, *Gospel of Luke*, 83.

[7] Borgman, *The Way According to Luke*, 27.

proclamation to Zechariah in Luke 1:13-17 is placed parallel to the proclamation to Mary in Luke 1:30-33 there are important elements of continuity and discontinuity that have ramifications for the whole text(ure). Dawsey places the proclamation to Zechariah next to the proclamation to Mary and notes that when it comes to the announcement of joy, 'Clearly Mary is excluded'.[8]

This exclusion is noteworthy and the text of Luke 1:26-38 is arguably emotionless apart from the emotion of fear. Mary responds to the blessing announcement in Luke 1:28 with fear: 'Greetings, O favored one, the Lord is with you'.[9] Even the angel's opening address to Mary in Luke 1:28 (χαῖρε) could be understood as a reference to joy instead of merely a greeting equivalent to 'hello'.[10] The difficulty with this position is that it makes Mary's response less than pious and her fear a direct rejection of the angel's command to rejoice. Regardless, the *emphasis* of Luke 1:26-38 is *not* on Mary's immediate joyful response to the visitation of the angel.

But why does joy appear in the Magnificat and not in the proclamation text to Mary? The answer to the problem of the absence of joy unfolds as we examine the visitation of Mary to Elizabeth's house in Luke 1:39-45.[11] This text bridges the proclamation text (Lk 1:26-38) with the Magnificat (Lk 1:46-56). In this text, the response of the baby (John the Baptist) in Elizabeth's womb to Mary's greeting is to 'leapt for joy' (Lk 1:44).[12] This could be (albeit woodenly) translated as: the baby in my womb '*joyfully jumped in extreme happiness*'. Both the verb and the noun communicate the emotion of joy.

The use of blessing language in Luke 1:42 is abundant but the emotion of joy and the object of the emotion of joy clarify the blessing. The object of the emotion of joy is the baby in the womb of Mary, as is clear in Luke 1:42: 'Blessed are you among women and blessed is the fruit of your womb!'. It is the presence of the baby in Mary's womb that is the cause of joy.

The separation of the emotions of fear and joy achieves a sense of discontinuity and development of the earlier reversal of Zechariah and Elizabeth. The theme of piety is established by Mary's fear in similar fashion to the description of the piety of Zechariah and Elizabeth. The theme of joy is

---

[8] Dawsey, *Lukan Voice*, 136.

[9] In Lk 1:29, the fearful thoughts or reasoning of Mary are tied together by the homonym-like juxtaposition of διεταράχθη καὶ διελογίζετο. This likely reflects Luke's poetic style, the purpose of which summarizes speech and action. Borgman, *The Way According to Luke*, 27 n2; S. Farris, *The Hymns of Luke's Infancy Narratives: Their Origin, Meaning, and Significance* (JSNTSup 9; Sheffield: JSOT Press, 1985), 151.

[10] De Long, *Surprised by God*, 139-141.

[11] De Long's case for viewing joy as present in the angelic greeting to Mary in Lk 1:28 hinges upon one word. Perhaps there is a *tension* between joy and fear. Luke's interest is on Mary's obedience, piety, and faithfulness to the 'word' of the Lord as presented through the angel (Lk 1:38). See De Long, *Surprised by God*, 143.

[12] The Greek of Luke 1:44 reads: ἐσκίρτησεν ἐν ἀγαλλιάσει.

established by Elizabeth's blessing upon the fruit of Mary's womb. The separation of the two emotions of fear and joy allows each emotion to achieve its own purpose.

Luke clearly chose to highlight the vocabulary of joy. The inner texture of Luke 1:26-66 uses contrast and repetition to draw attention to the emotion of joy. Robert Tannehill observes: 'Repetition has a persuasive effect. The events, characters, or assertions seem 'right' because they fit what is already known'.[13] In Luke 1:26-66 the emotion of joy as a response to the inauguration of the New Age seems 'right'. Joy embodies what God has done for Elizabeth, Mary, and Israel. The effect of this repetition is rhetorical and creates an abundance of emotion. Although Mary preserves her piety, there is no other emotion contending for attention in the visitation scene and the Magnificat. Here we have simply demonstrated that the inner texture of Luke 1:26-66 uses contrast to highlight the emotion of joy. Next, we will examine the emotion of joy in light of intertextuality or intertexture.

Joy and Intertexture

The central point I want to demonstrate in this section is: *Old Testament sources such as Isaiah provide coherence and meaning to the joyful reversals of the pregnancy/birth narratives of John and Jesus.* Our study of the relationship between the joy theme and intertextuality in Luke 1:26-66 begins with David Pao's argument that Luke 3:4-6 provides a hermeneutical key for Luke. We will examine the intertextual threads in Luke 1:26-66 to demonstrate that that the joy theme has its origins in Old Testament literature. This is the joy that plays a role in persuading the reader that God has inaugurated a new age. We will see that the joy theme draws from a variety of Old Testament texts, some of which come to the foreground. The foregrounded use of Isaianic themes provides meaning and coherence to the pregnancy narratives.

The very promise to Mary that ensures her reversal (from lowliness to honour) also provides details about the coming Davidic reign in Luke 1:32: 'the Lord God will give to him the throne of his father David'. Pao argues:

> These references to David's throne recall 'the statement in Isaiah 9 in which the imagery of the 'throne of David' is used to describe the reign of the eschatological figure during the restoration of Israel: 'His authority shall grow continually, and there shall be endless peace for the throne of David and his kingdom' (μεγάλη ἡ ἀρχὴ αὐτοῦ, καὶ τῆς εἰρήνης αὐτοῦ οὐκ ἔστιν ὅριον ἐπὶ τὸν θρόνον Δαυιδ καὶ τὴν βασιλείαν αὐτοῦ Isa 9:6[7]).[14]

By establishing an intertextual relationship between Luke 1:32 and LXX Isaiah 9:6, Pao provides evidence that there is a relationship between Jesus and David

---

[13] Tannehill, *Shape of Luke's Story*, 217.
[14] Pao, *Acts and the Isaianic New Exodus*, 136.

vis-à-vis the Davidic kingdom and the restoration of Israel.[15] What is important
to note in this study is that this intertextual relationship also provides a key to
understanding the nature of the joy theme in Luke 1:26-66.

The text of Isaiah 9:2-7 arguably begins with a reversal from darkness to
light (especially v.2). After the reversal is encapsulated, it is immediately
depicted in terms of the emotion of joy and rejoicing in LXX Isaiah 9:2:

> Most of the people, whom you have brought back in your *joy*, will also *rejoice*
> before you like those who *rejoice* at the harvest and in the same way as those who
> divide plunder (LXX Isaiah 9:2).[16]

The vocabulary for joy is based on the repetition of εὐφροσύνη and εὐφραίνω.
This passage (LXX Isa 9:2) is followed by three clauses that explain the
reversal and the reason for the joy: v.3) διότι ... v.4) ὅτι ... v.5) ὅτι παιδίον
ἐγεννήθη ἡμῖν, υἱὸς καὶ ἐδόθη ἡμῖν. In Isaiah 9, both the reversal from darkness
to light and the emotional rejoicing are rooted in the event of a son being given
by God.

This is significant because the first public words of Jesus in Luke 4 – a poem
borrowed from Isaiah – contain the 'kernel of all that is to follow in the story'.[17]
The assertion that the quotation of Isaiah provides a hermeneutical key or
'kernel' for the whole narrative is similar to this study's contention that the
emotion of joy is part of Luke's programme for persuading the reader about the
dawning new age as depicted in the Isaianic New Exodus. While this study is in
agreement that Jesus' quotation of Isaiah is programmatic, the quotation of
Isaiah by Jesus in Luke 4:18-19 is part of a trajectory begun much earlier. In
other words, the Isaianic New Exodus began with the pregnancy reversal
narrative of Elizabeth and Zechariah in Luke 1:5-25.

To recap, Pao argues that Luke 3:4-6 is paradigmatic for the Lukan corpus
and provides an Isaianic intertextual framework or hermeneutical key for all
that *follows it*.[18] The Isaianic intertextual thread is important for the whole of
Luke, including the preface and pregnancy narratives. Others agree that Isaiah
is programmatic in some manner. The question is how pervasive and backward
looking this is. We may summarize the position this way: *Old Testament
sources provide coherence and meaning to the joyful reversals of the
pregnancy/birth narratives of John and Jesus.* In order to demonstrate that an

---

[15] Pao, *Acts and the Isaianic New Exodus*, 136. For a note on the 'conglomeration' of
OT texts behind Lk 1:32-33 see D.W. Pao and E.J. Schnabel, *CNTUOT* (eds. G.K. Beal
and D.A. Carson; Grand Rapids: Baker, 2007), 260. Köstenberger concurs: 'The angel's
announcement to Mary focuses on the Davidic promise'. A. Köstenberger, 'Hearing the
Old Testament in the New: A Response', in *Hearing the Old Testament in the New* (ed.
S.E. Porter; Grand Rapids: Eerdmans, 2006), 274.

[16] *NETS*, Book of Esaias, 831.

[17] Borgman, *The Way According to Luke*, 26.

[18] Pao, *Acts and the Isaianic New Exodus*, 39.

Isaianic intertextual framework provides meaning for the emotional reversals from barrenness to birth, we will examine the intertexture of the reversals of Elizabeth and Mary.

Elizabeth's speech provides foreshadowing of John the Baptist's future ministry that will be characterized by joy (ἀγαλλίασις in Lk 1:44, 58). In the birth of John the Baptist, Elizabeth's neighbours and relatives are described as rejoicing (συγχαίρω) with her (Lk 1:58). There may be a reference here to the fact that John was related to the house of David.[19] What is important to note in this study is that joy is the dominant emotion and is exclusive to the birth account. The joy of John in the visitation is focused on the presence of Jesus in Mary's womb. Elizabeth's statements reveal her identification as a member of Israel who was seeking the Lord (κύριος). Elizabeth states in Luke 1:43 that Mary is: 'the mother of my Lord'. There is joy on a small scale as it is related to the immediate family of Mary and Elizabeth. But Luke takes care to widen the emotional impact to the community of Israel who are seeking the Lord. John's life and birth is characterized by joy on the individual and corporate levels.

There are several Septuagintal sources that likely stand in the background of John's birth in Luke 1:39-45. One possible intertextual source for Litwak suggests that Elizabeth's greeting to Mary echoes Deborah's words regarding Jael in Judges 5.[20] A second possible source is the birth of Jacob and Esau in Genesis 25.[21] In this view, the movement of the unborn babe 'foreshadows the future lot of the child'.[22] A third possible source is the laughter ('Isaac' means 'he laughs') that Abraham showed when he was told of Sarah's forthcoming pregnancy.[23] In this third view, Mary and Elizabeth function more typologically and their experience of 'divine reversal' is an echo of 'every barren woman in scripture'.[24]

A fourth possible intertextual source is the reference to joy in the immediate co-text of Malachi 3:1 that is referenced in Zechariah's prophecy in Luke 1:76: 'for you will go before the Lord to prepare his ways'. Zechariah's prophecy

---

[19] Talbert, *Literary Patterns, Theological Themes and the Genre of Luke-Acts*, 104.

[20] Litwak, *Echoes of Scripture in Luke-Acts*, 104. The 'blessing' of Deborah in Judges 5 comes in the form of a song; cf. Judg 5:1. In contrast, Luke 1:39-45 is distinctive in that it is not a song and stands in contrast with the Magnificat to follow. In addition, the length and exhaustiveness of the song of Deborah stands in discontinuity with Elizabeth's short blessing and greeting.

[21] C.H. Talbert, *Literary Patterns, Theological Themes and the Genre of Luke-Acts* (SBLMS 20; Missoula: Scholars Press, 1974), 105. Marshall notes that even if the text of Genesis does not portray a literal awareness of this movement in the womb by Rebekah, this was a rabbinical interpretation in *The Gospel of Luke: A Commentary on the Greek Text*, 80.

[22] Talbert, *Literary Patterns, Theological Themes and the Genre of Luke-Acts*, 105.

[23] The word used in the LXX for Abraham's action of laughing is γελάω.

[24] De Long, *Surprised by God*, 170-71.

provides further development of John's ministry of preparation and confirms this reading of joy in the pericopes related to him. This is likely an echo of LXX Malachias (Malachi) 3:1a: 'Behold, I am sending my messenger, and he will oversee the way before me'.[25] It must be acknowledged that this vocabulary for the emotion of joy or delight in LXX Malachi 3:1 (θέλω) is different from that used in Luke 1:44 (ἀγαλλίασις) and Luke 1:58 (συγχαίρω). And Malachi 3:1 is likely an interpretation of Isaiah 40:3.[26] However, there is undoubtedly a conceptual continuity and Luke as a writer seems quite comfortable using various vocabularies for similar emotions.[27] The image of John as the joyful prophet surrounded by a joyful community likely draws on several intertextual sources. At the very least Isaiah plays a role in the trajectory.

The emotional experience of John the Baptist along with his family and community at the presence of Jesus can be best understood in light of texts from Isaiah and Malachi. These two sources work together because Malachi 3:1 is an interpretation of Isaiah 40:3.[28] John is the one who will prepare the way and Jesus is the 'messenger of the covenant in whom you delight'. The question about the nature of John's ministry is specifically posed in Luke 1:66: 'What then will this child be?' Here is evidence of the rhetorical task Luke has taken up in respect to John. The reader is drawn into the narrative and takes up the same task of answering this question even as those who saw God's hand acting in the hill country of Judea had to answer it (Lk 1:65). At this point, it is helpful to bridge this study from John's birth to the Magnificat.

The structure of Mary's Magnificat in Luke 1:46-56 follows a similar structure to the pericope in Isaiah 9. There are several elements of continuity between Isaiah 9 and the Magnificat. First, they both begin with an image of reversal. In the case of LXX Isaiah 9:2 there is imagery of movement from light to darkness. In Luke 1:48 Luke immediately uses the imagery of the lowly servant (δούλη) to create the imagery of Mary's reversal. Second, both Isaiah and Luke immediately move from reversal to the emotion of joy. In both texts, the primary emotional response to God's action of bringing about a reversal is joy. Whether it is promise or fulfillment, the emotion of joy is the primary way the event is marked, with a series of explanatory clauses following.

A fully orbed exegesis of the text must also take into account the strong intertextual relationship between the Magnificat and the song of Hannah in 1

---

[25] *NETS*, Malachias, 821. The Greek reads: ἰδοὺ ἐγὼ ἐξαποστέλλω τὸν ἄγγελόν μου, καὶ ἐπιβλέψεται ὁδὸν πρὸ προσώπου μου.

[26] Pao, *Acts and the Isaianic New Exodus*, 42.

[27] Further evidence for an intertextual relationship between this text and Mal 3:1 is the possibility of an association between the 'leaping' of John in the womb and the presence of God's salvation. Green, *The Gospel of Luke*, 95 n6.

[28] Pao, *Acts and the Isaianic New Exodus*, 42.

Samuel 2.[29] Mary's Magnificat bears strong resemblance to the song of Hannah (1 Samuel 2)'.[30] A cursory comparison between the introductory lines of the two songs of LXX 1 Samuel 2:1-10 (1 Samuel is entitled 1 Kings or 1 Reigns in the Septuagint) and Luke 1:46-55 reveals strong elements of continuity and influence, particularly the emotion of joy.

> And she said, "My heart was made firm in the Lord; my horn was exalted in my god; my mouth was made wide against enemies; I was glad in your deliverance".[31] (LXX 1 Samuel 2:1-10)

> And Mary said, "My soul magnifies the Lord, and my spirit rejoices in God my Savior, for he has looked on the humble estate of his servant". (Luke 1:46-47)

The following quote by James Sanders explains the significance of this parallelism: 'The new kingdom announced by God in the first century, to be fully understood, must be seen in light of the kingdom introduced by God through Samuel, culminating in David'.[32] This is a provocative statement because it points to a progressive trajectory in the Jewish Scriptures that culminates in a Davidic kingdom. The Davidic promise of a new kingdom and a new age is developed by building on antecedent theology and history. Isaiah 9 provides strong evidence that it lies within this trajectory. In other words, although there is continuity between Luke 1:46-55 and 1 Samuel 2:1-10, there is also continuity between Luke 1:46-55 and Isaiah 9:2-7 because Isaiah develops and builds on elements present in 1 Samuel 2:1-10.

Such a claim requires an examination of how Isaiah 9:2-7 lies on the same trajectory of the Davidic kingdom as 1 Samuel 2:1-10. One piece of evidence of the development being argued for is that Hannah's song does not refer to the Davidic king except by a reference to a king ($\beta\alpha\sigma\iota\lambda\epsilon\acute{u}\varsigma$) at the end of the song in LXX 1 Samuel 2:10: 'He will judge earth's ends and gives strength to our kings and will exalt the horn of his anointed'.[33] However, Isaiah's song is much more specific and evidences development of thought about the Davidic king:

---

[29] There may also be a connection between emotional liturgical language in Luke and LXX Habakkuk 3:18. See Pao and Schnabel, 'Luke', *CNTUOT*, 261.

[30] J.A. Sanders, 'Isaiah in Luke' in *Luke and Scripture: The Function of Sacred Tradition in Luke-Acts* (eds. C.A. Evans and J.A. Sanders; Minneapolis: Fortress, 1993), 17; G.A. Kennedy, *New Testament Interpretation Through Rhetorical-Criticism* (Chapel Hill: North Carolina Press, 1984), 108.

[31] *NETS*, 1 Reigns, 249.

[32] Sanders, 'Isaiah in Luke', 17. Contrast with Bock who cites 2 Samuel 7:9-16 as the primary OT parallel source. Bock, *Luke: 1:1-9:50*, 113.

[33] *NETS*, 1 Reigns, 250. The English LXX title for 1 Samuel is 1 Reigns.

His sovereignty is great, and his peace has no boundary upon the throne of David and his kingdom, to make it prosper and to uphold it with righteousness and with judgment from this time onward and forevermore. The zeal of the Lord Sabaoth will do these things.[34] (LXX Isaiah 9:6)

This conclusion drawn is rather modest but is also necessary for the integrity of the claim that there is an intertextual relationship between Luke 1:32 and LXX Isaiah 9:6.[35]

The promised Davidic king (βασιλεύς) is more developed in Isaiah 9 (than the Davidic covenant in 1 Samuel) and likely provides informs Luke's theology. An exegesis of the text does not have to exclude either choice as informing and providing coherence to the Magnificat. By considering the antecedent theology behind Isaiah 9 that is related to 1 Samuel vis-à-vis the Davidic promise, intertextual relationships in the Magnificat can be reconciled. The rhetorical nature of the Magnificat is part of an attempt to persuade the reader that this reversal of Mary is part of the restoration of Israel.

This study fills a lacuna by demonstrating that in the same pericope of Isaiah 9 that is quoted in Luke 1:32, the emotion of joy is the first and primary response of the characters to the reversal of God. The Magnificat and the intertextual co-text of Isaiah 9:6 (the pericope of Isaiah 9) use the emotion of joy as an important way to identify that God has brought about reversal.[36] The joy theme ties all of the actions together while simultaneously appealing to the emotions of the reader.

When we consider intertextuality as part of the rhetorical strategy, we see that joy connects with other themes to evoke Israel's promises and interaction with YHWH. The Magnificat is largely about the 'restoration' of Israel.[37] Specifically, the explicit appropriation of Isaiah in Luke 3:4-6 places Isaiah in the foreground of other intertextual sources. Even in the Magnificat, where Isaiah plays second fiddle, its sound is strong. This use of Isaiah provides meaning and coherence to the joy experience of reversal of Elizabeth and Mary. This study concludes that Luke's text seeks to persuade the reader that a new age has dawned with the presence of a Davidic son and that this age consists of the joyful reversal of God that is establishing the fulfillment of the Davidic promise.

---

[34] *NETS*, Book of Esaias, 832.

[35] Pao, *Acts and the Isaianic New Exodus*, 136.

[36] De Long suggests that the portrayal of Zion as a woman giving birth in Isa 66:7-10 is one of the intertextual sources of Mary's divine reversal from barrenness to pregnancy (*Surprised by God*, 157). Given the Lukan penchant for drawing from several sources at once, this cannot be ruled out.

[37] Köstenberger, 'Hearing the Old Testament in the New: A Response', 274.

Joy and Sacred Texture

The sacred texture consists of those elements in the text that communicates something about the relationship between the human and the divine.[38] This texture is more integrative than the first two and represents the synthetic and progressive nature of the study. I will demonstrate that a study of joy and sacred texture results in conclusions that are similar to the conclusions drawn from the study of the sacred texture of Luke 1:5-25. *The emotion of joy is used by Luke in Luke 1:26-56 to persuade the reader that the God of Israel who brings about reversal of fortune should be the object of joy.*

The fact that the God of Israel who brings joy to his people is holy is apparent based on the inner texture of Luke 1:26-38 (the announcement pericope) and Luke 1:39-45 (the visitation pericope) that was analyzed above. Earlier this study concluded that the lack of the presence of joy in the former pericope and the jubilation in the latter creates parallelism as well as development of the earlier reversal of Zechariah and Elizabeth. The theme of piety and the concept of the fear of the Lord are established first. Even as Mary is commanded in Luke 1:30: 'do not be afraid', she does not begin a series of joyful and free exclamations. Mary seems to retain an element of fear. This is not terror but reverence as the angelic messenger speaks on behalf of YHWH. Mary simply responds to the reversal that is parallel to and even exceeds Elizabeth's own reversal from barrenness with (Lk 1:38): "Behold, I am the servant of the Lord; let it be to me according to your word'. The piety is evident in her humble response that contrasts with Zechariah's response that led to his temporary muteness. Rhetorically, she becomes a model for proper response and behaviour. As noted above, this contrasts with the following visitation pericope that is bubbling with the joy of the two pregnant women.

The inner texture intersects with the sacred texture because the very surface of the text associates emotion with the actions of God. The text exhibits development in the sense that holiness is immediately followed up with joy. This operates not only on the pericope level but also on the stanza level. This movement from austerity to joy is evident in the Magnificat (Lk 1:47) 'and my spirit *rejoices* in God my savior'.[39] The reader learns not only how to respond to God but the repetition connects emotion with *what* and *who* God is. Arguably, God is never described as having the emotion of joy himself in Luke 1:26-56. In Luke 1:47 the dative is used to articulate that God is the direct object of Mary's joy: τῷ θεῷ. This is followed by the appositional dative that

---

[38] 'This idea of the sacred is located in those references in the text to deity, holy persons, spirit beings, divine history, human redemption, human commitment, religious community, and ethics'. W.R. Tate, *Biblical Interpretation: An Integrated Approach*, 3rd ed. (Peabody: Hendrickson, 2008), 341. Here the focus is on emotion as a response to deity and divine history and its use in Luke's rhetoric.

[39] The Greek of Luke 1:47 reads: 'καὶ ἠγαλλίασεν τὸ πνεῦμά μου ἐπὶ τῷ θεῷ τῷ σωτῆρί μου'.

provides development: τῷ σωτῆρί μου (Lk 1:47). It is not possible to separate who God is from what he does. God is the object of joy as well as the Saviour. The two emotions of fear and joy are separated in each pericope to allow both to function as concurrent emphases.

Two of the three pericopes of Luke 1:26-56 (the visitation and the Magnificat) use the emotion of joy to communicate the proper response to the radical and unexpected nature of God's reversal. Even the pericope of the annunciation (Lk 1:26-38) that maintains a tone of austerity creates a muted connection to joy vis-à-vis the direct pattern between the reversal from barrenness to pregnancy as noted in Luke 1:36. The reader is well aware of the joy that Elizabeth expressed at her own reversal and expectation of joy is at least established. The reversal of Elizabeth and the joy resulting from the angel's annunciation to her create an anticipation of joy at the annunciation to Mary.

Each pericope is oriented around God's actions that are extraordinary. It is acknowledged that God is portrayed by Luke as sovereign and Luke is particularly interested in noting how God the Father works out all things in accordance with this plan.[40] The theocentric plan of God in Luke 1 is discernible based 'on the way in which events unfold at the behest of God and in accordance with His plan'.[41] The text itself demands that recognition be given to God for accomplishing what has come to pass. Joel Green notes, 'Elizabeth speaks to Mary of what had been spoken to her "by the Lord," thus emphasizing the fact that Gabriel had delivered God's own message'.[42] What may be added to this statement is that the plan of God is filled with joy. The emotion of joy relates to this plan due to the way the plan unfolds: through extraordinary acts of reversal.

These acts of God are so extraordinary and beyond the bounds of expectation that they are literally unbelievable.[43] This is particularly the case with Zechariah (Lk 1:8-23) whose unbelief (mingled with belief) was explored in the previous chapter. Although miracles were an integral part of both Jewish and Greco-Roman religions, Luke uses the contrast between Zechariah and Mary to communicate that not everyone's response to God's acts will be appropriate. Joel Green concurs: 'The contrast with Zechariah could scarcely be more stark: he did not believe but she did'.[44] Zechariah and Elizabeth's pregnancy involved God's supernatural empowerment to achieve pregnancy through natural means. However, in the case of Mary's reversal, the reversal

---

[40] I.H. Marshall, *Luke: Historian and Theologian* (Downers Grove: IVP, 1988), 104.

[41] Marshall, *Luke: Historian and Theologian*, 104.

[42] Green, *Gospel of Luke*, 96.

[43] For a note on the divine identity of the God of Israel and acting in a 'surprising' way in the Isaianic New Exodus see R. Bauckham, *God Crucified: Monotheism and Christology in the New Testament* (Grand Rapids: Eerdmans, 1998), 70-71.

[44] Green, *Gospel of Luke*, 96.

from barrenness to pregnancy is achieved through supernatural means (Lk 1:35): 'The Holy Spirit will come upon you, and the power of the Most High will overshadow you'. Most commentators find that Luke as an author is interested in using Mary's reversal as a model of belief in God's ability to do what he has promised but they do not explain the role for emotion. The emotion of joy dominates each reversal. For example, in the Magnificat it is the first and only emotion to explicitly appear. The exclusivity of the mighty acts of God and the emotion of joy establish a texture or thread that runs throughout the text.

God the Father is never explicitly described as joyful in this text but the sacred texture of the text reveals a connection between joy and God's mighty reversals through Luke's use of a theology that incorporates the Father, Son, and Holy Spirit as individual characters.[45] Such a connection between Luke's theology and joy is found in the visitation pericope (Lk 1:39-45). When Mary arrives in the town of Judah, Elizabeth is described in Luke 1:41 as 'filled with the Holy Spirit'. This description serves to explain the speech to follow that begins with a blessing upon Mary and her child (Lk 1:42) and a description of John's response in her womb. The previous appearance of the 'Holy Spirit' was in the annunciation pericope (Lk 1:35). The 'Holy Spirit' who was himself the 'power of the Most High' was the very same one who filled Elizabeth and empowered her speech. This empowerment is possibly 'prophetic' in the sense that her words foretold what God's actions would entail.[46] The exclamation that John the Baptist was filled with joy (ἀγαλλίασις) is directly attributable to the Holy Spirit who is the Most High God. This is admittedly not describing the Holy Spirit himself as joyful but the emotion becomes connected to him due to the inspiration behind the speech.

The emotion of joy is persuasive as it is not possible to conceive of the God of Israel doing 'mighty' things (Lk 1:49) without an equally appropriate response to God and his actions. There is a tension created by Luke as he intentionally separates the emotion of fear as a response to the holiness of God and the emotion of joy as a response to the mighty deeds of God. This is particularly apparent in the so-called absence of joy in the annunciation to Mary in Luke 1:26-38. As the text itself bears witness, this absence of joy is immediately followed by joy produced by the Holy Spirit in John the Baptist, Elizabeth, and Mary.

Joy and Ideological Texture

Rhetorical or ideological texture is the thread of the tapestry of the text that

---

[45] The Father in the parable of the prodigal son in Luke 15 is likely a circumlocution for God expressing joy. This passage is examined in chapter six.

[46] Marshall, *Gospel of Luke: A Commentary on the Greek Text*, 80.

consists of its effect.[47] Joy functions ideologically as opposed to psychologically because its force is community oriented. The beginning of the Magnificat is so personal (e.g. 'my soul' and 'my spirit') that 'readers here are listening in on someone else's song, a song in which they cannot directly share'.[48] What is significant is that as the poem continues, the personal focus expands to the corporate level.[49]

As the hymn progresses, the reversal motif based on the poles of humility and greatness (e.g. the slave girl and the mighty one) opens the poem up to 'all generations'.[50] The reader can indeed participate in the joys of the Magnificat because the blessings of her pregnancy are 'to Abraham and to his offspring forever' (Lk 1:55). Rather than posit such a strict dichotomy between the joyful introduction of the Magnificat and its development of the theme of reversal, it is better to understand the joy as strengthening the rhetorical power of the reversal throughout.

Luke uses the emotion of joy to convince the reader that YHWH has visited his people by reversing the condition of Mary and Israel in one act. This absence of joy in Luke 1:30-33 shifts emphasis 'away from the individual' to the social group of Israel.[51] On the contrary, it is *through* Mary that joy embodies what God is doing for Israel. This is evident in the promise of the angel who speaks of 'the throne of his father David' (Lk 1:32) and 'the house of Jacob' (Lk 1:33). The narrative does not skip Mary as it moves from the individual to the corporate. The relationship between Mary and Israel is tied together by the poetry of the Magnificat 'presents God's choice of the lowly mother and God's overturning of society as *one* act'.[52] Green also concludes that Mary's reversal from virginity (childlessness) to pregnancy is typological of what Israel is experiencing as a nation: 'Israel is estranged from God, under alien rule, oppressed. God's covenant with his people has not been realized fully'.[53] The intertextual pattern of reversal from barrenness to child-bearing the emotion of joy moves through Mary to all of Israel. Through this one act, Mary's reversal is Israel's reversal and joy belongs to both the individual as well as the collective people of God. One qualification is in order. Israel's barrenness and Mary's barrenness are not totally parallel in every way. Whereas Mary's barrenness is finally overcome, the plight of Israel is mixed with both rising and falling.

---

[47] W. Wuellner, 'The Rhetorical Genre of Jesus' Sermon in Luke 12:1-13:9' in *Persuasive Artistry: Studies in New Testament Rhetoric in Honor of George A. Kennedy* (JSNTSup 50; Sheffield: Academic Press, 1991), 93.

[48] Tannehill, *Shape of Luke's Story*, 43.

[49] Tannehill, *Shape of Luke's Story*, 43.

[50] Tannehill, *Shape of Luke's Story*, 43.

[51] Dawsey, *Lukan Voice*, 137.

[52] Tannehill, *Shape of Luke's Story*, 45. Emphasis his.

[53] Green, *Gospel of Luke*, 84.

The pericopae following Luke 1:5-25 where Elizabeth and Zechariah experience the reversal from barrenness to pregnancy are interconnected and development can be seen throughout. Luke 1:5-25 creates an anticipation of how Luke wants to shape the values of the reader according to the new age. The reversal of the young maiden and the priest reverses social expectations of piety and places emphasis upon the weak and pious rather than upon the professional 'clergy'. The narrative is developed in Luke 1:6-66 as Mary and her child are given prominence over Elizabeth and her son John.

Joy in Luke 1:26-66 follows the pattern of the reversal of Elizabeth and is articulated as both personal and corporate. In the visitation pericope the emotion of joy is connected to Elizabeth, John and the Holy Spirit (Lk 1:39-45). In the Magnificat, Mary's joy is personal (Lk 1:46-7) but also reflects what God has done for Israel (Lk 1:54). Likewise, in the birth narrative of John, the joy is specifically corporate and involves her neighbours and relatives (Lk 1:58): 'And her neighbours and relatives heard that the Lord had shown great mercy to her, and they rejoiced with her'. Joy is without doubt an emotion that involves psychological elements. However, in Luke its impact is always communal and therefore also ideological. In Luke 1:26-66 God has reversed the plight of the lowly maiden by giving a son to Israel who are themselves the sons (and daughters) of Abraham. What persuaded the individual in the narrative provides emotional energy that forces the implied reader and the implied community to consider what God has done.

As readers place themselves imaginatively within the narrative and listen to the joy of Mary, Elizabeth, John, and the Holy Spirit, they enter Luke's joyful upside-down world. This model of ideology builds on the idea that, 'Readers tend to place themselves imaginatively within the narrative and to listen to Jesus' words as addressed to themselves'.[54] An analysis of the ideological texture of Luke 1:6-66 must give adequate explanation of the presence of the joy theme that is found throughout the pericopae. In Luke 1:39-45 the emotion of joy impacts the reader as one is drawn into John's response to Jesus which is Elizabeth's response to Jesus which is the Holy Spirit's response to Jesus. This is immediately followed by the Magnificat (Lk 1:46-56) that draws in the reader so as to imitate her own joy and emotion at the presence of Jesus' coming bring salvation for her and the people of God. This analysis differs from John York who states, 'Throughout the poem [Magnificat], the emphasis is upon the action taken by God, and the poem thus demands that primacy be given to the acts of God, not conditions of the human characters'.[55] On the contrary, the conditions of human characters are crucial to Luke's emotional rhetoric. Building on the emotion of the reversal of Elizabeth the implied reader is brought into the song of the lowly maiden and her emotion pressures the reader to exalt the God of Israel who has brought these reversals about that

---

[54] Kurz, *Dynamics of Biblical Narrative*, 183.
[55] York, *The Last Shall Be First*, 53.

culminate in the Davidic son.

Ideology uses emotion in the narrative as the readers tend to place themselves imaginatively within the narrative and to listen and feel the words of those who have experienced the reversal of God. The repetition of joy frames the narratives and creates expectations as well as forces the reader and the community to consider their own response to God's reversals. According to Paul Borgman, 'hearing and speaking' are 'so crucial within this two-volume narrative and in the story-telling world of Luke'.[56] Likewise, Peter Mallen focuses on the 'listen, learn and do' pattern that is empowered by a 'rhetoric of perception'.[57] Both models do not take into account the role of emotion as playing a role in persuading the implied reader of the author's ideology. In Luke's story-telling world, hearing, speaking, *and feeling* are crucial.

The Reversal of the Shepherds at Jesus' Birth: Joy in Luke 2:1-21

The joy theme extends into the reversal of the shepherds as their role is woven into the birth of Jesus in Luke 2:1-21. As the anticipated son is born, the joy theme is arguably 'most prominent'.[58] The dawning of the new day of salvation is both temporal and typological: 'to you is born *this day* in the city of David a Saviour, who is Christ the Lord' (Lk 2:11). The use of 'this day' (σήμερον) indicates a temporal framework. This word is also reflective of a typological marker of turning points in salvation history as reflected in the renewal of the covenant with Moses in LXX Deuteronomy 29:9-15.[59] In the narrative that covers Jesus' birth, the emotion of joy is used to strengthen the rhetoric of reversal as the reader is persuaded that a new age has dawned and has culminated in the birth of Jesus.

The hermeneutical key to the reversal motif of Luke 2:1-21 is present on the surface of the text as Luke repeatedly identifies the shepherds (Lk 2:8, 15, 18, 20) as those who were the first witnesses at the birth of the one who is to sit on the throne of David over Israel. The reversal motif in Luke 2:1-21 is proleptic of the bi-polar reversals in Luke 6 where the poor are reversed and the blessings given to the poor are equated with woes for the rich.[60] Such a conclusion is also warranted in light of the rhetoric present in the bi-polar reversals between the priest Zechariah and the lowly maiden Mary. Against a

---

[56] Borgman, *Hearing the Whole Story of Luke-Acts*, 24.

[57] Mallen, *Reading and Transformation of Isaiah*, 165.

[58] Such is the conclusion of M.L. Strauss, *The Davidic Messiah in Luke-Acts: The Promise and its Fulfillment in Lukan Christology* (JSNTSup 110; Sheffield: Sheffield Academic, 1995), 78.

[59] Contra Resseguie who only attributes 'this day' in Lk 2:11 to a temporal reference. J.L. Resseguie, *Narrative Criticism of the New Testament: An Introduction* (Grand Rapids: Baker, 2005), 108-9. See a contrasting comment about the 'eschatological urgency' of the 'today' motif in Luke on p. 156.

[60] York, *The Last Will Be First*, 21.

social context in which shepherds were socially despised and associated with breaking the Mosaic Law, this would have been seen as nothing less than a dramatic reversal. However, the reversal of the shepherds in Luke 2:1-21 is one sided: the lowly are elevated and the shameful are honoured. While acknowledging the danger of being simplistic, the presence of joy in the reversal of the shepherds and the birth of Jesus is an immediate fulfillment to the promise of joy given in Luke 1:14 as considered in the previous chapter.

Joy and Inner Texture

The inner texture of Luke 2:1-21 indicates that joy is a major theme of Jesus' birth and the reversal of the shepherds. A cursory comparison of the two major pericopae of Luke 2:1-7 of the birth of Jesus and Luke 2:8-21 as the reversal of the shepherds will find that joy does not appear at all in the birth pericope. The birth of Jesus is technically emotionless as Luke reports the birth of Jesus in such an objective and fact-based way that the reader is reminded of his intention to write a διήγησις. The emotional response to the mighty deeds of God is rooted in a dialogical relationship with cognitive facts.[61] In the introductory chapter the connection between Luke's preface and his intention to write a persuasive history was made. The sudden and strong movement from the birth narrative into the reversal narrative distinguishes the latter and works on a rhetorical level as the reader is persuaded to respond as the shepherds to the presence of Jesus.

The first emotion to appear is not joy but fear. The angel of the Lord appears to the shepherds and fills them with fear (Lk 2:9). The angel specifically instructs the shepherds in Luke 2:10: 'fear not' (μὴ φοβεῖσθε). The fear is genuine emotion and is understood as the normal response to frightening circumstances.[62] But Luke uses this fear to demonstrate a piety that is more than just 'normal'. The fear appears first and establishes the character and quality of those who respond first to Jesus' birth. Those who are lowly *demonstrate* their lowliness. The piety theme is established through the shepherd's humble fear as they respond to the glory of the Lord encompassing them.[63] The presence of the piety prevents the emotion of joy to follow from being understood as flippant or irreverent. The emotions of fear and joy are not intermingled. Once the angel commands the shepherds to not fear, the narrative moves from the theme of piety to the theme of joy. It is specifically through the command not to fear and their obedience that piety is demonstrated. The division between the two themes of piety and joy brings emphasis to the repetition of the vocabulary in each pericope.

---

[61] Elliott, *Faithful Feelings*, 180.

[62] Elliott, *Faithful Feelings*, 201.

[63] 'In this world, we are breathing the air of first-century Palestinian Jewish piety'. Green, *Theology of Luke's Gospel*, 12.

The joy theme is integrated with actions such as praising, as exemplified in the reversal of the shepherds in Luke 2:8-21. The angel's proclamation and use of χαρά introduces the joy theme in Luke 2:10: 'and the angel said to them, Fear not, for behold, I bring you good news of great joy that will be for all the people'. The emotion of joy is then connected to the verb αἰνέω and the noun δόξα in Luke 2:13 and 2:14, respectively. The shepherds are then privy to the event that causes the angelic host to praise. Having found Mary and Joseph and having witnessed the baby Jesus in the manger, they returned with joy on their lips (Lk 2:20): 'and the shepherds returned, glorifying and praising God for all they had heard and seen, as it had been told them'. As a response to their cognitive knowledge and experience of seeing the fulfillment of God's promises, the emotion of joy appears with the verbs 'to glorify' (δοξάζω) and 'to praise' (αἰνέω). This supports the conclusion that a study of the joy theme must cover a relatively wide range of vocabulary.[64]

The repetition of the joy theme is in part conceptually based. The use of the superlative adjective μέγας in conjunction with joy in the angel's proclamation indicates that the birth of the baby Jesus marks the inauguration of God's new stage in history. Luke's intention is not simply to establish a historical fact; he intends to persuade the reader to respond to this information in an emotional way based on cognitive facts. Like the textual units analyzed thus far, development is established via the discontinuity or the separation of the two emotions of fear and joy. As in Luke 1:5-25 and Luke 1:26-56, the emotion of joy is repeated and amplified across the inner texture of Luke 2:1-21. Great joy is the only emotion that seems right and fits with what the implied reader already know thus far in the narrative.

Joy and Intertexture

This examination of the intertexture of Luke 2:1-21 will be brief and limited to connections between the joy theme and the previously established relationship to Isaiah. The reversal of the shepherds and their joy is best understood in terms of the already established Isaianic New Exodus.

The presence of the shepherds as the Davidic king's first subjects ties the baby Jesus to his role as the shepherd par excellence. The birth of Jesus is equivalent to the arrival of the one who inaugurates the Isaianic New Exodus that will be characterized as a time when the 'flock' of the People of God will be shepherded in accordance with LXX Isaiah 40:11: 'He will tend his flock like a shepherd and gather lambs with his arm and comfort those that are with young'.[65] Out of the 'city of David', the Davidic shepherd-king has been born

---

[64] Navone, *Themes of St Luke*, 71-3; O'Toole, *Unity of Luke's Theology*, 228.

[65] *NETS*, Book of Esaias, 854.

and is now attended to by lowly-yet-honoured, joyful shepherds.[66]

This conclusion should be held tentatively because Jesus is not portrayed as a shepherd 'but as one visited by shepherds.'[67] However, the use of the Davidic king language in Luke 2:1-4 implies that Luke is setting up an ideological challenge to Augustus' kingship on some level and directly connecting Jesus to the lineage of David through Bethlehem (Lk 2:4). Because David was a shepherd-king one can conclude that Luke understood Jesus as the shepherd-king. Thus, the text of the birth of Jesus and the reversal of the shepherds provides some evidence for a reading that can appropriate intertextual threads that support Jesus as both a shepherd *and* one visited by shepherds.

Further evidence is present of a direct intertextual connection between the joy vocabulary in Luke 2:8-14 and the repetition of joy vocabulary in Isaiah 9:1-3. The repetition of joy vocabulary (εὐφραίνω, εὐφροσύνη) occurs primarily in LXX Isaiah 9:2:

> Most of the people, whom you have brought back in your *joy*, will also *rejoice* before you like those who *rejoice* at the harvest and in the same way as those who divide plunder.[68]

The argumentation for this intertextual relationship between Luke 2:8-14 and Isaiah 9:1-6 LXX/MT is five-fold: (1) light in the midst of darkness, (2) joy, (3) birth of a child, (4) the presence of the Davidic messiah, and (5) an era of peace. The reference to the Davidic throne in LXX Isaiah 9:6 is one of the strongest ties between Luke 2 and Isaiah 9 because of its specificity. The strength of this connection should be tempered slightly by the fact that Luke 2 uses χαρά for joy while Isaiah 9 uses εὐφροσύνη. But even this should take into account Luke's wide semantic range for the emotion of joy and rejoicing, which is a frequent feature of Luke's style. Isaiah's promise of a Davidic heir will be characterized by joy in the nation and this is what Luke uses to describe shepherds. As the unclean shepherds respond in joy to Jesus they are participating in the promise that was given to Israel and those who were once last are now first. This is proof that the intertextual use of LXX Isaiah 9:1-6 by Luke furthers his rhetoric of reversal.

Luke uses joy 'to introduce a theme that will be prominent throughout Luke-Acts: God is to be praised for the joyful time of redemption has arrived'.[69] But

---

[66] Litwak concurs with Strauss that the phrase 'city of David' connects Jesus with Davidic lineage. Litwak, *Echoes of Scripture in Luke-Acts*, 95; Strauss, *Davidic Messiah in Luke-Acts*, 110-111.

[67] Pao and Schnabel, 'Luke', *CNTUOT*, 267.

[68] *NETS*, Book of Esaias, 831. The Greek reads: τὸ πλεῖστον τοῦ λαοῦ, ὃ κατήγαγες ἐν εὐφροσύνῃ σου, καὶ εὐφρανθήσονται ἐνώπιόν σου ὡς οἱ εὐφραινόμενοι ἐν ἀμήτῳ καὶ ὃν τρόπον οἱ διαιρούμενοι σκῦλα.

[69] Strauss, *Davidic Messiah in Luke-Acts*, 77. The Davidic connection to Bethlehem also appears in Micah 5:1-2 (4:14-51 MT). Pao and Schnabel, 'Luke', *CNTUOT*, 266.

this conclusion leaves a lacuna in terms of explaining the persuasiveness of the emotion of joy. Joy operates as a literary theme but also as a genuine emotion that exerts rhetorical pressure on the reader. The element of joyful emotion and the status reversal of the shepherds establish an emotional force that persuades the reader to arrive at the conclusion that Jesus is the messiah who brings the peace of salvation.[70]

The case for understanding joy as playing a role in Luke's intertextual-based rhetoric does not necessarily reflect his desire for an authoritative religious text that would justify Luke's claims about Jesus' birth.[71] Rather, Luke's use of the Old Testament and Isaiah in specific has to do more with his overarching framework. Intertextuality is used primarily to provide meaning and coherence rather than justification. By responding to Luke's narrative with joy, the reader (re-)enacts the drama of participating in God's salvation as promised in Isaiah.

Joy and Sacred Texture

The emotion of great joy in Luke 2:1-21 adds persuasive power to Luke's multifaceted picture of God. God's mighty deeds for Israel demand a response. In Luke 2:1-21 the joy theme both unifies Jesus with God as the source of joy and distinguishes Jesus from God as God the Father becomes the one who is glorified. With one exception in Luke, the object of the verb δοξάζω is always either God or Jesus.[72]

Jesus is the immediate cause of the great joy in Luke 2:10-11. The angel who meets the shepherds promises in Luke 2:10-11: 'Fear not, for behold, I bring you good news of great joy... who is Christ the Lord'. There is a sense in which the immediate cause of the great joy is the fulfillment of the promises given to Israel and the εὐαγγέλιον ties intertextually to the Isaianic New Exodus (compare with Isa 52:7). A good case can be made for an expanded joy theme that includes εὐαγγελίζω.[73] Syntactically, the great joy in the phrase in Luke 2:10 is parallel to the explanatory phrase in Luke 2:11 because of the conjunctions γὰρ and ὅτι. The syntax shows that the great joy is ultimately a response to the Christ the Lord.

In Luke 2:1-21, God is distinct from the baby Jesus but he is also the object of joy in Luke 2:13-14, 20. Luke's theology (which earlier referenced the Holy

---

[70] Borgman, *The Way According to Luke*, 28.

[71] This would be comparable to Köstenberger's statement about Paul and intertextual rhetoric: 'Since the Jewish sacred writings were already considered authoritative by many in Paul's audience, if the apostle could show that his teaching was consistent with, and in further application of, these writings, he would considerably increase the likelihood of his teaching being accepted by many in his audience (cf., e.g., 1 Tim 2:13)' in 'Hearing the Old Testament in the New: A Response', 259.

[72] The one exception being the 'word of the Lord' in Acts 13:48. Pao, *Acts and the Isaianic New Exodus*, 161.

[73] The Greek of Luke 2:10 reads: ἰδοὺ γὰρ εὐαγγελίζομαι ὑμῖν χαρὰν μεγάλην.

Spirit in Luke 1:35) allows him to speak of the baby Jesus as 'Lord' or κύριος (Luke 2:11) and θεός in Luke 1:14 as worthy of glory and praise. The Father the κύριος (Luke 2:15) and Jesus is the κύριος (Luke 2:11). The honours that God and Jesus share are slightly differentiated. We might say there is a unity and diversity in Luke's conception of God.

The use of joy is effective in persuading the reader about the divine and human nature of the baby Jesus and what his presence means for the salvation of the people of God. The response to the κύριος as God (the Father) is the same response to the κύριος as Jesus the baby king. It is not possible for Luke's readers to respond to the arrival of the Davidic king in a way that does not take into account that two characters in this narratival history receive the same honours.

Joy and Ideological Texture

The social world of the first century 'was defined around power and privilege'.[74] It is in this context that we should understand the birth narrative of Jesus. It is a narrative that is about 'confrontation' between the 'kingdom of God' and the 'kingdoms of the world'.[75] William Morrice relates the joy of the shepherds in Luke 2 to the prior scenes in which the lowly experienced a reversal: 'Luke shows the joy with which the incarnation was greeted by this small group of pious Jews, which included people like Mary and Joseph, as well as Elizabeth and Zechariah, the parents of John the Baptist'.[76] We must also add the shepherds to this list. Given this slight qualification, Morrice's observation concurs with the findings of this study. Luke's intention is not simply descriptive when he identifies the joy theme as simply 'positive reactions to the experience of God's salvific will'.[77] *Luke is not a passionless historian. On the contrary, the emotion of joy is one of his key tools of persuasion.*

The birth narrative of Jesus has a distinctly Jewish background *and* a Greco-Roman background.[78] The presence of a king would not go unnoticed in a Greco-Roman context. The child king who brings peace would have challenged those who viewed Caesar as the source of divine peace. Luke's contrast between Jesus as Lord and Caesar as Lord is likely deliberate but admittedly relies upon implicit connections.[79] But we should be careful of claims that Luke

---

[74] J.B. Green, *The Theology of the Gospel of Luke* (Cambridge: Cambridge University Press, 1995), 11.

[75] Wright, *Luke for Everyone*, 23.

[76] Morrice, *We Joy in God*, 16.

[77] O'Toole, *Unity of Luke's Theology*, 226.

[78] Brown, *Birth of the Messiah*, 416.

[79] S. Kim, *Christ and Caesar: The Gospel and the Roman Empire in the Writings of Paul and Luke* (Grand Rapids: Eerdmans, 2008), 80.

intends to 'replace' Caesar's peace.[80] This is an overstatement. The very fact that Luke simultaneously recognizes the *contemporaneous* rules of Jesus and Caesar in Luke 2:1-7 demonstrates that his Jesus-driven ideology is nuanced. Luke is trying to challenge the values of his readers but not to the exclusion of obeying Caesar as a political ruler. In the end it is the prolific use of Old Testament allusions and terminology that point to the dominance of the Jewish background of kingdom and kingship.[81]

Luke's intention is to persuade the reader that the new age has arrived in the baby Jesus. Such a goal comes with controversy. In Luke 2:1-21 the emotion of joy functions ideologically because it draws attention to the reversal of the shepherds who are the first to attend the birth of the shepherd-king Jesus who is to sit on the throne of David. The emotion of joy draws the reader into a confrontation with those who reject the presence of the inaugurated kingdom. The very act of God reversing the plight of the lowly and honouring those who are assumed to be undeserving of honour creates conflict.

The reversal of the shepherds not only establishes the nature of Jesus' kingdom and his rule as the shepherd-king but it anticipates a conflict between Jesus and those who have values associated with the world and are thus opposed to the values of the kingdom. Such a conflict appears immediately after Luke's programmatic text (Luke 4:16-30) where Jesus publically introduces himself and presents himself as the fulfillment of God's promises to Israel (Luke 4:24-27):

> And he said, "Truly, I say to you, no prophet is acceptable in his hometown. But in truth, I tell you, there were many widows in Israel in the days of Elijah, when the heavens were shut up three years and six months, and a great famine came over all the land, and Elijah was sent to none of them but only to Zarephath, in the land of Sidon, to a woman who was a widow. And there were many lepers in Israel in the time of the prophet Elisha, and none of them was cleansed, but only Naaman the Syrian". (Luke 4:24-27 ESV)

Here Jesus presents a series of events from the history of Israel in which God acted in such a way as to provide salvation to someone outside of the nation of Israel. The hermeneutical key to this pericope is the use of the 'acceptance' (δεκτός) vocabulary in Luke 4:24.[82] This passage lists instances in which Israel resisted YHWH and, as a result, YHWH was pleased to *accept* those outside of Israel. Israel had an exclusive relationship with God because of their redemption through the Exodus and the covenants with Abraham, Moses, and David. But their national election did not justify anger at God's grace toward those outside of their national boundaries.

The presence of this pericope so soon after the passage in Luke 2:1-21

---

[80] Kim, *Christ and Caesar*, 81.

[81] Bock, *Luke: Vol. 1*, 200.

[82] Pao, *Acts and the Isaianic New Exodus*, 79.

provides the best justification for a comparison reading that focuses on reversal. Luke's use of the reversal motif thus far is challenging and as ideological as his presentation of Jesus' speech in Luke 4:16-30.[83] Luke has framed the narrative since his prologue by presenting a series of Israelites who are on the bottom of the honour-shame scale (i.e. barren, poor, unclean, unaccepted).[84] Luke is painting a broader landscape that anticipates what Jesus says *in nuce* when he introduces himself in the public reading of Isaiah 61:1-2. This Isaianic passage ties together the presence of YHWH's salvation and the reversal of status of the poor, oppressed, blind.[85] The shepherds and their reversal of status as the first subjects present with the arriving of the king fit within this paradigm. There were many fruitful Israelites when the kingdom arrived but God chose the barren. The salvation of God arrived for all the people (λαός) of Israel but only shepherds were invited.[86] Whereas Luke 4:16-30 presents the two Isaianic themes of rejection by the Jews and contrast between Jews and Gentiles, the entirety of Luke's post-prologue narratives present the reader with similar themes in a larger framework.[87] Joy functions rhetorically as it tests the responsiveness of the reader to the presence of God's salvation in and through Jesus.

Conclusion

If ideology in the text is Luke's conscious 'enactment' of 'presuppositions, dispositions, and values held in common with other people', it is possible to understand this enactment of the pregnancy of Mary and the birth of Jesus with all of its associated reversals as persuasion.[88] As Luke seeks to persuade the reader that God has inaugurated a new age through the throne of David who will be called the Son of the Most High (Lk 1:32), his rhetoric is emotional or based in part on *pathos*. Emotion plays a crucial role not only in Luke's narrative world as mentioned above but in the social world. Joy functions as a cultural code that was an accepted social convention shared with his audience.

Burton Mack explains, 'persuasion finally rested upon the correlation between the construction that the speaker put on a particular case and those

---

[83] Mallen argues that Lk 4:16-30 is programmatic for Jesus and for themes in Acts. Specifically, the use of Isaiah in Jesus' sermon addresses 'the long-awaited era of New Exodus salvation' (*The Reading and Transformation of Isaiah*, 75).

[84] Shepherds were often associated with thieves and dishonesty; they were assumed to be outsiders according to the Mosaic Law. See R.E. Brown, *The Birth of the Messiah* (Updated ed.; New York/London: Doubleday, 1993), 420 n88.

[85] Pao, *Acts and the Isaianic New Exodus*, 74.

[86] York, *The Last Shall Be First*, 112 n6.

[87] Pao states: 'The significance of the Nazareth pericope lies not only in the Isaianic quotation but more importantly in the Lukan interpretation and qualification of this quotation' in *Acts and the Isaianic New Exodus*, 78.

[88] Robbins, *Exploring the Texture of Texts*, 95.

general cultural codes of conduct and value shared by the audience'.[89] The question then is: has Luke created a particular case for Jesus that is strong enough to warrant joy in the reader?

Whereas formal Greco-Roman rhetoric used emotion to summarize arguments, Luke begins with it, reflecting the Jewish influence of the Septuagint. Luke also uses the emotional narrative to call the reader to a decision or judgment about Jesus.[90] In the reversal pericopae of Luke 1:6-66, joy is used to establish the reversal as God inaugurates the new age through the pregnancy of Mary who will bear a son. This is then fulfilled in the birth of Jesus who is accompanied by shepherds who represent a larger motif of reversal from dishonor to honour. The presence of the shepherds with the baby Jesus represents the present fulfillment of what was promised in the new age. Yet the values of the kingdom and the new age are not always apparent in the presence of those who are dishonoured, poor, and lowly. This social context sets the stage for the rise and fall of many in Israel. Jesus' birth has been anticipated and has now arrived: he is the Davidic king and the saviour, the Lord (κύριος) who receives the same emotional response attributed to the Lord (κύριος) in the Septuagint.

---

[89] Mack and Robbins, *Patterns of Persuasion*, 38.
[90] Mack and Robbins, *Patterns of Persuasion*, 55.

CHAPTER 4

Joy in the Galilean Ministry of Jesus

The vignettes in Luke 1-2 introduced the reader to the ideas that will guide the narrative to follow. YHWH has visited his people and inaugurated a new age. This visitation has brought about events that reverse or overturn the fortunes of individuals as well as the whole people of God. In the previous chapter, we saw how peasants and shepherds are elevated while the piety of a priest is questioned. In this chapter we see that Jesus' Galilean ministry is characterized by joy.

Introduction

The air is still tingling with excitement and joy as the narrative moves quickly from the birth of Jesus to his ministry. Jesus' path is ultimately moving along a path toward Jerusalem but a long stretch of text is devoted to the Galilean ministry. The use of reversal continues in the Galilean ministry and is woven through the warp and woof of the whole narrative. For much of the narrative, Isaiah is the dominant source of intertextual relationships. In Luke 6:20-26, 'the same concept of reversal is present and several terms that also occur in Isaiah 61:1-3'.[1] This conclusion is helpful but requires a more robust theory about the emotional component of what it means to be 'blessed'. This is particularly important because the recipients of Jesus' salvation for Israel are often the social outcasts.[2] This will require a socio-rhetorical analysis that examines the various threads that are woven together in the text.

In this chapter we will examine three textual units from the Galilean ministry of Jesus as found in (1) the beatitudes and woes of the Sermon on the Plain (Luke 6:20-26), (2) the identification of Jesus by John the Baptist (Luke 7:22-23), and (3) the explanation of the parable of the sower (Luke 8:9-15). Each textual unit contains elements that are part of Luke's joy theme and rhetoric of reversal.[3] An analysis of these textual units will demonstrate that the emotion of

---

[1] Mallen, *Reading and Transformation of Isaiah*, 107.

[2] Mallen recognizes that Jesus' salvation results in a 'status reversal and restoration to community' but he does not examine how the emotion of joy provides the emotional force to move these reversals forward or how emotion challenges the reader (*Reading and Transformation of Isaiah*, 107).

[3] R. Grams' study of the rhetoric of Matt 23:1-39 cites Lk 6:24ff as an instance of prophetic speech that exemplifies epideictic argumentation that is characterized by an

joy provides emotional power to the persuasive tasks that these texts seek to achieve.

The Reversal of the Oppressed: Joy in Luke 6:20-26

Joy plays a central role in the reversals of the beatitudes and woes in Luke 6:20-26.[4] The beatitudes and woes are 'eschatological' because they 'put the future in tension with the present'.[5] Likewise, Luke 6:20-23 is a location in the Lukan corpus where the joy theme and the reversal motif intersect.[6] Rhetorically speaking, these verses function as the 'exordium for Luke's Sermon on the Plain'.[7] Even if we do not agree that Luke intentionally shaped his rhetoric according to technical specifications for Greco-Roman rhetoric, there is undoubtedly a rhetorical dynamic in the pericope.[8] Furthermore, the Sermon on the Plain repeats the 'form of bi-polar reversal encountered in the Magnificat'.[9] One side of this bi-polar relationship follows the Magnificat: the oppressed and lowly are to reinterpret their status in light of God's mighty deed in establishing a new Messianic age with the presence of Jesus.[10] The other side of the bi-polar relationship of Luke 6:20-26 comes in the form of the woes to those who are powerful and wealthy in this age: they must reinterpret their status with respect to their position about Jesus. In agreement with York, the pericope of Luke 6:20-26 exhibits a strong rhetoric of reversal.

There are substantial threads of continuity between the Sermon on the Plain and the vignettes that framed the narrative in chapters 1 and 2. Luke's goal is to persuade the reader to incorporate and exhibit the values of the new age as inaugurated through the coming of Jesus. A critical component of this task is

---

'increase in *pathos*' in 'The Temple Conflict Scene' in *Persuasive Artistry: Studies in New Testament Rhetoric in Honor of George A. Kennedy* (ed. D.F. Watson; JSNTSup 50; Sheffield: Academic Press, 1991), 60. We will not be examining relationships with classical rhetorical categories (i.e. epideictic rhetoric) but the use of pathos as it relates to emotional dimensions of the persuasive agenda of the narrative.

[4] The whole rhetorical unit likely stretches from 6:20 to 7:1 if one takes the narrator's interruptions as integral to the style. See Kennedy, *New Testament Interpretation Through Rhetorical-Criticism*, 64.

[5] York, *The Last Shall Be First*, 56.

[6] Bernadicou, *Joy in the Gospel of Luke*, 27.

[7] York, *The Last Shall Be First*, 56.

[8] In addition to the reversal motif, M.A. Powell notes three qualities of the Lukan beatitudes that support this study of Luke's rhetorical agenda including: (1) Luke uses the second person in order to stress application to the reader, (2) Luke uses a temporal distinction with the word 'now' (Lk 6:21), and (3) Luke introduces the reversal woe passages in *What Are They Saying About Luke?* (Mahwah: Paulist, 1989), 24.

[9] York, *The Last Shall Be First*, 56.

[10] F. Craddock notes: 'The pattern of reversed fortunes will reappear often in Luke; for example, recall Luke's beatitudes and woes (6:20-26)' in *Luke* (Louisville: WJKP, 1990), 30.

the appeal to the emotions. Current scholarship continues to support the conclusion that Jesus' Sermon on the Plain integrates a rhetoric of reversal. This 'complete reversal' of values is tied to the Magnificat: 'Mary's poetic vision of this upside-down reality is echoed here'.[11] But it is not clear how the rhetoric of reversal utilizes the emotional components of the text.[12]

Here we will demonstrate two things. First, the emotion of joy provides an important part of Luke's appeal to the emotions. Second, the emotion of joy ties the values of the new age to the prior introductory narratives.

Joy and Inner Texture

The examination of inner texture is concerned with the text itself and the use of vocabulary, key words, and repetition. The location of joy (χαίρω, σκιρτάω) in the textual unit of Luke 6:20-26 is in Luke 6:23a: 'Rejoice in that day, and leap for joy, for behold, your reward is great in heaven.[13] The statements are directed toward the disciples and the twelve but specifically address the state of those who are oppressed. In this section I will integrate the concept of being 'blessed' (μακάριος) into the broad conceptual and semantic pattern of Luke's joy theme.

A thick analysis of the joy theme in the inner texture of Luke 6:20-26 must account for the μακάριος vocabulary that is integral to the beatitudes. The structure of Luke's beatitudes presents us with a grouping of eight statements inclusive of an imperative that brings them to an emotionally oriented apex before transitioning into the woes in Luke 6:24-26. The epigrammatic form of the eight statements follows this pattern:

> blessed are those who [insert present adjectival quality],
> for you [insert a future state].

The variation between the present tense ownership of the kingdom in Luke 6:20, the future tense states in Luke 6:21-22 and the imperatives in Luke 6:23 indicate that Luke is intentionally creating tension between the present and the future.

The 'blessed' (μακάριος) vocabulary is widely regarded as having an emotional component.[14] The Greek usage of μακάριος was used to express the 'happy, untroubled state of the gods, and then more generally the happiness of the rich who are free from care'.[15] The ESV renders μακάριος in Luke 6:20-22

---

[11] Borgman, *The Way According to Luke*, 45.

[12] For another example see Mallen who characterizes Lk 6:20-26 as 'eschatological reversal' (*Reading and Transformation of Isaiah*, 106).

[13] The Greek text of Luke 6:23a reads: χάρητε ἐν ἐκείνῃ τῇ ἡμέρᾳ καὶ σκιρτήσατε, ἰδοὺ γὰρ ὁ μισθὸς ὑμῶν πολὺς ἐν τῷ οὐρανῷ.

[14] Bock, *Luke 1:1-9:50*, 571-72; N. Geldenhuys, *Commentary on the Gospel of Luke* (Grand Rapids: Eerdmans, 1977), 210.

[15] Marshall, *The Gospel of Luke*, 248.

as 'blessed'. In American English parlance, the word 'blessed' communicates divine favour of some kind and this likely captures a sufficient amount of Luke's intended meaning. The way that Luke structures the statements in parallel fashion and the use of the imperative form of χαίρω and σκιρτάω is evidence that one cannot be μακάριος without an accompanying emotional state.[16] There is a tension apparent because it is hard to understand how one can be μακάριος and also κλαίω. But in Luke 6:21 this 'weeping' will (future tense) turn into 'laughing' (γελάω). The emotive component on the lexical level creates tension in the discourse level. If we take a component approach to μακάριος then it is inclusive of favour and emotion.

The most likely explanation for the reluctance to include μακάριος vocabulary into the joy theme on a lexical or conceptual level is the lack of clarity surrounding the emotion of joy. For example, some have suggested the μακάριος vocabulary refers to a 'religious joy'.[17] We must remember that joy is simply an emotion.[18] The language of blessing is simply inclusive of subjective feelings or emotions.[19] The problem with 'eschatological joy' or 'religious joy' terminology is that it establishes nebulous preconditions for examining the use of joy in the Lukan corpus. The use of this terminology also creates the impression that joy is something other than an emotion. The emotion of joy does not have 'content'. To say that an emotion such as joy has an eschatological nature is nonsensical. The emotion of joy can have degrees of intensity and it is a cognitive response to an object or event. The only way to make sense of 'eschatological joy' is to say that it is an instance of the emotion of joy that is responding to a certain event that either is presently occurring, has begun to occur, or will occur in the future. France's point is well taken that simply glossing μακάριος with 'happy' may not capture the meaning of the text.[20] But one must not conclude that μακάριος vocabulary does not have an emotional component.

Further evidence for the importance of μακάριος vocabulary and emotion rests upon how Luke has already framed the narrative and connected the emotion of joy with εὐλογητός vocabulary in Luke 1:42. Here we assert substantial agreement with Joseph Fitzmyer who concludes that 'In effect, Jesus' beatitude echoes that of Elizabeth in [Lk] 1:42'. These earlier blessing proclamations are emotion laden. Fitzmyer's conclusion reflects an important

---

[16] With respect to the imperative form of σκιρτάω, there is an understood or supplied concept of joy (Nolland, *Luke 1:1-9:20*, 279).

[17] Hauck, 'μακάριος' *TDNT*, 4:367.

[18] Elliott, *Faithful Feelings*, 166.

[19] In comparison, J. Nolland finds that the *Assumption of Moses* 10:8 uses beatitudes to speak 'of a future state of happiness'. This emotional component of 'happiness' is also paralleled in the beatitudes of Tobit 13:14 in *Luke 1:1-9:20* (Volume 35A; Dallas: Word, 1989), 280.

[20] R.T. France, *The Gospel of Matthew* (Grand Rapids: Eerdmans, 2007), 161.

element of establishing Luke's rhetorical programme as evidenced by repetition. The use of the joy theme in the beatitudes and the repetition of the pattern of joyful blessing both provide evidence of rhetorical amplification.[21]

Even if we do not interpret the μακάριος language as emotional or related to the joy theme, the joy theme is clearly present in Luke 6:23. Joy appears at the height of the blessings and twice engages the reader with the use of the second person imperative (χαίρω, σκιρτάω).[22] The variation of vocabulary for joy is itself evidence that Luke intends to use the rhetorical amplification technique of accumulation (piling up words that are nearly identical in meaning).[23] Those who conclude that the series of blessings are devoid of the emotional sense of 'happiness' would have to agree that such a conclusion would serve to single out and highlight joy as the dominant feeling appropriate for the new age. The rhetorical function of joy is evident in the role it plays as a pole in Luke's double reversal scheme as well as being the only blessing to receive repetition.

This repetition of joy in the Sermon on the Plain should be understood as a continuation of the repetition that was used rhetorically in the introductory narratives that Luke used to frame the discourse in chapter one but an important dimension is added in Luke 6:25: not all joy is good! The second to last woe includes γελάω, which falls conceptually under the joy theme. There is joy to be found when one finds rejection based on one's relationship to 'the Son of Man' (Lk 6:22-23). The joy that God opposes is oriented to those who have present acceptance among 'all people' (Lk 6:26).

Whereas Luke used joy rhetorically to establish a reversal of values in Luke 1-2, this is a development that challenges present joy due to their objects that lie outside the Kingdom. The inner texture of Luke 6:12-26, and specifically of Luke 6:23, points to the importance of the emotion of joy in Luke's rhetoric of reversal.[24] The use of joy in the blessings and woes forces the reader not only to consider their response to God's new age. The reader must carefully consider the object of their joy.

Joy and Intertexture

The intertexture of Luke 6:12-26 is evocative of the covenantal setting in which Israel received the law through Moses. N.T. Wright suggests that Deuteronomy is the primary source for Luke's intertextual programme in this text: 'Four

---

[21] Witherington, *What's in the Word*, 59

[22] In the New Testament, the word σκιρτάω occurs in Luke alone. G. Fitzer, 'σκιρτάω', *TDNT* 7:401-402.

[23] Witherington, *New Testament Rhetoric*, 227.

[24] Resseguie notes that Luke's beatitudes are distinctively rhetorical and ideological and he also finds that this ideology is expressed in the reversals. He also links this rhetoric of reversal with the Magnificat in Lk 1:46-55. His study stands in agreement with many conclusions in this study but lacks an analysis of how the emotion of joy functions in this rhetoric of reversal (*Narrative Criticism of the New Testament*, 187).

promises, and four warnings, presenting in terms of Israel's great scriptural codes: in the book called Deuteronomy, there were long lists of 'blessings' for those who obeyed the law, and 'curses' for those who didn't.'[25] However, Wright continues to note the discontinuity in that Luke's programme entails a 'renewed Israel formed around him [Jesus]'.[26]

Wright's own observation about the importance of a renewed Israel furthers our argument that Isaiah's New Exodus provides a likely source for understanding his intertextual threads.[27] This observation is also significant because of Luke's interest in the apostles as the Twelve (δώδεκα) in Luke 6:13.[28] The description of the apostles as the 'twelve' is evocative of the New Exodus renewal of the twelve tribes of Israel.[29] Deuteronomy is present as an intertextual thread but it cannot fully account for the renewal motif. In addition to theme of the renewal of Israel, there is a strong theme of division present in Luke 6:12-26 as indicated by the use of blessings and cursing. This study argues that Deuteronomy's blessings and cursing are indeed important in the intertextual background of the Sermon on the Plain but Isaiah remains foregrounded.

There is evidence that the primary intertextual thread in Luke 6:12-26 is found in Isaiah 61:1-2.[30] Again, the prominent role of Isaiah 61:1-2 does not negate the influence of Deuteronomy or other texts. A study of the beatitudes in Matthew 11:4-6 and Luke 7:22-23 will demonstrate that the Old Testament allusions are 'broadly thematic as much as text-specific'.[31] The intertexture of Luke 6:12-26 reflects the difficulty in ascertaining the difference between echoes and allusions and the diverse threads of intertextuality that can be present in a given text. Indeed, there is no use of μακάριος language in Isaiah 61:1-2. But such vocabulary does appear in Isaiah 30:18 and Isaiah 56:1-2 as

---

[25] N.T. Wright, *Luke for Everyone* (London: SPCK, 2004), 71.

[26] Wright, *Luke for Everyone*, 71.

[27] Likewise, David Moessner cites Lk 6:23 as an instance in which 'Jesus' journey to death and rising up 'fulfills Moses and all the prophets'. This imagery supports a broader theme of exodus/death/departure. Moessner, 'Reading Luke's Gospel as Ancient Hellenistic Narrative', 139.

[28] D.H. Wenkel, "When the Apostles Became Kings: Ruling and Judging the Twelve Tribes of Israel in the Book of Acts," *BTB* 42:3 (2012): 114-23.

[29] Israel's self-identity was formed in relation to the exodus from Egypt (Exo 24:4). Interest in relating Israel's identity as to the twelve tribes is attested to in extra-biblical texts such as Sirach (44:23). Christian texts of the first-century continue this focus (Jam 1:1; Rev 7:4).

[30] The use of the Isaiah 61 theme attests to the authenticity of this saying. M.F. Bird, *Are You the One Who is to Come?: The Historical Jesus and the Messianic Question* (Grand Rapids: Baker, 2009), 101.

[31] Knowles, 'Scripture, History, Messiah', 69.

well as Psalm 146:5, 7-9.[32] These are all texts that likely lie in the background as Jesus draws from broad scriptural themes.

There is other data to consider before giving up on locating a specific foregrounded intertextual thread in Luke 6:12-26. The most important data is the double reversal pattern in the Lukan beatitudes that culminates in joy. The reversal is double or bi-polar because the rich will become poor and the poor will become rich (Lk 6:20, 24). This reversal pattern provides more than a literary function.[33] This reversal is indeed literary but also reflects the real nature of the new age that God has inaugurated. In the first-century societal structure based around the hierarchy of the wealthy, the Lukan message has important sociological ramifications. The covenantal setting orients the reader to the presence of a new age that has its own unique set of values. These values are established by the Sermon on the Plain. The covenantal blessings are suggestive of the covenant language from Deuteronomy that has been appropriated through Isaiah.[34] The preliminary work is now in place to comment on the use of the joy motif in Luke 6:12-26 and its intertexture.

As noted above in the study of inner texture, the emotion of joy occurs at the height of the blessings and engages the reader with the use of the second person. The inner texture of Luke 6:23 points to the importance of the emotion of joy in Luke's rhetoric of reversal. The key to understanding the role of Isaiah 61 for the Sermon on the Plain's blessings and woes is to consider more than just the first couple verses of Isaiah 61. The presence of the joy theme may indicate that although Jesus did stop reading after the first phrase of Isaiah 61:2, there is more of the passage to consider.[35] If this is the case it could be argued that Isaiah 61 was not only cited but transformed as parts of it were selected (e.g. the joy theme as found in Isaiah 61:3; 7; 10-11). The poetic Sermon on the

---

[32] M.P. Knowles, 'Scripture, History, Messiah' in *Hearing the Old Testament in the New Testament* (ed. S. Porter; Grand Rapids: Eerdmans, 2006), 69.

[33] York, *The Last Will Be First*, 21-22. This study concurs with York's assessment that the reversal pattern would have been recognizable in Luke's Greco-Roman milieu but is primarily related to the OT Septuagint antecedents. York, *The Last Will Be First*, 27; O'Toole, *Unity of Luke's Theology*, 50.

[34] V.K. Robbins also elaborates on the concurrent appropriation of Deuteronomy and Isaiah in Luke 4-7 in 'The Socio-Rhetorical Role of Old Testament Scripture in Luke 4–19', in *Z Noveho Zakona /From the New Testament: Sbornik k narozeninam Prof. ThDr. Zdenka Sazavy* (eds. H. Tonzarova and P. Melmuk; Praha: Vydala Cirkev cesko-slovenska husitska, 2001), 87-88.

[35] J.A. Sanders, 'Isaiah in Luke' in *Luke and Scripture: The Function of Sacred Tradition in Luke-Acts* (eds. C. Evans and J.A. Sanders; Minneapolis: Fortress, 1993), 23.

Plain establishes a reversal of joy and sorrow for those who are the recipients of God's favour (echoing Isaiah 61).[36]

While Isaiah 61 is likely the most prominent Isaianic intertextual thread, the New Exodus of Isaiah 40 also plays a formative role. The Sermon on the Plain presents two paths: a way of blessing (as beatitudes) and a way of cursing (as woes). This is highly suggestive of Luke's message of division within Israel and John's message that the one coming after him has a winnowing fork in his hand (Lk 3:17).[37] This builds on the conclusion that the New Exodus motif entails a remnant concept that uses a subdivision into a faithful community and those who were disobedient (e.g. wheat and chaff).[38] For the faithful, they are part of the restoration of Israel.[39] The pattern of division is more than suggestive in Luke 6:23 where the reference to the prophets who were killed in the past provides a template or pattern for understanding the Kingdom that Jesus preaches.[40] The pattern of division is such that 'the whole world is divided into two camps'.[41] This allusion to the Old Testament prophets is crucial to Luke's rhetorical strategy that is evident in our study of joy. The use of joy in the blessings and woes forces the reader not only to consider their response to God's new age. The reader must also carefully consider the object of their joy because joy in the present age and the values thereof can prove that one is not participating in the New Exodus.

Joy and Sacred Texture

Broadly speaking, the sacred texture of a text consists of the vertical dimensions that connect human life and the divine. The Lukan narrative has progressed since the pregnancy and birth narratives that sought to persuade the reader of what the God of Israel has inaugurated by visiting his people. The co-text that leads up to this point is particularly important for understanding the role of joy in Luke 6.20-26. In Luke 6:1-5, Jesus' speech reflects his status as a prophet like Moses. Jesus is a παράδειγμα ('example'). The vignettes (such as the plucking grain incident) are examples that exhibit Jesus' lordship as he speaks as one who is a greater prophet than Moses or Elijah (compare Lk 6:46; 9:7-9, 18-19).[42] Specifically, Luke's rhetoric takes an important turn in Luke 6:20 where Jesus begins a direct discourse after 'lifting his eyes'. Our focus

---

[36] Mallen makes strong connections between the 'salvation as reversal' motif in Luke 6 and Isaiah 61 and 65-66 but he does not integrate the emotional dimension into his study (*Reading and Transformation of Isaiah*, 106-108).

[37] Litwak, *Echoes of Scripture in Luke-Acts*, 194.

[38] Litwak, *Echoes of Scripture in Luke-Acts*, 194.

[39] Bird, *Are You the One Who is to Come?*, 147.

[40] Litwak, *Echoes of Scripture in Luke-Acts*, 135.

[41] O'Toole, *Unity of Luke's Theology*, 110.

[42] D.P. Moessner, *Lord of the Banquet: The Literary and Theological Significance of the Lukan Travel Narrative* (Harrisburg: Trinity Press International, 1998), 46.

will remain on the rhetoric of reversal that characterizes his speech.[43] Jesus' speech is on behalf of this kingdom that explicitly belongs to God.

What Jesus has previously enacted (as a παράδειγμα) is put into words in Luke 6:20-26. Previously, Luke portrayed Jesus as engaging God's law in a way that challenged the Pharisees interpretation of Jesus himself. There are several items that point to an understanding of the Lukan beatitudes as the establishment of a new set of laws or a new word from the κύριος. In Luke 6:12-26 we see that 'God is doing something quite new'.[44] Jesus is delivering a new word to the 'Twelve' and the crowds that forms a renewed law for a renewed Israel.[45] Perhaps one can conclude that this speech is related to the Isaianic New Exodus promise that is oriented around the λόγος going forth in LXX Isaiah 40:5b: 'and all flesh shall see the salvation of God because the Lord has spoken'.[46] The God of Israel is acting through Jesus by giving them a renewed word. Further evidence of the direct connection between Jesus' speech and the divine is seen in the first blessing in Luke 6:20 that promises the 'kingdom of God' to the poor.

But who are the 'poor'? Are they socio-economically, politically, or spiritually poor? Luke's division of the people into 'falling and rising' in Simeon's oracle likely establishes a hermeneutical key for this dilemma.[47] The 'poor' are inclusive of those who have any condition that allows them to see their need for divine reversal that comes about through Jesus.[48] The story of Zacchaeus is a 'rhetorical' narrative aimed at 'conversion' but there are likely implications for this reversal from being rich to poor for implied readers who have already become disciples.[49]

Jesus' speech of blessings and woes is explicitly oriented around bi-polar reversals. In this formula, X will be Y and Y will become X. The rhetorical power of this speech has moved from the παράδειγμα of the co-texts to a divinely given word from the Lord that reverses expectations and values. These new values are not only radical but they are also imperatival. Joy plays an important role in this rhetoric because it is the only thing explicitly demanded with an imperative in Luke 6:23. Technically speaking, the only thing demanded of the renewed Israel by the renewed word of the Lord is the

---

[43] Robbins' explains this as Luke's interest in the rhetoric 'of' the story rather than an interest in the internal discourse of the story Mack and Robbins, *Patterns of Persuasion in the Gospels*, 131. Here I seek to examine both by looking at the speech of Jesus as it relates to the rhetoric of the story.

[44] Wright, *Luke for Everyone*, 71.

[45] Wright, *Luke for Everyone*, 71.

[46] *NETS*, Book of Esaias, 853.

[47] York, *The Last Shall Be First*, 116.

[48] Mallen, *Reading and Transformation of Isaiah*, 107.

[49] M. Parsons, *Body and Character in Luke-Acts: The Subversion of Physiognomy in Early Christianity*, Grand Rapids: Baker, 2006), 106. For a connection between the 'poor' and the reversal motif see Nolland, *Luke 1:1-9:20*, 283.

emotion of joy. The emotion of joy is connected to God (in heaven) and the implied reader. This is evidence of what York calls 'the divine principle of reversal'.[50] The object of this joy is also critically connected to the sacred texture. The people of God are to rejoice and leap for joy because of the promise of future reward in heaven (Lk 6:23). The nature of this line of reasoning is rather cryptic.[51] This is best understood as epexegetically related to the second clause in Luke 6:23 (for so their fathers did to the prophets).

The disciples who suffer for Jesus will receive the same reward as the prophets who suffered beforehand.[52] But heaven is coming down to earth as Jesus' kingdom is being inaugurated.[53] The angels came from heaven (Lk 2:15) and the voice of God came from heaven (Lk 3:22). One can also understand Jesus as the 'authoritative voice of God' commanding joy from above.[54] Thus, the reward of those who are outcasts and are suffering comes from God and this divine status reversal has rewards that may be tangible now in terms of possessing the blessing of God.

Joy and Ideological Texture

The value of a socio-rhetorical approach that clarifies ideological textures is most apparent in texts that have a clear element of conflict and opposition.[55] The co-text of Luke 6:20-26 helps us to identity the nature of the conflict addressed by Luke's rhetoric. In Luke 6:1-11, Jesus comes into conflict with the Pharisees over the Sabbath. The Pharisees attack Jesus' disciples for plucking ears of grain in the cornfields (Lk 6:1). The focus of the conflict is the Sabbath, which functioned as one of the 'chief badges of identity' for Israel.[56] Here we concur with N.T. Wright's assessment that Luke is seeking to 'shape the growing community of his followers, to turn them into God's New Israel, the people who would live in God's New Age'.[57] The conflict is isolated to the Pharisees but extends through Luke's integration of socio-economic and religious-spiritual conditions. Luke's Sermon on the Plain addresses those who

---

[50] York, *The Last Shall Be First*, 183.

[51] Marshall agrees: 'The connection of thought with the final clause is not clear'. Marshall, *The Gospel of Luke*, 254.

[52] Similarly see Bock, *Luke 1:1-9:50*, 581-82;

[53] Although 'heaven' is a periphrasis for God, it is also a place from which God has broken into history. L.T. Johnson, *The Gospel of Luke* (Collegeville: Liturgical Press, 1991), 107 n23.

[54] Moessner, *Lord of the Banquet*, 122.

[55] Shillington, *Introduction to the Study of Luke-Acts*, 60.

[56] Wright, *Luke for Everyone*, 68; Kennedy also notes the significance of the hostility of the Pharisees who were likely present in the audience (Lk 6:2, 7). Thus, Jesus is addressing an audience that is both sympathetic and hostile (*New Testament Interpretation through Rhetorical Criticism*, 65).

[57] Wright, *Luke for Everyone*, 69.

are rich, full, and laughing. By addressing the elevated social strata, Luke is challenging the ideology of the old age by associating the blessings and honour of his kingdom with social dishonour. This effectively turns the social pyramid upside down.

Crucial to understanding Luke's ideological texture and use of joy in Luke 6:20-26 is identifying the audience of the Sermon on the Plain as the crowds and the disciples. The crowds are characterized by non-commitment to Jesus while the disciples have some level if commitment, whether partial or nominal.[58] Jesus clarifies the nature of the conflict when he associates being hated and martyrdom with being blessed. One commentator asks: 'If this is what God's favor looks like, who would want it?'[59] Those who hear Jesus are placed into two categories but these categories are reversed. The 'rich' are poor and the 'poor' are rich (or, the hated are loved). Jesus 'announces a reversal' that demands that one's 'life orientation' be seen in light of this conflict.[60] If Jesus is the 'New Moses', then one of his central demands is joy.[61] This study contributes to this paradigm of division and divine reversal by establishing joy as an important emotional component of the rhetoric of reversal.[62] In sum, emotion plays a crucial role in the conflict that characterizes this new age.

The Reversal of the Outcast: Joy in Luke 7:18-23

The use of μακάριος vocabulary builds on the beatitudes (and woes) found in Jesus' Sermon on the Plain (Lk 6:20-26). It is further evidence that Luke continues to use emotion to empower his text. The entire pericope of Luke 7:18-23 presents a 'summary' of Jesus' axiomatic and paradigmatic sermon in Nazareth in Luke 4:16-30.[63] During Jesus' ministry in Galilee, his fame begins to spread so much that John sends two disciples to inquire if Jesus is truly the messiah.[64] For our purposes, it matters very little if objections stand against this

---

[58] Marshall, *New Testament Theology*, 98.

[59] Borgman, *The Way According to Luke-Acts*, 46.

[60] M. Goheen, 'A Critical Examination of David Bosch's Missional Reading of Luke' in *Reading Luke: Interpretation, Reflection, Formation* (eds. C. Bartholomew, J.B. Green, A.C. Thiselton.; Carlisle: Paternoster, 2006; Grand Rapids: Zondervan, 2005), 246.

[61] The portrayal of Jesus as the 'New Moses' supports the conclusion that Luke appropriates the Exodus tradition. Moessner explains that Luke's portrayal of Jesus reflects Moses' prophecy of a 'prophet like me' (Deut 18:15-9) because Jesus gives 'life-giving words of God himself' (*Lord of the Banquet*, 46).

[62] R.J. Karris, *Luke: Artist and Theologian: Luke's Passion Account as Literature* (Mahwah: Paulist, 1985), 54.

[63] Green, *Theology of the Gospel of Luke*, 76; York, *The Last Will be First*, 120.

[64] It is plausible that John saw that Jesus' deeds were similar to Elijah's. See J.M. Dawsey, *The Lukan Voice: Confusion and Irony in the Gospel of Luke* (Macon: Mercer, 1986), 130.

reading of John the Baptist's initial interpretation of Jesus.[65] The joy theme is not strong in Luke 7:18-23 but it is present as this relates and builds on the presence of the joy theme in the μακάριος language used in the Sermon on the Plain. The concept of joy is also present in Jesus' use of the Isaianic language for reversals mentioned in his response to John.[66] The 'governing idea' or governing question in this pericope is: who is Jesus?[67] The one who understands who Jesus is and follows him will be joyful and blessed. The reversal motif demonstrates the type of thinking that is required to accept Jesus and the joy theme is used to reinforce this new outlook.

Joy and Inner Texture

Some recognize that the joy theme is present in the Sermon on the Plain but it is not widely recognized in the response to the messengers of John the Baptist (Lk 7:18-23).[68] The key question that must be answered with regard to the joy theme and the reversal of the outcast in Luke 7:22-23 is whether there is any emotion of joy meant by the vocabulary of μακάριος in the statement: 'And blessed (μακάριος) in the one who is not offended by me' (Lk 7:23).[69] The entry for μακάριος in *TDNT* states that this word refers to 'distinctive religious joy which accrues to man from his share in the salvation of the kingdom of God'.[70] The problem with this definition in the *TDNT* is that the 'word itself does not have this special meaning'.[71] The word μακάριος is indeed emotional but does not necessitate that it be used with the kingdom of God. The conclusion of our study of μακάριος in the Sermon on the Plain was that a component-based definition includes both blessing and the emotion of joy or happiness. Although it is used in Luke 7:18-23 in reference to the kingdom, it is important to recognize that its meaning is at least partially emotional. Luke 7:23 is an instance in which Jesus is referring to the emotion of joy or happiness.[72] This is significant for understanding the inner texture of Luke's rhetorical goals because it is evidence of repetition of the joy theme that has been developing throughout the Gospel.

---

[65] Bock, *Luke 1:1-9:50*, 657-58.

[66] Du Toit, *Der Aspekt der Freude im urchristlichen Abendmahl*, 28.

[67] Moessner, *Lord of the Banquet*, 101.

[68] For example, Navone's study does not cite Lk 7:18-23 in his chapter on the theme of joy. Navone, *Themes of St. Luke*, 75-76.

[69] For comments on the comparison of this pericope between Luke, Matthew, and Q see Kurz, *Reading Luke-Acts*, 190 n28.

[70] Hauck, 'μακάριος,' *TDNT*, 4:367.

[71] Elliott, *Faithful Feelings*, 165.

[72] Elliott, *Faithful Feelings*, 167.

Joy and Intertexture

Our focus is on the presence of the *makarism* in Luke 7:23 as it provides an (at least partially) emotional reversal of the outcast. The logic of Luke 7:23 is thus: the one who is not offended by Jesus is blessed (μακάριός). The intertextual source of the μακάριος language is most likely the Septuagint and not contemporary Greco-Roman sources. The usage of μακάριός reflects a reversal of values so different from normal Greek usage that 'this points to the New Testament's independence from Greek ideas'.[73] This is likely stating the conclusion too strongly. The very value of the reversal of expectation and its rhetorical power to challenge conventional thought is based on the assumption that the reader has a preconceived idea of what it is to be 'joyful'. In the case of Luke's Gospel this would entail being weak, poor, and humble.

There is a fairly strong consensus that the beatitudes and woes of Luke 7 are tied intertextually to a harmony of Isaianic texts, the strongest echoes reflecting Isaiah 35 and Isaiah 61.[74] Some conclude that Isaiah 61 is not significant for Luke.[75] On the other hand, it is likely that there is an 'Isaianic scheme' in this pericope that 'reflects the hermeneutical importance of Isaiah 61 for the identity of the early Christian movement'.[76] Another piece of evidence for viewing Isaiah as the strongest intertextual thread in this pericope is the use of the *makarism* in Luke 7:23 to summarize the Sermon on the Plain. This blessing in Luke 7:23 may summarize Jesus' sermon in Luke 4:21 as Jewish midrashic and homily patterns usually included a formulaic statement.[77]

In addition, Isaiah 35 is filled with the joy theme, which is particularly strong in Isaiah 35:1-7. This summary beatitude is highly evocative of the emotional and joy-driven reversal rhetoric of the New Exodus theme in Isaiah 35. One piece of evidence that links Luke 7 and Isaiah 35 is the theme of 'the Way' that is prepared for YHWH to come and his people to return.[78] This evokes the Exodus tradition that has been transformed by Isaiah (and others). This connection is reflected in Jesus' intertextual comment in Luke 7:27 about

---

[73] Elliott, *Faithful Feelings*, 169; Meynet, *Rhetorical Analysis*, 22.

[74] Pao and Schnabel, 'Luke', *CNTUOT*, 299-300; Pao, *Acts and the Isaianic New Exodus*, 74; Turner, *Power from on High*, 250; York, *The Last Shall Be First*, 120; Marshall, *Luke: Historian and Theologian*, 124; Bird, *Are You the One Who is to Come?*, 99. This string of pearls approach to intertextual citations reflects the pattern of Isaianic quotations in the messianic apocalypse (4Q521). The two most likely sources cited in 4Q521 are LXX Isa 35:5 and 61:1. Bird, *Are You the One Who is to Come?*, 146. It has been suggested that Jesus drew from a common tradition shared with 4Q521. G.J. Brooke, *The Dead Sea Scrolls and the New Testament* (Minneapolis: Fortress, 2005), 14, also 80, 262.

[75] C. Tuckett, 'The Lukan Son of Man' in *Luke's Literary Achievement: Collected Essays* (ed. C.M. Tuckett; JSNTSup 116; Sheffield: Academic Press, 1995), 217.

[76] Pao, *Acts and the Isaianic New Exodus*, 75.

[77] Kimball, *Jesus' Exposition of the Old Testament in Luke's Gospel*, 113.

[78] Pao, *Acts and the Isaianic New Exodus*, 53.

John: he has prepared 'the way'. In Luke 7:23 the rhetoric of reversal is strengthened and by the intertextual echoes of joy that are inherent in the blessing or *makarism* for those who accept Jesus.

Luke quotes Jesus as he presents the inaugurated new age that is characterized by a reversal of conditions for the people of God. There is even evidence of a bi-polar reversal wherein the poor become rich and the rich become poor in Jesus' response that contrasts the 'luxury' of the king's courts to the ministry of a prophet (Lk 7:25). The strongest point that can be made here is that the emotion of joy is present (to some extent) in Jesus' reference to Isaiah 61 and that this is used persuasively to support the conclusion that the new age of salvation has arrived in himself.

Joy and Sacred Texture

The importance of the sacred in Luke 7:18-23 is necessary to examine because Jesus intentionally describes his identity in terms of messianic categories: Jesus speaks the words of God.[79] In Matthew's version of John's inquiry of Jesus the messengers reported what they saw and heard.[80] Luke, on the other hand, records Jesus' instructing the messengers to relay the mighty works he has been doing. What is significant about this is that the works that Jesus has done are all divine reversals. Throughout the narrative, the emotion of joy has been integral to divine reversals as Luke uses them to persuade the reader about who he is. Although there the presence of emotion is not as strong as in other pericopae, there is a strong rhetorical presence that is indicated by the string of questions that Jesus puts to the crowds (Lk 7:26). By establishing the blessing and joy that comes to the one who accepts Jesus, the reader knows how to answer these questions from Jesus. At the very least, these questions help one to see that Jesus is 'more than a prophet' (Lk 7:25-6). This messianic framework is preparatory for understanding that Jesus speaks the words of God.

Luke records Jesus' offer of joy after he explains his ministry of mighty deeds. By referring to his mighty deeds, Jesus provides both tangible evidence for who he is and a Scriptural key for understanding his ministry based on Isaiah 61 and other texts. One must conclude that Jesus embodies the divine promises given to Israel; he is the fulfillment.[81]

The narrator uses the title 'Lord' for Jesus although human characters generally do not refer to Jesus as 'Lord' in his lifetime.[82] Luke's Christology

---

[79] Bird, *Are You the One Who is to Come?*, 29.

[80] Marshall, *Luke: Historian and Theologian*, 43.

[81] 'Jesus confirms that he is more a prophet like Elijah; he is the one who embodies the divine promises to be given to the unfortunate of society'. York, *The Last Shall Be First*, 120.

[82] Marshall, *New Testament Theology*, 175.

consists of recognizing that the earthly Jesus was the Lord although he was unrecognized as such before his death and resurrection.[83]

The very invocation of John the Baptist invites the reader to think in terms of those who have aligned themselves with John through repentance and those who have not. The sacred texture is important to consider because Luke explicitly refers to the 'purpose of God' when the narrator explains in Luke 7:30: 'but the Pharisees and the lawyers rejected the purpose of God for themselves, not having been baptized by him'. The rational of the narrative is explained; the Pharisees and lawyers were not aligned with John and therefore rejected Jesus.[84] Here is a picture of what it means to be scandalized by Jesus' words. The rejection of John and his words of repentance become a picture of what it means to reject Jesus. Such people will lose the joyful-blessing. The primary emotion driving this is based on the emotion connected to μακάριός. This foil sets up the rhetoric that drives the reader to align themselves with Jesus' words from God and repent.

Joy and Ideological Texture

The joy theme appears in the μακάριος vocabulary at the end of Jesus' reply to John the Baptist.[85] Like the other uses of the joy theme, this instance comes after Jesus answers John's disciples with a picture of his kingdom that totally reverses expectations. Jesus is connected to the outcasts (the blind, lame, lepers, deaf, etc.; Lk 7:21-23). Having articulated that his kingdom work is based on the inclusion of outsiders, Jesus responds (Lk 7:23): 'And blessed is the one who is not offended by me'. This concluding comment by Jesus is also 'foreboding' because it assumes that there are those who oppose Jesus' inclusion of the outcasts.[86] This statement develops the division theme that has been present since the introductory narratives. David Pao concurs with this in essence when he states that 'This qualification of the jubilant message of Isaiah 61:1-2 serves to make sense out of the significant opposition of the Jews against both the early Christian movement and its "founder"'.[87] For our purposes, it is the element of emotion that strengthens Luke's rhetoric of reversal and division.

It is the reversal of the outcasts that clarifies Jesus' ministry. The radical nature of this ministry requires that he address those who take a stance against him and his work. The reason for the confusion about Jesus' identity is that his ministry did not fit neatly into preconceived types or characters. In *some sense*,

---

[83] Marshall, *New Testament Theology*, 175.

[84] Contra Borgman, this text makes it unlikely that Jesus was anticipating that John himself would take offence at Jesus (*The Way According to Luke-Acts*, 62).

[85] R. Brawley, *Centering on God: Method and Message in Luke-Acts* (Louisville: WJKP, 1990), 49.

[86] Kurz, *Reading Luke-Acts*, 24.

[87] Pao, *Acts and the Isaianic New Exodus*, 80.

Jesus is not the 'exalted king of Israel' even though he is the Son of David; nor is he conquering the Roman Empire even though he is the New Joshua.[88] This thesis has merit because it was not clear to John who Jesus was until he asked Jesus directly. But the cause for confusion is better placed in the nature of the people whom Jesus was calling into his kingdom. Here, the quotation of Scripture by Jesus serves as the hermeneutical key to understanding his deeds and his kingdom. In Luke 7:22-23 Jesus answers John that his ministry is reversing the status of the least. Jesus' ministry to lepers and the like is the real problem with Jesus' identity.[89]

The pericope of Luke 7:18-23 creates a not-so-subtle ideology against those who are rich, strong, and proud. The opponents of Jesus are left unstated by his closing comment. Yet it is easiest to imagine that they are those who are the opposite of those whom he is ministering to in Luke 7:22-23. The most natural opponents of Jesus who find his ministry a scandal will be those who are not in need of physical healing or spiritual healing (Lk 7:21). The presence of the *makarism* creates an obvious inverse: those who are scandalized by Jesus' ministry to outcasts will not be joyfully-blessed. And to participate in this programme is to participate in joy. Jesus' kingdom is a scandal (σκάνδαλον) and this requires that he directly engage those who posture themselves against the kingdom. The ideological nature of Luke's rhetoric is directly connected to the emotional state of the reader who is willing to accept Jesus and his kingdom of outcasts. In the *makarism* or blessing in Luke 7:23, joyful-blessing is the reward for accepting Jesus' ministry to the outcasts. *By presenting the possession of Jesus' joyful-blessing as a matter of controversy, Luke uses it to posture Jesus against his opponents.*[90]

The Reversal of the Would-Be-Doer: Joy in Luke 8:9-15

The use of joy in the Parable of the Sower is the exception that proves the rule. Whereas all the other instances of joy are used positively, the use of joy in Luke 8:13 is surprisingly negative.[91] The key to understanding this idiosyncrasy is that Luke never divides hearing from doing. Jesus' deeds are cause for celebration. Yet those who follow Jesus must critically examine the presence of joy in light of one's endurance in obeying the word. As Jesus' ministry in

---

[88] Dawsey, *Lukan Voice*, 152.

[89] 'Luke more than the other evangelists stresses Jesus' offensive behavior to the 'righteous'. J.A. Sanders, 'Sins, Debts, and Jubilee Release' in *Luke and Scripture: The Function of Sacred Tradition in Luke-Acts* (eds. C.A. Evans and J.A. Sanders; Minneapolis: Fortress, 1993), 89.

[90] Tannehill, *Shape of Luke's Story*, 260.

[91] Navone states that through poverty and renunciation of the world only 'then can the word of God produce Christian joy'. It is not clear if this comment on Lk 8:13 reflects the nature of an instance of joy which is temporary and fails during testing. Navone, *Themes of St. Luke*, 76.

Galilee progresses, he encounters a mixture of responses.[92] For both Greco-Roman parables and those shaped primarily by their Jewish context, the content of the parable is important.[93] This is particularly true for the Parable of the Sower. This parable reflects the variety of responses to Jesus' message about the kingdom while maintaining a connection between hearing and doing and feeling.

The kingdom of God is coming through the 'seed' of the word of God. Because of its proximity, one must align with the kingdom or be aligned against it. For those who hear the word (receive the seed), there are deceptions that can come along and fool the would-be-doer of the word. This negative use of joy simultaneously commends a positive alternative through the power of emotion.[94] Here joy operates as the reversal of the reversal that comes about in the kingdom.[95] There is an ideal state of affairs wherein hearing is mixed with obedience. Yet, one of the greatest dangers is joy. Its presence can persuade one that he or she is an ideal recipient of the seed of the word when in fact the emotions are not mixed with obedience.

Joy and Inner Texture

The parable of the sower utilizes an element of reversal of expectation by associating joy with a disciple who falls away. The reference to joy appears in reference to the seed that lands on the rock (Lk 8:6 and Lk 8:13). This seed or preaching of the 'word of God' is initially described as (Lk 8:6): 'and some fell on the rock, and as it grew up, it withered away because it had no moisture'. Jesus then explains the parable to the disciples in secret. The issue here is that time demonstrates that the would-be disciples are not mixing hearing the word of God with action. Initially there are positive signs that include the presence of 'joy' (χαρά) and 'faith' (πιστεύω). The end, however, is 'desertion, defection or apostasy'.[96]

---

[92] Green, *Gospel of Luke*, 327.

[93] Witherington, *New Testament Rhetoric*, 41.

[94] This rhetorical goal is similar to John Nolland's interpretation of the unclean spirit who leaves the residence and returns with seven worse companions (Lk 11:24-26). Nolland understands this as a warning against 'deception' that comes with 'apparent improvement in one's lot'. Conceptually Nolland is describing Luke's rhetoric when he explains that Luke has '*commended*' a 'positive alternative'. J. Nolland, 'The Role of Money and Possessions in the Parable of the Prodigal Son' in *Reading Luke: Interpretation, Reflection, Formation* (eds. C. Bartholomew, J.B. Green, and A.C. Thiselton; Grand Rapids: Zondervan, 2005), 184.

[95] Karris' comments are suggestive of a reversal of a divine reversal as the seed which should reverse the evil of hunger is reversed itself through deception and falling away (*Luke: Artist and Theologian*, 55).

[96] C.C. Black, *The Rhetoric of the Gospel: Theological Artistry in the Gospels and Acts* (St. Louis: Chalice, 2001), 106. Compare ἀφίστημι in Acts 5:37-38; LXX Jeremiah 3:14; 1 Maccabees 11:43.

The use of this language reflects Luke's connection between the joy theme and salvation. There is also an ecclesiological function detectable in Jesus' use of joy in this parable; the ones who possess faith and joy are reflecting good signs that they are disciples. The sign or marker of genuine faith and repentance is 'joy'. This connection is necessary for the parable to function as a challenge to the reader. There are assumptions based on the connection between joy and discipleship or even membership in the kingdom. The explanation of the seed that falls on the rock is challenging precisely because one assumes that it is entirely positive when the word of God produces the fruits of joy and faith. The positive language is bait for the sudden switch (reversal) that results in falling away (Lk 8:13). The presence of faith and joy is not absolute if it is not followed in time by perseverance under trial. Joy must have 'roots' in persevering obedience or it is not genuine.

Joy and Intertexture

The reason for Luke's use of 'joy' (χαρά) for the second soil in Luke 8:13 is best understood in light of Luke's rhetorical programme of reversal of expectation. The citation of a part of Isaiah 6:9-10 is suggestive of Luke's desire for the reader to understand this parable in terms of his overall Isaianic programme.[97] Like Isaiah 6:9-10, the response in Luke 8:10 'illustrates the obduracy of God's people towards the word of the Lord proclaimed by his messengers'.[98] The objection may be raised that in the Septuagint, Isaiah 6:9-10 'does not refer to judgment' but rather they 'are a description of the obduracy of the fathers'.[99] But this conclusion does not make good sense of Jesus' explanation to the disciples that incorporates ἵνα (Lk 8:10) to indicate purpose. Jesus teaches in parables *in order* to produce the blindness and deafness of Isaiah 6:9-10. But this is not an either/or dilemma. One can understand the citation of Isaiah 6:9-10 as an allusion to the obduracy of Israel's former leadership and as a framework for understanding the judgment they now experience in the present.

---

[97] Pao denies that the reference to Isa 6:9-10 is an 'explicit Isaianic quotation' because he vigorously argues that Luke reserves the place for an explicit quotation till Acts 28. Yet, Pao acknowledges that this intertextual reference is 'taken' from Isa 6:9. The language in Lk 8:10 (βλέποντες μὴ βλέπωσιν καὶ ἀκούοντες μὴ συνιῶσιν) is such a strong parallel with Isa 6:9-10 (Ἀκοῇ ἀκούσετε καὶ οὐ μὴ συνῆτε καὶ βλέποντες βλέψετε καὶ οὐ μὴ ἴδητε) that it is hard to conclude that Luke has omitted an explicit reference. One can agree with Pao that the strongest reference to Isa 6:9-10 is in Acts 28. It may be best to conclude that this reference in Luke 8 is weaker so as to foreshadow a clearer instance of hardening in the future (i.e. Acts 28). Pao, *Acts and the Isaianic New Exodus*, 105.
[98] Litwak, *Echoes of Scripture in Luke-Acts*, 186, also 194.
[99] Litwak, *Echoes of Scripture in Luke-Acts*, 187.

It is also likely that focus on the 'word of God' is related to the importance of the 'word of God' in LXX Isaiah 55:10-11. The key to the parable is the explanation that the 'seed is the word of God' (Lk 8:11).[100] The reference to χαρά in both Luke 8:13 and LXX Isaiah 55:12 supports this relationship. Such a conclusion must be tempered by the fact that the χαρά in Luke 8:13 is only temporary and represents misleading evidence of God's word at work. On the other hand, this logic also works in favour of a connection. Luke may be re-contextualizing joy as something that should be genuine. This also frames the word and joy in terms of the Isaianic New Exodus.[101] The very fact that joy has the power to persuade the hearer of the 'word of God' means that joy which is not accompanied by perseverance is dangerous. The connections between Isa 55:10-11 and the parable of the Sower now include the theme of joy as well as the references to 'seed' and the 'word'.[102]

The use of χαρά for the second soil in Luke 8:13 can be located in the broad scope of Luke's continual interaction with Isaianic themes. The parable is strong evidence of the persuasive power of the emotion of joy. This power is so potent that the one who possesses it can be deceived.[103] The joy theme intersects with the theme of division as Luke portrays those who follow the Way as those who are faithful. *Joy can mislead those who hear the word of God if it does not endure along with perseverance in obedience.*

Joy and Sacred Texture

The place of God in the parable of the Sower is rather indirect. The 'word' that is received with 'joy' (χαρά) in Luke 8:11 is nothing other than the 'word of God' (ὁ λόγος τοῦ θεοῦ). The parable of the Sower reinforces the connection between Jesus' ministry and the word of God. Green comments that Jesus is 'the one who discloses and brings to fruition the divine purpose, in the face of which response is not only possible but mandatory'.[104]

A comparison between the parable of the Sower in Mark and Luke reveals that Luke emphasizes the identification of the seed with the 'word of God'.[105] This not only establishes the importance of the word for the ecclesiastical function of supporting the remnant or faithful community but it also prepares the reader for the growth of the word in Luke's second volume. The language of fruitfulness in the parable of the sower envisions a community that 'not only is judged by its fruit but is itself a manifestation of the fruitfulness of

---

[100] Pao and Schnabel, 'Luke,' *CUOTNT*, 305.

[101] Pao, *Acts and the Isaianic New Exodus*, 171.

[102] Pao, *Acts and the Isaianic New Exodus*, 171.

[103] It is quite possible that this negative use of joy mirrors the concept of 'false joy' present in Israel in Stephen's reference to the golden calf incident in Acts 7:41. See Morrice, *Joy in the New Testament*, 97.

[104] Green, *Gospel of Luke*, 327.

[105] Pao, *Acts and the Isaianic New Exodus*, 170.

Yahweh'.[106] The parable of the sower is a foundational parable that 'describes the shape of the community that he [Jesus] is calling into being'.[107]

This proposal above must be tempered with the reality of demonic opposition to the word of God and the kingdom of God. The community envisioned here is a community in conflict. Luke 8:12 is likely an instance that disproves Hans Conzelmann's theory of a 'Satan-free' period in Jesus' life.[108] The on-going demonic activity must prompt those who are seeking the kingdom to retain a hermeneutic of suspicion toward the emotion of joy because of its deceptive power. To reject his word is to reject the purpose of God. This is why it is so important to understand the power and deception of joy mixed with faith that does not endure under trial.

Joy and Ideological Texture

The conflict and opposition that characterize the Parable of the Sower seems to be two-fold. These two arenas of conflict are also related. First, there is an internal conflict that takes place within the would-be-doer. This is evident in the language of 'belief' that has no 'root' in Luke 8:13. Second, there is an external conflict that reveals the depth of the root. This is also evident in Luke 8:13 as the temporal condition: 'in time of testing [they] fall away'. In order to understand the ideology and conflict in view, the question arises as to the nature of this 'testing' (πειρασμός). It may be best to see the meaning of πειρασμός as very indefinite. Green interprets it in this vein: the 'purpose of God, then, may be countered or opposed in a host of ways within the Gospel, and by a plurality of characters'.[109] And any opposition is attributable in some manner as demonic opposition.[110] This is supported by the fact that πειρασμός is used to designate testing from the realm of Satan in Luke 22:28, 40, 46.[111] Ultimately, the conflict manifests itself as the rejection of God's message and messengers. The testing may mean death as the citation of Isaiah 6:9 associates the contemporary first-century situation with Israel's history of rejecting prophets.[112] Thus, fulfillment is used rhetorically to persuade the reader to respond to the word in a way that perseveres and takes root.[113]

The ideology of the Parable of the Sower is likely targeted to include a community that is facing trials as well as to 'others' in whom it brings about hardening. The Parable of the Sower is designed to illumine some and harden

---

[106] S.C. Keesmaat, 'In the Face of the Empire' in *Hearing the Old Testament in the New Testament* (Grand Rapids: Eerdmans, 2006), 200.

[107] Keesmaat, 'In the Face of the Empire', 200.

[108] Kimball, *Jesus' Exposition of the Old Testament*, 94-95.

[109] Green, *Theology of the Gospel of Luke*, 34.

[110] Green, *Theology of the Gospel of Luke*, 34.

[111] Green, *Theology of the Gospel of Luke*, 66.

[112] Litwak, *Echoes of Scripture in Luke-Acts*, 186-87.

[113] Witherington, *New Testament Rhetoric*, 38.

others. Joy is close to the centre of Luke's rhetorical strategy to overturn the values of the world and replace them with faith in Jesus that produces the reversed values of the Kingdom. For most of Luke's Gospel, the repetition of joy encourages 'a feelingful participation meaning'.[114] In the parable of the Soils, because the emotion of joy is almost universally connected to an appropriate response, thus it serves as a perfect foil. The fact that the person with joy ultimately falls away presents a reversal of expectation. This brings the reader back to a place of disorientation.[115] The place of re-orientation has already been established in the narratives that framed the Gospel as Mary's obedience and joy function as a παράδειγμα to follow. One must carefully consider how they are responding to hearing the word of God, particularly in light of trials.[116]

Conclusion

This chapter examined three textual units from the Galilean ministry of Jesus as found in (1) the beatitudes and woes of the Sermon on the Plain (Lk 6:20-26), (2) the identification of Jesus by John the Baptist (Lk 7:22-23), and (3) the explanation of the Parable of the Sower (Lk 8:9-15). It is clear that the joy theme that was established in the early narratives of the Gospel of Luke continues to resonate throughout the text. Luke's use of Isaiah remains an important source for providing the framework of divine reversal and joyful response to Jesus' preaching of the kingdom. Some Isaianic passages are more important than others are, yet the whole remains a 'blueprint' for his corpus.[117]

In the Sermon on the Plain, joy is not only commanded but it is directly connected with the treasure in heaven that functions as an incentive. This proves that Luke uses the emotion of joy to challenge one's stance or position toward the world and toward the 'word' that Jesus and his disciples are sowing. Jesus concludes his statement to John the Baptist with a *makarism* that can be understood to have a joyous emotional component. This statement by Jesus to John echoes the Sermon on the Plain and amounts to a summary statement. In the Parable of the Sower, the rhetorical force of joy is most clearly seen. It is assumed that the experience or possession of joy in conjunction with some type of faith is so strong that it has the potential to deceive. Each use of joy can be connected directly to Luke's use of the rhetorical device of reversal of expectation.

---

[114] Tannehill, *Shape of Luke's Story*, 33.

[115] Resseguie, *Narrative Criticism of the New Testament*, 33-38.

[116] This contrasts with Mary's joy that was present with her obedience at hearing God's word. The theme of joy relates to the rest of Luke's narrative via 'intersignification'. Karris, *Luke: Artist and Theologian*, 55.

[117] B.J. Koet, 'Isaiah in Luke-Acts' in *Isaiah in the New Testament* (eds. S. Moyise and M.J.J. Menken; NY/London: T&T Clark, 2005), 79.

Joy has been the primary emotion that Luke used to frame the narrative of Luke-Acts in the narratives following the prologue. This chapter broadly follows Jesus in his Galilean ministry as we examine the persuasiveness of joy in light of Luke's themes of reversal in the framework of the Isaianic New Exodus.[118] During Jesus' ministry in Galilee, his opponents are not yet strongly associated with the elite power brokers.[119] Yet conflict has arisen and the narratives reflect an ideological stance. The joy theme exhibits significant development in that its rhetorical effect is understood as so strong that Luke cautions against reliance upon it. If joy is not understood properly by the implied reader it is a fallible indicator of one's participation in the kingdom.

---

[118] R. Grams' study of the rhetoric of Matt 23:1-39 cites Lk 6:24ff as an instance of prophetic speech that exemplifies epideictic argumentation that is characterized by an 'increase in *pathos*' in 'The Temple Conflict Scene', 60.

[119] Green, *Theology of the Gospel of Luke*, 14.

Chapter 5

Joy on the Journey of Jesus to Jerusalem

In this chapter we see the truth that those who follow Jesus will reflect the divine principle of reversal as defined in Luke 1:47-55: the last shall be first.[1] Depending on their response, the reader participates in the rising and falling of many. In this way, the emotion of joy functions as a device that provides an emotional force (*pathos*) to the rhetoric of reversal.

Introduction

As the narrative in Luke's Gospel progresses the reader becomes accustomed to the continual stream of reversal of expectations. But the continuity of reversals is plagued by the law of diminishing returns as the reader adjusts to them. In order to facilitate continued results, elements of the narrative that were clearly established as positive are themselves reversed *in some sense*, including the emotion of joy. Whereas the emotion of joy was clearly established as a positive and desired response to Jesus and God's salvific work, the journey of Jesus to Jerusalem requires some clarifications and qualifications. Luke's rhetoric is not empty of emotion.[2] The emotionally charged rhetoric of reversal continues to communicate the upside-down values of the kingdom with certain nuances.

This chapter continues the thesis that joy is integral to Luke's persuasive task as expressed in his rhetoric of reversal. This chapter examines the joy theme in two textual units. The first occurrence is in the return of the seventy-two disciples in Luke 10:17-24 and the second is in the trio of joyful parables that occur in Luke 15 (the Parable of the Lost Sheep, Lost Coin, and the Lost [Prodigal] Son). It is widely recognized that the joy theme occurs throughout these two textual units. Many commentators and studies have developed the notion that joy is one of the desired results of this gospel. However, the emotion of joy is not only the *end*; it is also the *means* because it is integral to the persuasive reversals that challenge the ideology of the reader. On the journey to Jerusalem, Jesus must ensure that the joy that accompanies his kingdom is carefully qualified so that it does not become triumphalistic and a

---

[1] York, *The Last Shall Be First*, 171.

[2] Contra Spencer who argues that *pathos* is the least relevant dimension to Luke's rhetoric (*Rhetorical Texture and Narrative Trajectories*, 52).

barrier to the cross itself.

The Reversal of the Joyful Disciples: Joy in Luke 10:17-24

Jesus has just announced his notice of determination to travel to Jerusalem in Luke 9:51. The journeying motif has dropped out of view in Luke 10:17-24 but remains in the background as the narrative framework.[3] The return of seventy-two disciples (the seventy is used here interchangeably) from their journey of kingdom expansion is marked by a reversal or overturning of expectations.[4] Joel Green identifies Luke 10:17 as an instance where joy is 'related to the advent of salvation' and he describes this as 'eschatological celebration'.[5] This terminology is confusing and may even hinder an understanding of this joy as normal emotion. For our purposes, it is necessary to explain that the emotion of joy is identical to 'non-eschatological' joy while the object or reason for such joy is unique. Furthermore, the normality of this emotion is important because Luke's rhetorical strategy integrates the emotion of joy into his motif of reversal.[6] Here, in the pericope of Luke 10:17-24, Luke uses reversal to overturn misunderstandings about power and joy in the kingdom.[7] This reversal of expectations develops the nature of the deliverance of YHWH: Jesus is the κύριος who has authority over the forces of evil.

---

[3] Bernadicou notes that the mission of the Seventy connects the significance of the travel narrative to Jerusalem to the disciples. It is not clear why he does not account for the joy theme in Lk 10:17-24 (*Joy in the Gospel of Luke*, 23).

[4] There is a well-known textual variant in Lk 10:1 and 10:17 that is equally divided between seventy and seventy-two. Mallen, *Reading and Transformation of Isaiah*, 192 n146. Mallen suggests that a change from 72 to 70 is most likely. In addition, the fact that 72 is divisible by 12 (the number of reconstituted Israel in Lk 6:13) concurs with this. It is also possible that Luke's portrayal of Jesus as the New Moses supports a parallel between the seventy-two in Luke 10 and the seventy-two elders sent out by Moses in Num 11:16-30. Pao and Schnabel suggest that the textual problem cannot be solved by such conceptual parallels ('Luke', *CNTUOT*, 316). However, when textual variants are attested to in significant manuscripts on either side, it seems reasonable to give weight to conceptual parallels even if they are not definitive. Metzger is so confident that internal evidence points to seventy-two that he suggests that it be printed without brackets around the number two. B. Metzger, *A Textual Commentary on the Greek New Testament* (2nd ed.; NY/London: United Bible Societies, 1994), 126-27.

[5] Green, *Theology of the Gospel of Luke*, 110.

[6] Litwak, York, and Minear all specifically cite Lk 10:20-24 as one of many instances of overturned expectations or reversal. Litwak, *Echoes of Scripture in Luke-Acts*, 127; York, *The Last Shall Be the First*, 24; P.S. Minear, *To Heal and to Reveal: The Prophetic Vocation According to Luke* (NY: Seabury, 1976), 19-30.

[7] The connection between joy and signs of power is also found in Acts 8:8. Moessner, *Lord of the Banquet*, 241 n.207.

Joy and Inner Texture

Jesus' response to the returning disciples in Luke 10:17 is a further example of Luke's on-going use of reversal as a rhetorical device. Evidence of Luke's intentional use of the joy theme is apparent when one compares Luke 10:21 with Matthew 11:25 which omits any reference to joy.[8] The aorist active form of the verb (ἀγαλλιάω) is rare and is likely related to the noun ἀγαλλίασις in framing narratives of the Gospel (Lk 1:14 and Lk 1:44).[9] The reversal in this text involves the Seventy-Two disciples and their victory over the demonic powers. The disciples have joy (χαρά) when they return. Jesus demands they have joy (χαίρω) not because of their victories but because their names are in the book of life.[10] The emotion of joy is integral to this rhetoric of reversal. Joy is the only emotion and indeed the only description that marks the return of the seventy-two.

Because the joy theme has been so pervasive throughout the Gospel, the reader is conditioned to expect that it is positive. Luke has used characters such as Mary and Elizabeth as models of faith who respond to the work of God with joy. The emotion of joy is a key component of how Luke influences and persuades the reader to incorporate the values of the kingdom that Jesus preaches. One qualification has already arisen in the Parable of the Sower in Luke 8. But even that parable presents the emotion of joy as the assumed default response by a person who has heard the 'word of God' and produced faith. The danger is that this joy is deceptive because once this person goes through testing (πειρασμός); he falls away because his faith does not endure.

Following Jesus and working in his kingdom does require joy. It is the proper emotion but its proper use depends upon its object.[11] The misunderstanding of the disciples must be carefully framed at this point. Jesus' rebuke of the disciples does not mean that the disciples did not understand his

---

[8] C.A. Evans, 'Jesus and the Spirit: On the Origin and Ministry of the Second Son of God' in *Luke and Scripture: The Function of Sacred Tradition in Luke-Acts* (eds. C.A. Evans and J.A. Sanders; Minneapolis: Fortress Press, 1993), 30.

[9] York, *The Last Shall Be First*, 47.

[10] S. Vorwhinde argues that Jesus' joy is of a different nature altogether than the disciples because of the use of ἀγαλλιάω in Lk 10:21 versus the use of χαίρω in Lk 10:20. His argument rests on a faulty view of emotions as he appeals to the 'religious exuberance' of Jesus (p. 130). What Vorwhinde neglects is that Jesus himself commanded the disciples to have joy using χαίρω in *Jesus' Emotions in the Gospels* (London: T&T Clark, 2011), 130. Vorwhinde appeals to *BDAG* but *BDAG* itself demonstrates parallel usage of ἀγαλλιάω and χαίρω in James 4:9. This note appears on the definition of χαρά in W. Bauer, *A Greek-English Lexicon of the New Testament and Other Early Christian Literature* (ed. F.W. Danker; 3rd ed.; Chicago: University of Chicago Press, 2000), 1077.

[11] For a discussion about the notion of commanding or requiring emotion see Elliott, *Faithful Feelings*, 141.

sayings *per se* (compare with Mark 8:33).[12] Rather, the disciples rejoiced in their use of power and the subjection that the evil powers show them (Lk 10:20a). This rejoicing reflects a triumphalism that does not represent the ultimate reversal of the cross that Luke anticipates on this journey to Jerusalem.[13] The proper object of emotion is described by Jesus: 'that your names are written in heaven' (Lk 10:20b). This reference to a divine record likely signifies divine acceptance or election. The existence of such a record was widespread in the Old Testament and contemporary Jewish literature.[14] This book of life likely reflects a remnant theology and divine election such as is reflected in Isaiah 4:1-4 and Daniel 12:1-3. The passive form ἐγγράφω in conjunction with ἐν τοῖς οὐρανοῖς refers to divine action.[15] This concept of election from the Old Testament remnant theology would explain how this could be understood as divine acceptance.[16] The observation that the disciples are exalted to heaven while Satan is cast down is suggestive of a bi-polar reversal.[17] The object of joy is the elect status of the disciples that has been established by God.

This following pericope furthers the joy theme and begins with Jesus rejoicing (Lk 10:21). In order to relate this directly to the reversal of the rejoicing disciples, a temporal qualification is noted: 'in that same hour' (Lk 10:21). This is the same hour as the seventy-two disciples return from their journey. The scene of the victorious seventy-two sets the stage for Jesus' teaching about the proper object of joy. The object of Jesus' rejoicing is 'the presence of the kingdom'.[18] Since the disciples have not been tested according to this new instruction, Jesus' rejoicing in 'these things' most likely refers to the kingdom victories won through healings and the submission of demonic

---

[12] Kurz, *Reading Luke-Acts*, 150.

[13] The repetition and summarizing statement that refers to 'subjection' in Lk 10:20 makes it unlikely that Jesus was rebuking the seventy for attempting to make a name for themselves as Borgman suggests (*The Way According to Luke*, 85).

[14] Old Testament references include: Exo 32:32; Isa 4:3, 34:16; Dan 12:1. Contemporary Jewish references include: *Jub.* 19:9; 23:32; 30:19-23; 36:10; *1 Enoch* 47:3; 98:7 104:1; 108:3, 7; 1QS 7:2; 1QM 12:2. Stein, *Luke*, 310. Marshall provides references for earthly lists of God's people in Neh 7:5, 64; 12:22; Ps 86.5-7, Ezk 13:9 (*The Gospel of Luke*, 430).

[15] Marshall, *Gospel of Luke*, 430.

[16] Nolland states that the divine record provided the seventy-two with 'an assured place in the kingdom of God' but it is not clear how this relationship would have been established. John Nolland, *Luke 9:21-18:34* (WBC Vol 35b; Dallas: Waco, 2002), 566. Bock contends that this book indicates that 'the evil one's power cannot remove their secure position'. In order for Bock's explanation to relate the divine book to the benefit of security requires an antecedent concept of election in *Luke 9:51-24:53* (BECNT; Grand Rapids: Baker, 1996), 1009.

[17] Bock, *Luke 9:51-24:53*, 1009.

[18] Dawsey, *Lukan Voice*, 147.

powers.[19] But this must not be understood as Jesus rejoicing in the very thing that he forbids the disciples to rejoice in. Rather, the direct object of Jesus' rejoicing is explained in the hiding and revealing activity of the Father (Lk 10:21-24). This hiding and revealing of the Father is based on a 'pattern of reversal [that] stands at the center of Jesus' view'.[20]

The reader first has their expectations reversed as the seventy-two disciples are rebuked. Then Jesus explains that rejoicing is proper when the disciples rejoice that their names are written in heaven. The narrative retains the power to confront the reader by challenging any identification between the joy of the disciples and the joy of the reader.

Joy and Intertexture

It is significant that the Lukan narrator describes the travelling of the disciples as 'on the way' (ὁδός) in Luke 9:57.[21] The likelihood that Luke intended to build upon this intertextual theme of the path or way of the New Exodus is strengthened by Jesus' appearance as a New Moses who is able to provide an authoritative interpretation of the Scriptures of Israel, even in opposition to the established scribes and interpreters.[22] Even further evidence of an Isaianic framework comes from the notable statement from Jesus that he had seen Satan fall like lightning from heaven.[23] The deliverance of Israel from the evil forces likely builds on this cosmic victory framework as the disciples experience victory as they minister in Jesus' name. Jesus has already explained that he views his ministry as one of freedom for those in captivity vis-à-vis Isaiah 61

---

[19] Brawley suggests that the referent of 'these things' is 'the particular relationship of Jesus with God and the same type of relationship of the disciples with God' (*Text to Text Pours Forth Speech*, 9). This explanation does not seem specific enough to address the specificity of the occasion. Specifically, the disciples have seen the power of the kingdom of God and only in this sense have they seen Satan's fall.

[20] Dawsey, *Lukan Voice*, 147.

[21] Kurz, *Reading Luke-Acts*, 52.

[22] Litwak explains 'Luke's audience knows that this new Moses has the authority and validation from God to provide an authoritative interpretation of the Scriptures of Israel' (*Echoes of Scriptures in Luke-Acts*, 60). Moessner proposes that Jesus functions as a 'prophet like Moses' in Luke-Acts (*Lord the Banquet*, 47). Only a new Moses can lead God's people through a new Exodus.

[23] The fall of Satan inaugurates the triumph of Jesus' kingdom; the defeat of the soldiers means the defeat of their master will soon follow. It is hard to identify a clear referent for Jesus' vision in Lk 10:17. Marshall describes Jesus' vision as 'metaphorical' (*Luke: Historian and Theologian*, 137 n1). However, the reference to 'eyes that see' in Lk 10:23 may indicate that Jesus has somehow actually witnessed the subjection of the demons. The notion of 'seeing' has tangible referents even though spiritual warfare is involved. Discussion subsequent to Marshall has generally gone for a visionary experience.

(Lk 4:18-19).[24] In this pericope joy plays a crucial function in providing emotion for the reversal of how power is to be understood in Jesus' kingdom.

The echo alludes to LXX Isaiah 14:12 where cosmic evil forces are related to the nations: 'How is fallen from heaven the Day Star, which used to rise early in the morning! He has been crushed into the earth who used to send light to all the nations!'[25] The text of Isaiah 14 contains a taunt song against the king of Babylon after the restoration of Israel (Isa 14:1-2). The likelihood that Isaiah 14 is a prominent intertextual source in Luke 10:17-24 is increased by the reference to Isaiah 14 in the prior pericope (Lk 10:13-16).[26]

Jesus' power over the forces of evil and Satan is related to the Isaianic New Exodus. Luke's use of Isaiah 14:12 provides a unique background for portraying the lordship of the risen Jesus.[27] The lordship of the risen Jesus flows from the lordship of Jesus before his passion and resurrection. This is further developed in the sacred texture of this pericope. What remains to be developed is how the joy theme and the reversal of expectations work to further this goal of establishing Jesus' lordship.

Luke does not seek to persuade the reader about the nature of Jesus' lordship apart from his kingdom. To understand Jesus' lordship means that one has understood how to participate in the on-going kingdom. Luke's selection of Jesus' statement about the falling of evil forces by the seventy as they minister in his name references Isaiah 14:12 in order to clearly communicate how important these series of victories are. Once the reader understands that this is nothing less than the beginning of the downfall of Satan, the joy of the disciples is framed in cosmic terms.[28] This significant downfall sets up the reader to quickly associate the victory with the initial joy reported in Luke 10:17. Given this framework, the imperative 'do not rejoice in this' (Lk 10:20) strikes the reader in a distinct way. This kingdom is not characterized by values of this

---

[24] This text from Isaiah sets up the 'pattern' of Jesus' ministry according to Mallen, *Reading and Transformation of Isaiah*, 73-75. Thanks to J. Maston for pointing out the connection with Luke 10.

[25] *NETS*, Book of Esaias, 835. The following statement from Jesus in Lk 10:19 that explains the authority he has given to the Seventy may be related to Ps 91:13. Our focus remains on intertextuality as it relates to Isaiah. For a note on the relevance of Ps 91:13 see Evans, 'Jesus and the Spirit', 43.

[26] The echo of Isa 14:13,15 in Lk 10:15 probably reflects 'the exegetical tradition where the language of Isaiah 14 was used to refer to the opponents of the righteous sufferer in texts such as Wisd 4:18-19, *1 Enoch* 46, 2 Maccabees 9 and others'. C. Tuckett, 'Isaiah in Q,' in *Isaiah in the New Testament* (eds. S. Moyise and M.J.J. Menken; NY/London: T&T Clark, 2005), 58.

[27] Pao, *Acts and the Isaianic New Exodus*, 209; Pao and Schnabel, 'Luke', *CNTUOT*, 318.

[28] Pao and Schnabel, 'Luke', *CNTUOT*, 318. J. Maston has pointed out that this inaugurated eschatology could have arguably begun when Jesus resisted Satan in the wilderness. Perhaps it would be best to understand Luke 10 as providing a pivot point in which the disciples begin to participate in this victory.

world and Jesus' lordship demands a reversal of values. Intertextuality and the joy theme give way to the rhetoric of reversal as the New Exodus programme is established.

Further evidence of the connection between the rhetoric of reversal and the Isaianic framework is found in Luke's word play with 'seeing' and 'hearing' in 10:23-24. Luke 10:23 has three verbs in common with Isaiah 6:9-10. Luke also references Isaiah 6:9-10 in Luke 8:10 and Acts 28:26-27. Another parallel occurs in the fourth servant song of Isaiah 52:15 where the uniqueness of God's redeeming work through his servant will surprise kings.[29] I would like to suggest that this is not an either/or choice. The surprising nature of God's work does indeed provide a parallel between Luke 10:24 and Isaiah 52:15. But the reference to Isaiah 6:9-10 in the near co-text of Luke 8:10 cannot be dismissed.

A comparison between Luke 8:10 and Luke 10:23-24 will demonstrate that Luke is likely working with Isaiah 6:9-10 in both texts:

> To you it has been given to know the secrets of the kingdom of God, but for others they are in parables, so that 'seeing they may not see, and hearing they may not understand'. (Luke 8:10)

> Blessed are the eyes that see what you see! For I tell you that many prophets and kings desired to see what you see, and did not see it, and to hear what you hear, and did not hear it. (Luke 10:23-24)

The best explanation for Luke's word play on 'seeing' and 'hearing' in Luke 10:23 is that he wants to demonstrate that the disciples are continuing to exemplify the reversal of the dull and deaf Israel of Isaiah 6:9-10. It is only fitting that as Satan falls, the disciples rise. God is at work in the people of God that they might truly see and hear as the reconstituted Israel. Thus, Isaiah 6:9-10 is present as an intertextual thread in Luke 10:23. As indicated by Luke's use of intertextual threads in earlier portions of his Gospel, he often transforms Old Testament texts by integrating various texts together. This is sometimes referred to as 'conflation'.[30] This makes it difficult to distinguish which echo is louder than the others. At the very least, we must acknowledge that Luke has a pattern of using several allusions or echoes close together. Given this pattern, it is plausible that Luke is using both Isaiah 6:9-10 and Isaiah 52:15 in the word play on 'hearing' and 'seeing' in Luke 10:23-24.

Klyne Snodgrass comments on the use of Isaiah 6:9-10 in the synoptic parables that they are 'to be understood not literally but forcefully'.[31] What my study has developed is the power and force of emotion as Luke deploys his rhetoric of reversal. This intertextual relationship establishes the divine

---

[29] Pao and Schnabel, 'Luke', *CNTUOT*, 319.

[30] Koet, 'Isaiah in Luke-Acts', 86.

[31] K.R. Snodgrass, *Stories with Intent: A Comprehensive Guide to the Parables of Jesus* (Grand Rapids: Eerdmans, 2008), 161.

principle of reversal upon which the emotion of joy operates.

Joy and Sacred Texture

Luke-Acts regularly employs the 'divine principle of reversal'.[32] What remains undeveloped is how this divine principle relates to Jesus. The pericope of Luke 10:17-24 provides significant development of how the divine principle of reversal that began in the reversal of the barren women in the framing narratives is related to Jesus. The use of the divine name κύριος for Jesus creates a relationship with the God of Israel. The emotion of joy plays a central role in developing this relationship.

The joy theme functions in relationship to the 'motif of disclosure' so that Jesus communicates the joy of the God of Israel.[33] There are three persons present in Luke 10:17-24 who share in the divine identity. Jesus' very statement about giving the disciples power over Satan is highly suggestive that he himself is included in the divine identity that has power over Satan. Jesus' own power over Satan is simply assumed whereas the disciples must rely upon a gift of empowerment. In addition, Jesus received the status of 'Lord' and 'mighty works' are now done in his name.[34]

Jesus is repeatedly referred to as the κύριος. It is through the 'name' of Jesus that the demons are subject to the Seventy and the use of the title κύριος reflects this early Christology.[35] In the text of Luke 10:17-24, two seemingly contradictory affirmations on the authority of the Father and the Son must be reconciled through the reality of filiation.[36] What has gone unexplored is how the emotion of joy works in conjunction with this title. The different vocabulary for joy (χαρά in Lk 10:17 and ἀγαλλιάω in Lk 10:21) reflects a single theme but are not limited to a simple thematic connection between Luke 10:17 and 10:21.[37] When we integrate the joy theme into a study of the title κύριος, we see that the reader is confronted with emotion.

The principle point of Jesus' possession of the Holy Spirit is not that he may defeat Satan, but that he can rejoice in the revealing and concealing action of the Father (Lk 10:21-24). To overhear Jesus 'in prayer is to encounter *something* of God's character and purpose'.[38] On the basis of Luke's own use of the joy theme and the prominence he gives it, this 'something' is inclusive of joy. As Jesus reveals the Father, the joy of the Son reflects the joy of the Father. The concept of the joyful Father will be developed further in the three 'lost'

---

[32] York, *The Last Shall Be First*, 183.

[33] Green, *Theology of the Gospel of Luke*, 60.

[34] Marshall, *New Testament Theology*, 192, 200.

[35] Rowe, *Early Narrative Christology*, 135.

[36] Meynet, *Rhetorical Analysis*, 330.

[37] Rowe, *Early Narrative Christology*, 136.

[38] Green, *Theology of the Gospel of Luke*, 60. Emphasis mine.

parables in Luke 15.

Because joy is integral to understanding Jesus, it is integral to understanding the Father. This is because Jesus reveals the Father. Or, one might state that to oppose Jesus is to oppose the Father. The danger Jesus faces due to opposition is reflected in the private explanation of Jesus' rejoicing in Luke 10:23-24. The sacred texture of Luke 10:17-23 portrays a joyful Jesus who reveals a joyful Father — but only to those who have been chosen (v.22) and are blessed (v.23) to see (v.23) and hear what many prophets and kings have previously desired (v.24). There is undoubtedly some lack of understanding on the part of the disciples and this is reflected in their lack of understanding about Jesus' need to die in Luke 18:34. The polarized schema of understanding vs. not understanding does not seem to explain the fact that Luke does not state that the disciples do not understand Jesus in Luke 10:23-24.[39] Rather, there is a *progressive* understanding of Jesus that is fulfilled after the resurrection. Thus, it is best to understand the 'babes' who receive knowledge as the disciples in Luke 10:17-24.

This text reveals an inner and outer circle that also reflects reversal of the sociological norms: the disciples who are chosen are like 'little children' who receive the secrets of the kingdom whereas kings are left on the outside. It is the children who are mature and the adults who are immature. The explanation of Jesus' joy is only revealed to the outsiders who are now on the inside.

Joy and Ideological Texture

The connection between Luke's rhetoric of reversal of values and an ideological stance against a certain perspective on power is clearly evident in the return of the seventy-two disciples. The kingdom of God comes with power that is greater than even John the Baptist displayed (Lk 7:28). The ministry of the seventy-two in Jesus' name is equivalent to that of ambassadors who are announcing the presence of a kingly reign that is characterized by a 'thrilling' amount of power.[40] Joy is the one element that characterizes both good and evil stances toward the power that the disciples possess as the kingdom begins to be unveiled. This joy follows the 'New Exodus' pattern of joy established by Jesus himself in his sermon based on Isaiah 61. Jesus is the Spirit-anointed proclaimer of freedom and good news.[41] Isaiah 61:3-4 describes the 'year of the Lord's favour' as a time of 'gladness' and 'praise' to God. Participating in this New Exodus means following Jesus' pattern of Isaianic ministry and emotionally engaging the Way.

As noted above, Luke uses reversals so thoroughly that he even reverses what the reader thinks has already been established in the early discourses that

---

[39] Brawley, *Centering on God*, 42.

[40] Moessner, *Lord of the Banquet*, 141.

[41] Mallen, *Reading and Transformation of Isaiah*, 75.

frame the narrative as a whole. The reader expects the joyful disciples to be responding appropriately. This is because joy was used without qualification in sections such as the infancy narratives. Now a qualification is presented. The response of joy over power should be rejected in favour of the Lukan reversal that finds joy in the weakness that appropriates God's mighty salvation. This is a problem in light of the power that the disciples now possess. The 'towns' that reject the Seventy have rejected Jesus and therefore have rejected God (Lk 10:16). There is a close connection between Satan and the towns of Israel. The towns that receive the Seventy are evidence that demons are now in subjection to the power of the kingdom. As the power of the kingdom grows the disciples must understand that this does not allow for a view of joy that is not conditioned by humility. The reason this power cannot be the object of rejoicing is that a triumphalistic notion of the kingdom will hinder a proper understanding of the cross which will finalize this victory over Satan.

The most important narrative clue as to the ideological focus of the mission of the Seventy is Jesus' reference to 'prophets and kings' in Luke 10:24.[42] Although Jesus refers to Chorazin, Bethsaida, and Capernaum, the geographical background is simply the 'road' that connects town to town (Lk 10:4).[43] The instruction not to greet anyone on the road makes the unnamed towns more prominent. The road must be travelled but it cannot be used as a ministry venue itself.

The 'prophets and kings' to whom Jesus refers are not likely close contemporaries of the Second Temple period but rather the prophets and kings of Israel's salvation history. They are the only ones who would have 'desired' to see the power of God's kingdom but did not (Lk 10:23-24). They are the rulers of Israel who rank beneath John the Baptist, who is the greatest of all of them. The power of the Seventy inaugurates an expansion of the Kingdom which is greater than any previous king or prophet who ruled amongst the people of God. The ideology of 'kings' is not political and the 'towns' are limited to Israel. Yet the lack of specificity in the narrative allows the warning against triumphalism to remain broadly applicable to the implied reader.

Luke's record of the mission of the Twelve and the Seventy is not restrictive and concerns Luke's audience as implied readers.[44] Luke requires a joyful response from those who seek to imitate Jesus (who reflects the Father). And this joyful imitation is likely rooted in Isaiah as well. The text of Luke 9:51-10:24 may be summarized thus: 'To journey with Jesus means to participate in the self-unveiling of his authority as the Son as he advances to Jerusalem'.[45] My study provides further nuancing: to journey with Jesus means to participate with joy in the work and kingdom of the Father and not in exercises of

---

[42] Resseguie, *Narrative Criticism of the New Testament*, 88.

[43] This may relate to Luke's designation of 'the Way' that he develops later in Acts.

[44] Mallen, *Reading and Transformation of Isaiah*, 192.

[45] Moessner, *Lord of the Banquet*, 142.

authority that reflect the triumphalism of the kingdoms of this world. Whereas other studies connect the lordship of Jesus with the typology of a Moses-figure who will provide an Exodus-like deliverance, it must be stated that the means of persuading the reader of this is a rhetoric of reversal empowered by the emotion of joy.[46]

The Reversal of the Lost: Joy in Luke 15:1-32

The next literary unit that reflects the joy theme is the trio of parables in Luke 15. It is widely recognized that the short vignettes or stories in Luke's Gospel are interrelated. The following observation is easily verified: 'The Lucan parables about lost objects all have the theme of rejoicing'.[47] But is not always clear why the emotion of joy is present. For some, the reason for this 'pious expression' of joy is 'not entirely clear'.[48] But, in each of these parables the emotion of joy is central to understanding how the parables operate as reversal narratives.[49] The act of including the outcast in the community presents an occasion for joy. We can also connect this pattern of reversal in Luke 15:1-32 with the larger Lukan theme of salvation.[50] In contrast to the emphasis on the duty of disciples in Mark, the Gospel of Luke uses the idea of reversal from lost to found to justify Jesus' mission to sinners such as tax collectors who 'typify the unconverted'.[51] Most exegetes develop Luke 15 in terms of apologetic language that is defensive rather than rhetorical or persuasive. Although these two types of language are not conceptually far apart, the use of the former can create a barrier to understanding the rhetorical function of joy in these three reversals.[52] Specifically, this study will develop the use of joy as it provides emotional energy to the rhetoric of reversal. It will be demonstrated that joy empowers the reversals that stress the inclusivism that characterizes the New Exodus.

The logic of the parables places an imperative upon the reader: to be void of the emotion of joy that is based upon God's kingdom is to exist in a state that is

---

[46] Moessner, *Lord of the Banquet*, 315.

[47] O'Toole, *The Unity of Luke's Theology*, 80.

[48] F. Bovon, *Das Evangelium nach Lukas* (4 Vol.; EKKNT; Zurich: Benziger Verlag, 1989), 3:33.

[49] Resseguie labels reversal of fortune narratives 'u-shaped plots'. Reflecting the findings of this study in chapter two, he finds similarity between reversals and Greek literary techniques; he finds the parable of the Prodigal Son to be a specimen of a u-shaped plot (*Narrative Criticism of the New Testament*, 205). Resseguie's work does not specifically explain the rhetorical function of emotion.

[50] Mallen, *Reading and Transformation of Isaiah*, 149.

[51] Marshall, *New Testament Theology*, 106; so also Moessner, *Lord of the Banquet*, 164.

[52] Bernadicou's study makes a direct connection between Luke's use of reversal and joy but he fails to see how the emotion makes this rhetorical technique persuasive (*Joy in the Gospel of Luke*, 27).

contrary to heaven. In the series of reversal parables that move from lost to found, the emotion of joy is central to the task of persuasion. These parables function at least on two levels.[53] The implied reader who is already a disciple of Jesus is persuaded to accept the lost or outcast and the implied reader who is not a disciple is persuaded to take up the task of repentance.[54] Both parties are identified in Luke 15:1-2. The tax collectors and sinners represent inclusiveness as indicated by Luke's description: 'drawing near to hear him'. The Pharisees and scribes are described as 'grumblers' (Lk 15:2) who reject Jesus' inclusivism (receiving sinners and engaging in table fellowship with them). It is hard to exclude repentance as a central feature of this pericope.[55] Simply stated, this trio of parables is about restoring 'lost' outcasts to God's community.[56]

Joy and Inner Texture

Luke 15 follows Jesus' address to the crowds (Lk 14:23-35) and the reaction of the Pharisees (Lk 15:1-2).[57] Specifically, the Pharisees and scribes are 'grumbling' about Jesus' association with sinners who reflect the dishonourable, lawless, and unclean. The rhetoric of reversal in the parable of the Lost Son (Lk 15:11-32) raises the question: how does the joy theme function in these three parables? Several keywords create solid relationships between the three parables in Luke 15 including 'finding' that which was 'lost'. Other keywords such as 'heaven' establish the restoration of sinners before God (Lk 15:7, 10, 18b, 21).[58] *In this section we will see that joy is one of the keywords that link the three parables together.*[59]

The repetition of the joy theme across the three parables reflects Luke's use of lexical repetition as a rhetorical technique.[60] The joy theme not only ties these three parables together in the narrative of Luke's Gospel, the theme also reflects Luke's continued use of emotionally charged reversal to persuade the reader. In order for linguistic elements to have a rhetorical function, they must

---

[53] Green finds that the last of the three parables in Luke 15, is '*imploring* us to examine in what ways we might be refusing to celebrate the welcoming of the apparently unfaithful into the family' (*Theology of the Gospel of Luke*, 124).

[54] Tannehill uses the concept of rhetoric when describing joy in these parables as he refers to 'motivation'. The text of Luke's Gospel seeks to motivate and therefore requires a methodology suitable for rhetorical analysis (*The Shape of Luke's Story*, 93-94). Tannehill does not examine the power of emotion or how intertextual citations impact the joy theme or its ability to motivate the reader.

[55] Borgman, *The Way According to Luke*, 177.

[56] Borgman, *The Way According to Luke*, 177.

[57] York, *The Last Shall Be First*, 145.

[58] Moessner, *Lord of the Banquet*, 129.

[59] York only relates these three parables via the keywords 'lose' and 'find'. For a discussion of keywords see chapter one (*The Last Shall Be First*, 146).

[60] Bernadicou notes that the frequent repetition of joy is connected with the repetition of invitation and participation (*Joy in the Gospel of Luke*, 16).

be in relationship with one another.[61] In Luke 15, the joy theme works on two levels. First, the joy theme operates on a lexical level that connects the theme to the framing narratives of the Gospel and beyond. Second, it provides *pathos* for the rhetoric of reversal at the discourse level.

The inner texture of these three parables is important to explore because, while they are often grouped together, the connection between reversal and the emotion of joy is rarely explored. This is curious because both reversal and joy are clearly present in all three as movements from lost to found.[62] In the first parable of the Lost Sheep, a man leaves the ninety-nine to find his lost sheep and bring it home. He brings the sheep home rejoicing (Lk 15:5). When he returns home he calls upon his friends and neighbours to rejoice with him (Lk 15:6). An explanatory aside is given to establish this joy as reflecting God's joy through the language of 'heaven' in Luke 15:7. Likewise, in the second parable of the Lost Coin, a woman searches her home until she finds her lost silver coin. Once the coin is found, the woman calls upon her friends and neighbours to rejoice with her. Again, an explanatory aside is given to establish this joy as reflecting God's joy as evidenced in the 'angels of God' (Lk 15:10). The third parable of the Lost (Prodigal) Son is much longer and developed. It 'ends with the focus on the younger son's return and father's joyous acceptance'.[63] Joy is not only the end (that which is required), is it also the means (its presence adds persuasive power to these three reversals from lost to found).

Joy and Intertexture

Unfortunately, there is very little analysis of intertextuality as it relates to the joy theme in the trio of 'lost' parables of Luke 15.[64] The contention of this study is that Isaiah is a likely intertextual source for Luke's joy theme. The emotion of joy provides emotional power to Luke's rhetoric of reversal as it reflects the reversals inherent in the Isaianic New Exodus.

The best argument against reading Deuteronomy 21:15-22:4 or even Ezekiel 34 as the *dominant* intertextual parallel to Luke 15 is the dominant presence of the joy theme.[65] Previously, pains were taken to demonstrate how the infancy narratives following the prologue framed the discourse or provided a

---

[61] Meynet, *Rhetorical Analysis*, 182.

[62] 'The third parable in the literary unit expands on the theme of joy over finding that which was lost, no longer dealing with possessions lost and found, but persons'. York, *The Last Shall Be First*, 148.

[63] York, *The Last Shall Be First*, 152.

[64] Kimball suggests that Lk 15:11-32 consists of 'creative alterations' with the LXX as a 'likely source' but he does not specify anything beyond this (*Jesus' Exposition of the Old Testament*, 20); Pao and Schnabel, 'Luke' in *CNTUOT*, 341-43.

[65] Ezekiel 34 does not employ the joy theme at all. Against Robbins, it is best to understand this passage as a likely source of intertextuality that lies in the background ('The Socio-Rhetorical Role of the Old Testament Scripture in Luke 4-19', 89).

framework for understanding themes to follow. It is on the basis of this that the joy theme can be understood as an intertextual thread that proceeds through Luke 15. The joy in Luke 15 is not to be understood apart from the joy and its intertextual dimensions in the framing narratives.[66] This relationship can be demonstrated on a lexical basis by the way that Luke uses vocabulary for joy in Luke 15:6, 9, 24 (χαίρω, συγχαίρω, εὐφραίνω) that reflects the same vocabulary used in Luke 1:14 (χαρά, χαίρω). The repetition invites the reader to read these parables in light of what Luke has already established previously in the narrative.[67]

The three parables as told by Jesus in Luke 15 are framed by the explanation in Luke 15:1-2. Jesus is eating with sinners and is opposed by the Pharisees and scribes. When Jesus is restoring sinners, the Pharisees and scribes refuse to participate.[68] If an exegesis of Luke 15 takes the framing work of Luke 1-2 seriously, the presence of the joy theme must not stand isolated. Luke has already established an intertextual relationship between the restoration of sinners and the joy theme.

The presence of this rhetorical pattern based on the repetition of evocative keywords does more than stress a point. The repetition is evocative of Luke's framing narratives which are in turn evocative of his intertextual framework. We must recall that 'Luke uses intertextual echoes to frame his discourse'.[69]

This foundation allows one to conclude that the joy theme in the trio of parables in Luke 15 is about the restoration of sinners. This restoration likely reflects the fact that the primary intertextual source in Luke's Gospel is Isaiah. Several Isaianic texts seem to play a role in this trio of vignettes.[70] The last parable may echo the original Exodus narrative as Israel is deemed YHWH's firstborn son (Exo 4:22). The discontinuity with this would be that the firstborn son in Luke's parable is painted negatively or at least with a questionable disposition. Nevertheless, Isaiah as a whole places a strong emphasis on restoring the lost. The restoration of sinners in Israel appears in the LXX of Isaiah 11:12; 27:13; and 49:14-16. Of particular importance is the parallel between YHWH gathering the 'lambs' in Isaiah 40:11 – the key text for the

---

[66] This is similar to Resseguie's notion that 'Verbal repetition thematically links narratives that on first glance appear to be unrelated' (*Narrative Criticism of the New Testament*, 42).

[67] The importance of early narratives and their impact on shaping narrative trajectories is the focus of P.E. Spencer's study of Jesus' speeches during his Galilean ministry. The thrust of my argument is focused on a different textual unit than that of Spencer but utilizes the same concept: the early part of the narrative shapes hermeneutical appropriations later in the narrative (*Rhetorical Texture and Narrative Trajectories*, 4).

[68] Green states, 'the father's reference to his younger son as "this brother of yours" is presented as an invitation to restoration' (*Gospel of Luke*, 586).

[69] Litwak, *Echoes of Scripture in Luke-Acts*, 171.

[70] Thanks to H. Morrison for pointing out several parallels between Isaiah and Luke 15.

New Exodus that describes the restoration of Israel.[71] There is also a conceptual parallelism between being 'lost' (ἀπόλλυμι) in Luke 15:6, 8, 24 and Israel's charge that God has 'forgotten' them in LXX Isaiah 49:14.[72] This parallelism may extend to the use of ἀπόλλυμι in LXX Isaiah 49:20. An additional parallelism may lie in the similarity between the lost 'sheep' carried home on *shoulders* (Lk 15:5) and the 'sons' and 'daughters' carried home to Israel on bosoms and *shoulders* from amongst the nations (Isa 49:22).[73]

In Isaiah (11, 40, and 49) and Luke 15, the joy theme plays a role in a rhetorical exchange. In both texts, the lost are restored in a reversal of circumstances that results in joy. If this intertextual thread is present, the joy theme plays a rhetorical role in evoking not only the framing work that Luke has done in the infancy narratives but the inauguration of the restoration of Israel.[74]

Joy and Sacred Texture

The first two parables of the lost sheep and coin are oriented around a strong polarity between heaven and earth. In the first parable, there is joy in heaven when a sinner repents (Lk 15:7). In the second parable, the joy of the angels of God over the sinner who repents (Lk 15:10) is also geographically located in heaven. The pattern of similitude between the three parables allows the reader to infer that this is also appropriate for the parable of the lost son. It is only appropriate that the parable of the Lost Son locates joy in the father (Lk 15:32) who is understood as the heavenly father.[75]

The trio of parables portrays God as joyful. God is joyful over repentant sinners (15:7, 10)'.[76] The emotional force of these three parables is such that it communicates something about how God should be perceived: 'This is how God thinks about these people and what God wants to do for them'.[77] To be 'God-like' is to be joyful. The joy that is in heaven should be reflected on earth.[78] The older son is a foil that exemplifies the wrong type of reception of sinners. The language of joy is widely recognized but it is not often understood

---

[71] K.E. Bailey points to parallels between Luke 15 and Isa 40:11 but he does not develop the New Exodus motif or the joy theme in *The Cross and the Prodigal: Luke 15 Through the Eyes of Middle Eastern Peasants* (Downers Grove: InterVarsity, 2005), 32.

[72] The LXX Isa 49:14 reads: Εἶπεν δὲ Σιων Ἐγκατέλιπέν με κύριος, καὶ ὁ κύριος ἐπελάθετό μου. For the English see *NETS*, Book of Esaias, 862.

[73] Thanks to J. Maston at Highland Theological College for pointing this out.

[74] Litwak explains that Luke's intertextual echoes tell 'his audience to expect a narrative which shows continuity with people and events in Israel's past (*Echoes of Scripture in Luke-Acts*, 110).

[75] O'Toole, *Unity of Luke's Theology*, 116.

[76] Brawley, *Centering on God*, 123.

[77] Morrice, *Joy in the New Testament*, 95.

[78] O'Toole, *Unity of Luke's Theology*, 116.

or explained how joy relates to the persuasive or rhetorical nature of these parables.

For Luke, the logic of the rhetoric works this way: Jesus is doing the work of God and God rejoices in this work. Therefore, embracing this work with joy is to be 'God-like'.[79] To joyfully embrace God's work requires that one accept and conform to Jesus' work because he has already been established as sharing the divine identity of YHWH (Lk 10:17-24). Whereas the norms of honour and shame provide a cultural standard for understanding the nature of outcasts and 'sinners' (Lk 15:2), these norms must be overturned and reversed. Luke seeks to persuade the reader to participate in the new 'upside down' world by representing God and his joyful embrace of repentant sinners. What goes unnoticed by commentators is how this emotion of joy plays a central role in Luke's rhetorical programme. Jesus has provided a series of parables in order to shape those who hear into disciples who reflect God himself. This is no dry and emotionless activity. The emotion of joy is not only the only emotion present, it is the central emotion and the emotion that provides the hinge for the contrast between those who oppose Jesus (the scribes and Pharisees) and those who embrace repentant sinners and eat with them.

Joy and Ideological Texture

Luke uses joy to develop a picture of those who are for God and those who are against God. In similar function to the framing infancy narratives, the rhetoric of reversal stands in contrast to forces of social and religious power as exemplified in the Pharisees and scribes (Lk 15:1-2).[80] In Luke 1:5-25 the juxtaposition of the young maiden (Mary) and the priest (Zechariah) sets the stage for understanding Mary's paradigmatic response to God's salvific actions. Likewise, in the parable of the Lost Son the juxtaposition of the younger brother and the older brother establishes a conflict with which the readers could associate themselves (with the addition of the father breaking social norms of honor to express his joy). The *pathos* or emotion that is present in these three parables is personal but also corporate. The breadth of this speech by Jesus is evident as Luke describes him calling 'all tax collectors and sinners' (Lk 15:1). The power struggle between Jesus and the Pharisees and scribes is a matter for the whole community.

The progressive movement of the three parables helps the reader understand that the shorter parables of the Lost Sheep and the Lost Coin can stand on their own but are enhanced by the longer parable of the Lost Son. The hermeneutical demands that derive from the rhetoric of the parables are based upon the clear

---

[79] Green states, 'these parables are fundamentally about God, that their aim is to lay bare the nature of the divine response to the recovery of the lost' (*Gospel of Luke*, 573).

[80] For a discussion on institutional forms of power in Jerusalem and ideology see Robbins, *Exploring the Texture of Texts*, 113-14.

repetition of joy and the repeated requests of the characters that others should join them.[81] The arrangement of the three parables demands the reader answer the question: do you rejoice with God at the prospect of a sinful and repentant person being added to the kingdom that Jesus preaches?[82] This positioning entails a reversal of expectations itself: the one who was lost (the younger son) is now found and the one (the elder son) who was always 'found' is at risk of being lost.[83] The 'rhetorical effect' of this section of text in Luke's Gospel is based on the acceptance of outcasts as seen in the trio of parables.[84]

The community of the Way must accept a repentant outsider even as God himself has sought after and accepted them. Those who are characterized by wealth or status as insiders and continue to trust in 'self-righteousness or ethnic descent' are 'excluded from salvation' as outsiders.[85] *The one who is lowly is to be exalted and the exalted are to be made low.*

Conclusion

The joy theme which began in the first narratives of the Gospel of Luke takes on more and more nuances. One of the developments evident in Luke 10:13 is the continued use of joy as integral to Luke's rhetoric of reversal. Prior studies have noted that Luke's reversal theme in Luke 10:17-24 where the lowly are exalted and the exalted become lowly reflects the framing narratives from the infancy narratives of Luke 2.[86] What has not been connected together is the relationship between this rhetoric of reversal and the joy theme. The entire reversal of expectation rests upon the reader hearing of the disciples' joy and expecting that this is an appropriate response. Indeed, this response has been conditioned by Luke's own use of the joy theme and the continued use of joy to confront the reader with the upside-down values of Jesus' kingdom. Luke's Gospel seeks to evoke the emotion of joy even as it utilizes it as a means of persuasion. The reader cannot help but emotionally engage the narrative through rhetorical devices such as reversal and repetition. As the journey to Jerusalem anticipates the cross, the victorious disciples must learn that success in spiritual battles must not lead to triumphalism.

Reversal is one of Luke's primary rhetorical techniques for confronting the reader because of the dissonance it creates in one's world-view (or, kingdom-view; or messiah-view).[87] Others have recognized that the 'topos of reversal' is

---

[81] For a helpful discussion about the danger of forcing too much theology out of parables see Snodgrass, *Stories with Intent*, 137.

[82] Navone, *Themes of St. Luke*, 85.

[83] Navone, *Themes of St. Luke*, 84.

[84] Snodgrass, *Stories with Intent*, 94.

[85] Mallen, *Reading and Transformation of Isaiah*, 108.

[86] Borgman, *The Way According to Luke*, 85.

[87] Resseguie, *Narrative Criticism of the New Testament*, 38.

'Luke's way of replacing common representations of the world with a new one'.[88] To this we may add that the reversal motif is rhetorical and ideological. *By placing the emotion of joy at the centre of the reversal motif it provides emotional power that would otherwise be absent.*

---

[88] Resseguie, *Narrative Criticism of the New Testament*, 188.

Chapter 6

Joy in the Persecution and Vindication of Jesus

In the previous chapter, we examined how Luke provided important nuances for the joy theme. One important qualification is this: partaking in the joy of the kingdom of God cannot equate to triumphalism. With this qualification in place, Luke proceeds to use joy as an integral part of his rhetoric of reversal. Luke is now able to present a joyful resurrection and vindication of Jesus.

Introduction

In the conclusion of the Third Gospel the emotion of joy continues to play an important and prominent role in how Luke seeks to persuade the reader about the nature of Jesus' persecution and vindication. The narratives that framed the discourse established expectations for the readers, including the expectation that joy is evidence of the fulfillment of God's promises and that one's own emotions are related to participation in the new age. The emotion (*pathos*) of joy cannot bear the entire weight of describing one's response to YHWH. With this qualification in place, Luke proceeds to use it as an integral part of his rhetoric of reversal. Luke is now able to present a joyful resurrection and vindication of Jesus.

It is not hard to see that Luke the joy theme in the final chapter is 'highlighted'.[1] Recent studies on the Lukan corpus have not clarified why this is.[2] Some even deny that emotion is important. For example, Patrick Spencer states that *pathos* or emotion is the least relevant aspect of Luke's rhetoric programme.[3] In spite of such claims, a socio-rhetorical analysis of the persecution and vindication of Jesus at the end of Luke's Gospel will demonstrate that emotion plays a large role in the rhetoric of reversal.

As the journey of Jesus to Jerusalem concludes in Luke 19, the path to the cross (persecution) and resurrection (vindication) begins in earnest. We will examine three instances of the joy theme as it relates to three instances of reversal. (1) The first reversal relates to Jesus' persecution as he rides triumphantly into Jerusalem on a donkey. Here, joy empowers a rhetorical

---

[1] Morrice, *Joy in the New Testament*, 95.

[2] York's analysis of the rhetoric of reversal does not extend into the final pericopae of Luke's Gospel (*The Last Shall Be First*).

[3] Spencer, *Rhetorical Texture and Narrative Trajectories*, 52.

picture of kingship. (2) In the second reversal, the emotion of joy is a central feature that stands in contrast to the unbelief and lack of understanding that characterizes the disciples. (3) The third reversal places the emotion of joy as reversing the judgment that had come upon Jerusalem and the temple. The conclusion opens the door to the second volume of Luke's corpus and to the reader who desires to participate in the newly inaugurated kingdom. *Here I intend to show that the rhetoric of reversal in the persecution and vindication of Jesus draws upon the emotion of joy as a source of persuasive power.*

The Reversal of Kingship: Joy in Luke 19:28-40

In the scene of Jesus' Triumphal Entry, the rhetoric of reversal is once again intertwined with the Isaianic New Exodus as it relates to the restoration of Israel vis-à-vis the Davidic throne.[4] Jesus' entry into Jerusalem is kingly yet humble and lowly, as is evidenced by his use of the donkey's colt. This is the apex of the journey motif and the movement toward Jerusalem.[5] The presence of the New Exodus motif is evident in the fact that Jesus is riding this colt on his way to celebrate the Passover, albeit a Passover to end all Passovers.[6] The New Exodus is achieved 'through his own Passover action on the cross'.[7] The Triumphal Entry constitutes an overturning-of-expectations scene because of the way it depicts Jesus' kingship and anticipates the ultimate reversal of the cross.[8] The restoration of the Davidic kingdom is not 'literal' in the sense that it is not a 'political entity'.[9] But how were the readers to arrive at the conclusion that this Davidic kingdom was spiritual in nature? Luke's use of emotions is part of his rhetorical toolkit. The spiritual nature of the kingdom is reflected in the emphasis on personal and internal characteristics such as repentance, faith, and joy. The joyful response of the people to the upside-down triumphal entry in Jerusalem reflects Luke's intention to communicate that this Davidic restoration first operates internally or spiritually.

Joy and Inner Texture

The joy theme has already appeared just prior to this textual unit (Lk 19:28-40) in the narrative of Zacchaeus (Lk 19:1-10). Even if one disputes how the

---

[4] Kim, *Christ and Caesar*, 92.

[5] Kurz, *Reading Luke-Acts*, 54.

[6] Wright, *Luke for Everyone*, 229.

[7] Wright, *Luke for Everyone*, 230.

[8] Seyoon Kim prefers to see the triumphal entry as 'not a real celebration of his enthronement on earth' because his kingship is rejected. But it is precisely because his kingship is rejected by men that God is able to establish his cosmic kingship through the cross. The triumphal entry is indeed a 'real celebration' and it reflects an inaugurated eschatology rather than a triumphalistic eschatology (*Christ and Caesar*, 155).

[9] Kim, *Christ and Caesar*, 100.

pericopae within Luke relate to each other, it is difficult to deny that the various genres of prophecy, narratives, and parables in the sequence from Luke 18:31 to 19:45 are related to each other from a literary perspective.[10] One important relationship is the presence of the joy theme in the Zacchaeus narrative and the bridge it provides to the rest of the joy theme. Due to space limitations this study will not be able to fully analyze the presence of the joy theme in the Zacchaeus narrative.[11] Nevertheless, there are two important points that arise from the Zacchaeus narrative that are relevant for understanding joy and the inner texture in the Triumphal Entry (specifically Lk 19:37).

First, the same vocabulary of joy which occurs in Luke 15 also occurs in Luke 19:6 (χαίρω) and in Luke 19:37 (χαίρω). The vocabulary of Luke 19:37 reflects the use of joy vocabulary in the pericope of the shepherds' praising God in Luke 2:13, 20.[12] This provides strong threads of connection to the joy theme throughout the Lukan corpus.[13]

The second relevant point connecting the Zacchaeus narrative to the Triumphal Entry is Luke's deployment of rhetorical techniques to engage the reader. The imagery of Zacchaeus as a person of small stature is rhetorically powerful because it would have persuaded Luke's audience that this man was indeed an outcast or sinner. This physiognomy as integral to the reversal as 'Luke turns the tables' as Zacchaeus becomes accepted by Jesus.[14] The widely held conclusion that the Zacchaeus narrative employs rhetorical features provides analogical evidence for developing Luke's rhetoric in the adjacent text of the Triumphal Entry. The interplay of physical attributes and the rhetoric of reversal is convincing and substantiated by evidence from the Greco-Roman and Jewish dimensions of the Hellenistic world. However, it does not account for the presence of the emotion of joy as a component of this rhetorical agenda in the Zacchaeus narrative. We must also notice that this instance of the rhetoric of reversal is adjacent to the Triumphal Entry. This is analogical evidence that simply strengthens the pattern and likelihood that Luke's technique of reversal continues in the Triumphal Entry narrative.

---

[10] Meynet, *Rhetorical Analysis*, 297.

[11] Navone cites the joy theme in Lk 19:1-10 as the last instance of joy in the Lukan travel narrative (*Themes of St. Luke*, 85); Bernadicou does not cite the joy theme in the Zacchaeus narrative or the triumphal entry (*Joy in the Gospel of Luke*).

[12] Robert Stein does not make any connection to other instances of the joy theme and he does not develop any narrative or rhetorical implications (*Luke*, 480).

[13] Navone does not cite Lk 19:37 as an instance of the joy theme (*Themes of St. Luke*, 86). De Long argues that the joy theme in the Triumphal Entry is, after the infancy narratives, the 'second "loudest" expression of the praise motif thus far in the Gospel' (*Surprised by God*, 225).

[14] Parsons, *Body and Character in Luke and Acts*, 108. In similar fashion, Robbins observes that physical bodies function similar to locations such as temples or homes inasmuch as they are political spaces ('Bodies and Politics in Luke 1-2 and Sirach 44-50', 826).

The emotion of joy in the Triumphal Entry stands in contrast with the sadness of Jesus over the fate of Jerusalem which did not recognize its king.[15] While all of the four Gospels narrate Jesus' entry into Jerusalem, only Luke mentions the disciples praising God with joy in Luke 19:37: 'the whole multitude of his disciples began to rejoice and praise God with a loud voice for all the mighty works that they had seen'.[16] George Shillington (who assumes Markan priority) suggests that Luke departs from Mark's Gospel due to a desire to maintain continuity between the 'unqualified multitude of Jerusalemites' and their sudden 'burst' of song for Jesus on the donkey.[17] However, this analysis places too much weight on a single word. The existence of a large group (ἅπαν τὸ πλῆθος) of disciples who would have been informed enough about Jesus to respond in praise can be justified by the reference to the seventy[-two] in Luke 10:1, 17.

Luke's desire to explicitly insert the emotion of joy is arguably another important aspect of his redaction rather than simply the identification of the crowd who shouted to Jesus as he rode in. The use of joy in the Triumphal Entry strengthens his rhetoric of reversal and fits in naturally with the adjacent pericopae.[18]

Joy and Intertexture

According to the socio-rhetorical method, an analysis of intertexture examines the presence of 'outside' texts that are woven into the present text (of Luke-Acts).[19] Luke's attempt to persuade the reader that Jesus is the fulfillment of the Scriptures rests in part upon an appeal to the emotions. The emotion of joy is used to persuade the reader that the Scripture is being fulfilled. God has promised that joy will occur when his promises are fulfilled. *The argument that the Scriptures are being fulfilled is not exclusively logical.*

One of the central arguments that this study presents is that the joy theme as a whole (as it runs throughout the Lukan corpus) is derived primarily from Isaiah's own joy theme. The narrative also draws the reader into the narrative world so that the implied reader's emotions are drawn toward joy.

The intertexture of the Triumphal Entry scene in Luke 19:28-40 is an amalgamation of echoes and quotations that cannot be easily isolated or separated from the whole. The clearest quotation that is related to the joy theme is the joyful cry of the 'disciples' (Lk 19:37) who say 'blessed is the King who

---

[15] Marshall, *New Testament Theology*, 138.

[16] The Greek of Luke 19:37 reads: χαίροντες αἰνεῖν τὸν θεὸν φωνῇ μεγάλῃ.

[17] Shillington, *Introduction to Luke-Acts*, 111.

[18] The presence of Luke's rhetoric of reversal in this pericope is strengthened by the use of 'pattern reversal' where the humble are exalted in the adjacent textual unit of the Emmaus road account (see Lk 24:25-26). Dawsey, *Lukan Voice*, 141.

[19] For a discussion of appropriating this aspect of the socio-rhetorical approach as articulated by V.K. Robbins see Shillington, *Introduction to Luke-Acts*, 53.

comes in the name of the Lord! Peace in heaven and glory in the highest' (Lk 19:38). This quotation is almost certainly from Psalm 118:26 (LXX 117:26).[20] There is a 'loud volume for the book of Psalms in Luke'.[21] Nevertheless, this study will focus on the Isaianic intertextual connections because this is the central source for connecting Luke's account with Israel's history.[22] In this vein, a less clear intertextual echo is related to the joy theme as Jesus responds to the Pharisees who seek to silence the joyful praising: 'teacher, rebuke your disciples' (Lk 19:39).

This challenge to the praise that Jesus is receiving as he enters Jerusalem is met with a statement that helps to explain the function of the joy theme. Jesus responds (Lk 19:40): 'I tell you, if these were silent, the very stones would cry out'. It is best to understand the referent of this masculine plural demonstrative pronoun οὗτοι as the disciples (also masculine plural). Jesus' actions demand a joyful response. When Jesus' response is taken as a 'straightforward metaphor' he is invoking images of creation responding to the coming of God.[23] The reference to the 'stones' crying out in joy locates Jesus' actions in terms of the cosmos and nature as a whole. Thus, the joy theme is related to the fulfillment of the Scriptures, particularly Isaiah 55:12.

The relationship between Luke 19:40 and Isaiah 55:12 is admittedly conceptual in nature (rather than lexical). Jesus' statement that οἱ λίθοι κράξουσιν may simply be a collective way of echoing the 'mountains' and 'hills' in Isaiah 55:12 that will rejoice (εὐφροσύνη, χαρά) as YHWH reverses the curse (thorns will give way to the cypress tree, etc.). It should be noted that the verb for 'shouting' (κράζω) does not appear in Isaiah 55, although this is paralleled conceptually by references to 'clapping' in LXX Isaiah 55:12 (ἐπικροτέω). The fact that this section of Isaiah refers to the future fulfillment of the Davidic covenant (Isa 55:1-5) strengthens the likelihood that it provides a basis for a promise-fulfillment reading of Jesus' actions as he comes into Jerusalem. Luke's interest in using Isaiah to 'vindicate' Jesus is the best explanation for the use of Isaiah 53:12 in Luke 22:37: 'and he was reckoned with the transgressors'.[24] Luke's interest in using historical sources to provide 'certainty' (Lk 1:4) makes it reasonable to assume that his quotation of Jesus places these words on Jesus' lips. One might reasonably assume that Jesus said more than his sources recorded. The selective nature of the quotations of Jesus

---

[20] Pao and Schnabel, 'Luke', *CNTUOT*, 355; Litwak, *Echoes of Scripture in Luke-Acts*, 103n146.

[21] Litwak, *Echoes of Scripture in Luke-Acts*, 103n146.

[22] For an introduction to the Psalms in Luke-Acts see P. Doble, 'The Psalms in Luke-Acts' in *Psalms in the New Testament* (eds. S. Moyise and M.JJ. Menken; London: T&T Clark, 2004), 83-118.

[23] Pao and Schnabel, 'Luke', *CNTUOT*, 356.

[24] C.A. Evans, 'Prophecy and Polemic: Jews in Luke's Scriptural Apologetic', in *Luke and Scripture: The Function of Sacred Tradition in Luke-Acts* (eds. C.A. Evans and J.A. Sanders; Minneapolis: Fortress Press, 1993), 201.

allows us to speak of Luke's interest in Isaianic quotations while also affirming that the quotation is presented in the text as Jesus' own statement. Similarly, the joy theme is necessary because it fulfills scripture and therefore vindicates Jesus' actions.[25]

The intertextual relationship is strengthened by temporarily returning to the Zacchaeus narrative in Luke 19. The reference to 'today salvation has come...' in Luke 19:9 reflects a Lukan pattern that signals the arrival of an eschatological moment of divine intervention.[26] This concept of 'today' as a day of salvation occurs in Luke 2:11 and 4:21. It is possible that the repeated use of 'today' in Luke's Gospel (including Lk 19:9) echoes or evokes the pattern of Israel after the Exodus. The significance of the 'today' theme: 'Clearly, "today" encompasses past, present and future decisions faced by Israel in all manner of places'.[27] The use of 'today' evokes an event for Israel where they must choose life or chose death, blessing or cursing. Jesus' presence requires that one become lowly and accept his salvation or remain 'honourable' by refusing to repent.

What I want to suggest is that macro-level and micro-level indicators point to an intertextual relationship between the joy in the Zacchaeus narrative and Isaiah. The rhetorical indicator occurs directly in the pericope: this is a significant 'today' of salvation for Zacchaeus. The macro-level indicator is the presence of strong connections with Isaiah established earlier such as Luke 4:16-30. Most importantly, the text of Isaiah 61 cited in Luke 4:16-30 has direct references to praise and joy (δόξα, εὐφροσύνη). The text of LXX Isa 61:3 reads: 'so that those who mourn for Sion be given glory instead of ashes, oil of joy to those who mourn'.[28] The concept of joy also appears in Isaiah 61:7, 10. The joy theme in Isaiah is likely the source of Luke's joy theme.[29] If Luke intends to use the narrative of Zacchaeus to persuade the reader of the arrival of the 'today' of the salvation of sinners in accordance with Isaiah, then the joy theme likely plays a role. Understanding the joy in Luke 19:9 in this manner requires a nuanced argument, and it remains rather tentative, but it also draws directly on significant intertextual relationships and signals.

Returning to the Triumphal Entry, we see that the presence of the emotional cries of the disciples as Jesus enters Jerusalem functions rhetorically as an

---

[25] The use of the OT to vindicate Jesus' actions is also expressed by B.J. Koet who finds that Jesus 'quotes scripture to justify his action' in purging the temple (Lk 19:4/Isa 56:7/Jer 7:11). This conclusion also supports the thesis that Luke uses the Old Testament rhetorically. Koet, 'Isaiah in Luke-Acts', 86.

[26] Resseguie, *Narrative Criticism of the New Testament*, 156.

[27] J.G. Millar, *Now Choose Life: Theology and Ethics in Deuteronomy* (NSBT 7; Grand Rapids: Eerdmans, 1998), 77.

[28] *NETS*, Book of Esaias, 871. The Greek text reads: δοθῆναι τοῖς πενθοῦσιν Σιων δόξαν ἀντὶ σποδοῦ, ἄλειμμα εὐφροσύνης τοῖς πενθοῦσιν.

[29] Isaiah 12:3 indicates that the arrival of the New Exodus calls for a personal response of joy. I.D. Friesen, *Isaiah* (Scottdale: Herald Press, 2009), 103.

intertextual reference to the joy that must accompany the visitation of God. The stones that would cry out in joy reflect not only the New Exodus restoration activity of Isaiah 55:12 but Zechariah 9:9. Much of the scholarly literature does not point out that Zechariah urges 'joy' in response to the arrival of Israel's king on a young donkey.[30] It is plausible that the donkey immediately evoked messianic fulfillment and the arrival of a Davidic shepherd king from several sources.[31] The presence of joy is not optional and it plays an explanatory role as well as a persuasive one.

The joyful shouts explain that this king riding on a colt is indeed the arrival of the King of Israel. The rhetorical function is exemplified by Jesus' own use of the joy theme as he responds to the challenge of the Pharisees. If the joy could be silenced then this event would lose part of its authenticity as the fulfillment of God's promises. The use of Zechariah remains in the foreground while Isaiah likely remains in the background. *Luke uses an amalgamation of themes and keywords that evoke scripture to persuade the audience.*

Joy and Sacred Texture

The sacred texture of the text of Luke 19:28-40 consists of the vertical dimensions that connect human life and the divine. The sacred texture is an important feature of the rhetoric of the Triumphal Entry. The very presence of joy is persuasive because the presence of it is part of a full-orbed rhetoric about Jesus and his kingdom.

The pericope makes clear that God (θεός) is the object of the praise and joy of the disciples (Lk 19:37). However, the object of praise is inclusive of Jesus as well. The two-fold repetition of the statement 'the Lord has need of it' (Lk 19:31, 34) creates an ambiguity. In the first case the word κύριος can refer to Jesus and in the second case κύριος can refer to God. As Jesus draws near on the donkey the disciples praise God for 'all the mighty works'. Jesus is then identified as the 'king' who is inaugurating the peace of heaven on earth (Lk 19:38). This distinct use of the title 'Lord' during the earthly ministry of Jesus is unique to Luke, but most likely it refers to Luke's proto-Trinitarian theology that reflects the unique 'relationship between Jesus and the God of Israel'.[32] God remains distinct from Jesus as the object of praise but Jesus is also identified as YHWH, making him also the object of praise. Kavin Rowe's study concludes that the 'ambiguity is thus finally irresolvable exegetically: the "both/and" of the κύριος resonance presses the point that the colt is God's colt precisely in that it is Jesus' colt'.[33]

---

[30] De Long, *Surprised by God*, 229.

[31] Bird, *Are You the One Who is to Come?*, 125, also 133.

[32] Rowe, *Early Narrative Christology*, 217; also see Marshall, *Luke: Historian and Theologian*, 167.

[33] Rowe, *Early Narrative Christology*, 163.

Jesus is the 'Lord' which makes him YHWH. This ambiguity about Jesus and God sharing the identity as YHWH allows the narrative to support the concept that Jesus is a recipient of the joy and praise of the disciples. Rowe wants to argue that the 'visitation of Jesus is the presence of God coming to Jerusalem as κύριος'.[34] But it is not clear what rhetorical tools are employed to achieve this end. This connection between the joy theme and the sacred texture adds richness to Rowe's study because it provides an emotional basis for accepting Jesus as Lord and king. Objectively the emotion of joy is evidence that God's promises have been fulfilled (or have begun to be fulfilled). Subjectively, the emotion of joy works together with the reasonableness or logic of Luke's argument. It draws the reader into the narrative world so that the implied reader must consider the kingdom in their own context.

The joy theme is rhetorically linked to the sovereignly determined plan of God.[35] This is particularly clear in the Triumphal Entry because Jesus explains that if the disciples did not cry out in joy, God would cause the stones to do so (Lk 19:40). This explanation occurs in the context of a challenge from the Pharisees. Having setup this rhetorical situation the theoretical joy of the stones implies that this rejoicing is required and is part of God's plan. Joy is necessary because it is part of the fulfillment of prophecy.[36]

The very notion that stones might cry out in joy if the Pharisees would have their way reinforces the stance that what God can do for Israel is beyond their expectations. This parallels the rhetorical features of interactions established in the framing birth narratives in Luke 1. The importance of challenging the ability of YHWH to act on behalf of his people was brought out in the reaction of Zechariah that initially left him unable to speak. Moreover, YHWH will be faithful not only to his promises as indicated by scripture but he will be faithful to provide praise surrounding the establishment of his king in Zion. Participation in the joyous shouting of praise at Jesus' entry into Jerusalem provides evidence of belief in the upside-down ways of God.[37] The dialogue between Jesus and the Pharisees continues to use the extraordinary to challenge the reader.

---

[34] Rowe, *Early Narrative Christology*, 166.

[35] The will or plan of God encompasses a wide range of vocabulary including βουλή and θέλημα. A dominant feature includes the use of 'must' (δεῖ). For a short overview see A. Marten, 'Salvation Today' in *Reading the Gospels Today* (Grand Rapids: Eerdmans, 2004), 112-13. Also, see J.T. Squires, *The Plan of God in Luke-Acts* (ed. S.E. Porter; Cambridge: Cambridge University Press, 1993), *passim*.

[36] Moessner suggests that the concept of 'stones crying out' may be an intertextual reference to the stones of ruin in Habakkuk 2:11. However, the stones in Habakkuk 2:11 seem to cry out in pain and anger, not in joy (*Lord of the Banquet*, 205).

[37] De Long emphasizes that the response of joy (praise) by the disciples is 'elemental' to God's actions as Jesus approaches Jerusalem (*Surprised by God*, 226). The analysis here supplements De Long's conclusions by demonstrating that these surprising deeds of God are understood in terms of reversal.

Joy and Ideological Texture

The study of ideological texture takes into account the position or posture of the text as it relates to conflict that draws the reader into the narrative and consequently into their contemporary dilemma.[38] The conflict in the Triumphal Entry involves the disciples, the Pharisees, and Jesus. The disciples respond with joy to Jesus while the Pharisees do not. Moreover, they even object to the praise. Sociologically this is a reversal of the status of the educated, honourable religious leaders of Israel who reject their own king. Those who are 'high' have fallen. Those who respond to Jesus are not educated disciples of a formal rabbi. They constitute people like Zacchaeus who are 'short of stature' (Lk 19:3) and are powerless in contrast to the Pharisees. Those who are high are now low and those who are lowly are now esteemed as followers of the king of Israel. This bi-polar reversal reflects the 'rising and falling of many in Israel' as predicted by Simeon (Lk 2:34).[39]

The presence of the emotion of joy on one's lips provides the determining piece of evidence as to one who has begun to participate in the kingdom. Jesus' entrance into Jerusalem demands joyful praise and the very rocks would cry out in praise if the disciples did not (Lk 19:40). This 'contrast' or bi-polar reversal reflects the introductory framing narratives where lowly disciples rejoice in Jesus while people of status resist and complain.[40] It is not hard to see how this provides two alternative paths to Jesus that one may participate in. The use of the emotion of joy operates as an integral part of Luke's rhetoric of reversal that challenges the reader to understand Jesus as king and Lord.

The Reversal of Heart and Mind: Joy in Luke 24:36-49

The rhetorical situation of Jesus' appearance in Luke 24:36-49 turns on Jesus' recognition of the 'thoughts' of the disciples (Lk 24:38). Jesus knows that 'doubts' about himself have arisen in the minds of the disciples. The word διαλογισμός in Luke 24:38 also occurs in Luke 5:21-22, 6:8, and 9:47-48. It often refers to thoughts that Jesus is challenging or seeking to change.[41] Brawley points out that Jesus engages the thoughts of his disciples only when they function partially as 'antagonists'.[42] Toward the end of this textual unit these doubts are specifically identified as Jesus engages their 'minds' about the necessity of his resurrected body, his suffering, and the universal good news of forgiveness of sins.

The reversal from doubt to faith in Luke 24:36-49 is part of the broader

---

[38] Shillington, *Introduction to Luke-Acts*, 54.
[39] York, *The Last Shall Be First*, 42.
[40] Borgman, *The Way According to Luke*, 94.
[41] York, *The Last Shall Be First*, 115n3.
[42] Brawley, *Centering on God*, 132.

pattern of reversal (rising and falling) that was clearly articulated in Simeon's oracle.[43] The rhetorical agenda of this unit is turning doubt into faith. This rhetorical situation is directly related to the major reversal (albeit one the reader has been prepared for) of the resurrection: 'the Lord has risen indeed!' (Lk 24:34).[44] The risen Jesus provides the disciples with what they need to understand his suffering and their own mission.[45] Those who move from doubt to faith must not stop there. The rhetorical process is complex as the narrator explains that 'Jesus opened their minds to understand the Scriptures' (Lk 24:45).[46] This is a reversal of both heart and mind. The rhetorical context involves the 'heart' that must be emotionally moved.[47] The rhetorical context also involves the 'mind' that must be persuaded in faith that Jesus is the fulfillment of the promises made in the Old Testament. The reversal is not only for the disciples. The mission of the disciples is now as broad as the nations (Lk 24:47). Joy is not only the goal in the sense of a transformed 'heart', it is also the means. As this complex rhetorical situation is developed through the concluding narratives, the theme of joy provides the *pathos* or emotional power needed to bring these reversals about.

Joy and Inner Texture

The textual unit of Luke 24:36-49 reflects the joy theme specifically in Luke 24:41. The use of joy appears idiomatic in the difficult phrase in Luke 24:41: 'And while they still disbelieved for joy and were marveling'.[48] The idea here may be that the disciples were 'stunned'.[49] Here the narrator is explaining the emotions and thoughts of the disciples who initially were 'startled' and 'frightened' when Jesus appeared among them (Lk 24:37). The sudden move

---

[43] York, *The Last Shall Be First*, 115. De Long does not use the language of 'reversal' but also concurs that 'narrative tension' is resolved as the disciples finally arrive at full recognition of Jesus and his work (*Surprised by God*, 245).

[44] Kuhn recognizes the reversal motif in the resurrection but does not connect it to the rhetorical challenge to unbelief that plays out in the following passages in Lk 24:36-49 (*Heart of Biblical Narrative*, 43). Rowe provides helpful comments on the 'reversal' motif in Lk 24 but does not encompass rhetorical and affective dimensions of the text in his study (*Early Narrative Christology*, 194-95).

[45] Brawley, *Centering on God*, 80.

[46] Witherington argues that this pericope contains a reference to a 'definite limit' to the OT and that it was closed rather than open. This is evidence of the rise of canon consciousness (*What's in the Word*, 155).

[47] Resseguie's rhetorical analysis of Lk 24:25-27 notes the importance of this reference to the 'heart' (καρδία). The καρδία is the seat of the physical, spiritual, and mental life. The failure of the disciples is not only intellectual it is also affective or emotional (*Narrative Criticism of the New Testament*, 83).

[48] The Greek of Luke 24:41 reads: ἔτι δὲ ἀπιστούντων αὐτῶν ἀπὸ τῆς χαρᾶς.

[49] Navone, *Themes of St. Luke*, 86.

from fear to joy reflects what Karl Kuhn calls 'affective dissonance'.[50] The rhetorical effect upon the reader is jarring and places an emphasis on the emotional state of the characters.

This emphasis on the emotional state of the characters is compounded by the fact that the disciples are pictured as discussing the Emmaus road (Lk 24:36) but then become speechless. They do not really understand the risen Jesus.[51] The result of this juxtaposition is a mixture of fear, joy, and misunderstanding. This sets up the need for the scriptures to be interpreted by Jesus so that the disciples can interpret Jesus from the scriptures. The inner texture reveals that Luke wants to challenge the reader about their understanding of Jesus. At the same time the disciples are confused but remain in a state of joy. This establishes the framework for Luke to direct the hearts and minds of the disciples to the 'paradigm-shattering' nature of the resurrection.[52]

Joy and Intertexture

The pericope of Luke 24:36-49 is the *locus classicus* where Luke refers to Jesus and the Hebrew Scriptures. The literature surrounding Jesus' statements about the relationship between himself and the Scriptures is vast. The concern of my study is to demonstrate that part of Luke's use of the Septuagint, particularly Isaiah, is rhetorical. Luke's use of the joy motif is evocative of themes that originate in the Septuagint. As noted above, the textual unit of Luke 24:36-49 reflects the joy theme specifically in Luke 24:41. There is no indication that there is any intertextual echo or quotation present in the narrator's explanation of the thoughts of the disciples outside of the use of χαρά. There are two interpretive tasks that must be taken here.[53] First, it will be helpful to consider what Luke's own statements about intertextuality add to the broader scope of study. Second, we must consider how the single word χαρά evokes an entire theme in which Luke has already provided a hermeneutical framework for the whole.

One aspect of Luke's use of the Septuagint is rhetorical: it is a source of information that has the capacity to persuade the reader about Jesus and his kingdom. This pericope (Lk 24:36-49) is particularly important for justifying the socio-rhetorical approach of this study and the interest in the connection between intertextuality and rhetoric. The socio-rhetorical approach reflects Luke's own interests in the text in so far as he understands that the Old Testament (Septuagint) itself serves a 'legitimizing function'.[54] The narrative of

---

[50] Kuhn, *Heart of Biblical Narrative*, 51.

[51] Litwak, *Echoes of Scripture in Luke-Acts*, 123.

[52] Rowe, *Early Narrative Christology*, 188.

[53] This is broadly similar to the two fold task of (1) promise/fulfillment and (2) apologetics as identified by H. Conzelmann. For an explanation see Kimball, *Jesus' Exposition of the Old Testament*, 24.

[54] Green, *Theology of the Gospel of Luke*, 31.

Luke-Acts takes up the Scriptures of Israel vis-à-vis the Septuagint and deploys it or renews it in light of Jesus.[55] This is rooted in Luke's own use of Jesus' speech in Luke 24:36-49. Jesus first explains that he 'fulfills' everything in the Old Testament (in the Law of Moses, the Prophets, and the Psalms, Lk 24:44). The narrator explains that the problem to be overcome is that the disciples must have their minds opened in order to 'understand' (Lk 24:45). Jesus' speech continues with the formula 'it is written...' (Lk 24:45).[56] The entire pericope is peppered with a broad but centred approach that connects Jesus to the Old Testament. This provides a retroactive hermeneutical key: any use of the Old Testament is legitimizing or evidence that can be used to persuade the reader of who Jesus is and what his kingdom is about.[57]

What is neglected is how the presence of the joy theme in Luke 24:41 provides an explanation of how the scriptures are to be used. Jesus' explanation of the relationship between himself and the Old Testament is given to the disciples while they are in a mixed state of disbelief, joy, and astonishment (Lk 24:41). This state itself is a continuation of the initial fear (Lk 24:37). This is highly suggestive of the need for joy as one seeks to understand Jesus and the 'Scriptures'. This narrative context must be kept in mind when understanding Jesus' explanation. The Gospel of Luke as a whole is filled with instances of rejection of Jesus and the 'obstacles to its potential recipients'.[58] One of the neglected obstacles that must be overcome is the lack of joy (*pathos*) that is present with lack of understanding (*logos*) and lack of faith in who Jesus is (*ethos*). Intertextuality must evoke joy because the Old Testament is the 'promise' that Jesus fulfills.[59]

The presence of the joy theme in Luke 24:41 (χαρά) evokes the whole that has already been firmly established in Luke 1 and developed throughout. The concept of reading in light of the entire co-text is not without precedent in Lukan studies. One can read the Parable of the Lost Son (Lk 15:11-32) 'within its larger narrative co-text' so that one can understand the 'expanded meaning' in the father's final words to his elder son.[60] The larger co-text provides the joy theme with expanded meaning. Specifically, the joy theme frames Jesus' explanation of the disciples mission (Lk 24:46-49).

Luke ties the 'consummation' or restoration of the (spiritual) Davidic

---

[55] Shillington, *Introduction to Luke-Acts*, 54.

[56] For comments on introductory formulae in Luke see Kimball, *Jesus' Exposition of the Old Testament*, 53.

[57] Rowe employs a similar procedure (called 'narrative hindsight') as he connects the Spirit's operations in Luke 1 with Luke 24 (*Early Narrative Christology*, 39).

[58] Green, *Theology of the Gospel of Luke*, 31.

[59] For Luke, 'the totality of Scripture is behind the story of Jesus'. Pao, *Acts and the Isaianic New Exodus*, 85.

[60] Green, *Theology of the Gospel of Luke*, 35.

kingdom with gospel preaching to 'all nations, beginning in Jerusalem'.[61] As the narrative unfolds, the disciples receive this while in a state of joy (amidst other emotions). Once the mission of the disciples to preach repentance and forgiveness of sins to 'all nations' is framed in terms of joy, the intertextual dimension can be understood. There are parallels between the mission to 'all nations' in Luke 24:46-47 and the universal concepts of being a 'light to the Gentiles' in Isaiah 49:6.[62] In addition, there is another Isaianic parallel between 'power from on high' in Luke 24:49 and the promise of 'a spirit from on high' in Isaiah 32:15.[63] These conclusions would support the likelihood that the joy theme is related to the Isaianic New Exodus.

Previously Luke introduced the universal programme of salvation in the 'dramatic reversal' in the explanation of John the Baptist's use of Isaiah 40:3-5 that articulates the Isaianic New Exodus which provides for 'all flesh' to 'see the salvation of God'. Thus, the universal mission of the disciples in Luke 24:36-49 reflects the universal mission of the New Exodus in Luke 3:4-6/Isaiah 40:3-5.[64] This relationship rests upon the literary relationship between intratextual connections and intertextual connections. The strength of these relationships is supported by both frequency (as repetition) and narrative prominence (occurrence in framing narratives). The occurrence of joy in Luke 24:41 is only significant as an intertextual thread when seen in light of the whole co-text. It provides a framework for understanding how a disciple should approach understanding the scriptures. The narrative encourages one to stand marvelling and interpreting the scriptures with joy, even if this is mixed at first with unbelief.

Joy and Sacred Texture

The sacred texture of a text is simply a way of referring to the intersection of human life and the divine. As the disciples are discussing their interaction with Jesus on the Emmaus road, Jesus appears to them. What follows is a meal scene in which the joy theme interacts with other themes such as fellowshipping and banqueting. What often goes unnoticed is that the joy theme is used to frame this meal scene in Luke 24:41. The state of joy in Luke 24:41 provides the emotional framework that is required to reverse the state of unbelief to belief (Lk 24:41) and to create an understanding of God's divine plan (Lk 24:45).

This concept of divine necessity and fulfillment of God's divine plan is widely recognized. The bulk of the discussion lies outside the scope of this study, although some brief comments are in order. There is a strong element of divine necessity that Luke attaches to the suffering, death, and glorification of

---

[61] Kim, *Christ and Caesar*, 162.

[62] Pao, *Acts and the Isaianic New Exodus*, 86.

[63] Pao, *Acts and the Isaianic New Exodus*, 122.

[64] Puskas, *Conclusion of Luke-Acts*, 103n121.

Jesus.[65] The element of divine necessity flows from what has been 'written' in the Scriptures (Luke 24:46). Joel Green explains the relationship succinctly:

> Luke ties the story of Jesus into the story of Israel; they are bound together in hermeneutical association so that Luke's audience is advised to return again and again to the Scriptures of Israel in order to appreciate more fully the significance of the story of Jesus.[66]

This reversal from unbelief to belief is necessary for the disciples to integrate into the 'overarching Lukan plotline of God dispensing salvation'.[67] The pericope of Luke 24:36-39 is tied to this plotline or plan of God as explained by Jesus on the Road to Emmaus in which the narrators explain that Jesus appeared 'as they were talking about these things' (Lk 24:36).

The reference to the mixed state of confusion and joy (Lk 24:41) appears after Jesus shows the disciples his hands and feet (Lk 24:40). This evidence confirms the question raised by Jesus appearance: who or what is Jesus? The rhetorical issue revolves around the identity of Jesus as Luke creates a connection between the plan of God and Christology. Jesus' physical body confirms that he is truly a person. The closing chapter of Luke can be summarized as movement 'from a restricted somatic existence to an unrestricted somatic existence'.[68] Jesus' sudden presence among the disciples confirms that his body is different in some sense (it is glorified and resurrected). The new age has physically broken into this age. The reference to 'his hands and his feet' in Luke 24:40 refers specifically to the injuries incurred on the cross. This is the same Jesus who was crucified. The identity of Jesus is critical and must be addressed. All expectations of the power of death have been reversed in the person of Jesus. Again, the reversal from unbelief to belief and misunderstanding to understanding occurs in the disciples who are indeed confused but also exhibit joy. Joy is integral to a faith that is seeking understanding. Luke frames Jesus' appearance in terms of *joy seeking understanding*.

Joy and Ideological Texture

The conflict that gives rise to Luke's ideological concerns is not between Jesus and his opponents as exemplified by the Pharisees. Here, the conflict arises within the disciples and is characterized by a tension between belief and unbelief in who Jesus is and what he has accomplished. Furthermore, if we

---

[65] Marshall, *New Testament Theology*, 142.

[66] Green, *Theology of the Gospel of Luke*, 31.

[67] Spencer, *Rhetorical Texture and Narrative Trajectories*, 80. Spencer cites Lk 24:13-49 as part of the call to discipleship. He does not examine how emotion plays a role in this call or in the overarching plot.

[68] Rowe, *Early Narrative Christology*, 189.

recognize the use of χαίρω in Luke 22:5 and 23:8 as referring to the joy of Jesus' opponents, namely the chief priests and Herod, we begin to see who really gets the 'last laugh'.[69] Thus, the joy of the disciples may stand in contrast with the opponents of Jesus who found joy in his death. The basic 'story line' in Luke 24 is about the 'disciples' transformation'.[70] In this story line, the emotion of joy is vitally important because it serves his 'rhetorical and pastoral ends'.[71]

Within the larger textual unit of Luke 24:1-53 are three sub-units that contain a 'threshold moment'. This 'threshold moment' is a pivot point at which the disciples move from 'misunderstanding to understanding'.[72] This is very similar to the concept that this study has labelled as 'reversal'. Karl Kuhn asks the simple but penetrating question: 'what's the rhetorical payoff?' His answer is,

> Through his shaping of this threshold moment Luke invites his audience to recognize and push aside such foolish doubt within themselves, to embrace the reality of Jesus' resurrection and ongoing ministry, and then also to join the disciples in living lives of joyous praise and witness (vv.44-49, 50-53). The affective dimensions of Luke's portrayal serve his rhetorical and pastoral ends.[73]

Kuhn's analysis echoes the thesis of this study, albeit on a much more limited scale and without an examination of certain features such as intertextuality. What is clear is that Luke is not just interested logic and historical facts: he is interested in a response to the risen Lord.[74]

The Reversal of Jerusalem: Joy in Luke 24:50-53

Luke wraps up his Gospel in a short ascension scene. The Gospel of Luke that began with joy in the Judean hills ends with joy in Jerusalem (Lk 24:52-53). Many have noted the uniqueness of this ascension scene but its importance is not always clear.[75] Here we must ask the question why Luke, more than any

---

[69] Thanks to H. Morrison for pointing out these passages. It is likely that some do not recognize the presence of the joy theme in Lk 22:5 and 23:8 because of the lack of lexical repetition (for example John Painter omits Lk 22:5 and 23:8 in 'joy' in his article in the *Dictionary of Jesus and the Gospels*, 394-96). However, from a narrative perspective, having two opponents (one being collective) that are finding joy in Jesus is relatively significant.

[70] Kuhn, *Heart of Biblical Narrative*, 34.

[71] Kuhn, *Heart of Biblical Narrative*, 35.

[72] Kuhn, *Heart of Biblical Narrative*, 34.

[73] Kuhn, *Heart of Biblical Narrative*, 35.

[74] Bernadicou, *Joy in the Gospel of Luke*, 28.

[75] Mallen, *Reading and Transformation of Isaiah*, 144.

other gospel, places such emphasis on Jerusalem.[76] What is central to Jesus' revelation of himself on the road to Emmaus in the previous pericope (Lk 24:28-35) is 'the New Exodus that would be accomplished in Jerusalem'.[77] The return from exile motif or New Exodus is based on the concept of the restoration of Israel.[78] Previously the emotion of joy has been used to incorporate an emotional force into Luke's rhetoric of reversal.[79] To participate in the new age inaugurated by Jesus requires that the reader accept and exhibit values that are congruent with a king who rides a donkey and who was first attended to by unclean shepherds. Jesus' entrance on the donkey identifies Jerusalem as the city of the restored (or, partially restored) Davidic monarchy. The city of Jerusalem is 'where the prophecies find their fulfillment.'[80] Because Jesus is exalted the city of David is exalted and the temple becomes a place of praise.

The textual unit of Luke 24:50-53 functions in three ways. First, it functions as the conclusion of the whole Gospel. Second, it functions as the fulfillment of Jesus' cleansing of the temple and his reference to the Old Testament promise regarding the temple being a 'house of prayer' (Lk 19:45). Third, it anticipates the second volume of Luke's corpus. *Rhetorically, the joy theme provides evidence and emotional power that a reversal has taken place with regard to Jesus and the temple in Jerusalem.*[81]

Joy and Inner Texture

As the culminating and final pericope of the entire Gospel, this section explicitly and implicitly ties together a plethora of themes and narrative threads. The focus of this study remains on the joy theme as it appears again in the use of χαρά (Lk 24:52) and εὐλογέω (Lk 24:53). The joy theme may be an *inclusio* that encompasses the entire Gospel.[82] Indeed, the presence of the joy

---

[76] S.W. Hahn, 'Kingdom and Church in Luke-Acts: From Davidic Christology to Kingdom Ecclesiology' in *Reading Luke: Interpretation, Reflection, Formation* (eds. C.G. Bartholomew, J.B. Green, and A.C. Thiselton; Carlisle: Paternoster, 2006; Grand Rapids: Zondervan, 2005), 303.

[77] Wright, *Luke for Everyone*, 298.

[78] N.T. Wright, *The New Testament and the People of God* (London: SPCK, 1992), 268-79; Mallen, *Reading and Transformation of Isaiah*, 14.

[79] Surprisingly, York's study of the rhetoric of reversal in Luke does not examine the textual unit of Lk 24:50-53 (*The Last Shall Be First*).

[80] Puskas, *Conclusion of Luke-Acts*, 108.

[81] This follows a trajectory begun in the early scenes of Luke's Gospel. Robbins provides a helpful summary statement: 'The Jerusalem Temple remains a place of God's power, but a new story of "important persons" begins to "tell" the Temple in ways that present decisively new challenges for the story of Israel' ('Bodies and Politics in Luke 1-2 and Sirach 44-55', 838).

[82] Bernadicou, *Joy in the Gospel of Luke*, 29.

theme in the last pericope of Luke's Gospel is striking.[83] The presence of the joy theme is noted by Paul Bernadicou: 'an aura of increasing joy encircles this last chapter [of Luke]'.[84] This 'encircling' or repetition of the emotion of joy provides narrative amplification. The appearance of joy vocabulary strengthens its importance as a major theme that runs from the introductory framing narratives to the conclusion.

There is a textual variant in Luke 24:53 with two major readings including αἰνοῦντες καὶ εὐλογοῦντες versus αἰνοῦντες.[85] External evidence tipped the scale for the UBS committee in favour of the latter variant. Regardless of the variant one favours, the element of the emotion of joy is present in either αἰνέω or εὐλογέω.[86] The joy of the disciples is depicted in two ways in the closing ascension pericope (Lk 24:50-53). The narrator describes the disciples' response to Jesus' departure as having 'returned to Jerusalem with great joy' (Lk 24:52). The identification of the temple as the final geographical location of the joyful disciples of the vindicated Jesus creates a strong *inclusio* between the conclusion and the framing narrative of Zechariah in the temple (Lk 1:8-23).[87]

A minor debate has taken place over the presence of a priestly function as Jesus raises his hands in blessing in Luke 24:50. This is important to consider because of the way in which Jesus may be reversing the earlier failure of Zechariah in the temple. There may indeed be a reversal relationship between Jesus' priest-like blessing in Luke 24:50-53 and Zechariah's inability to pronounce a blessing on the congregation in Luke 1:21-22. Bradley Chance notes that Jesus does not function primarily as a priestly messianic figure for Luke. Yet Chance is willing to give Jesus a 'priestly colouring'.[88]

What goes unnoticed is the role that the joy theme plays in this relationship.

---

[83] Bernadicou, *Joy in the Gospel of Luke*, 29; Marshall, *Luke: Historian and Theologian*, 203.

[84] Bernadicou, *Joy in the Gospel of Luke*, 28.

[85] The two readings for Luke 24:53 likely arise from a 'conflation' of εὐλογοῦντες and αἰνοῦντες. For our purposes, it is important to note that of the three possibilities, all have an element of rejoicing that connects with the joy theme. Metzger gives εὐλογοῦντες from sources such as **P**[75] and א a 'B' rating for 'almost certain'. See Metzger, *Textual Commentary*, 163.

[86] J.P. Louw and E.A. Nida, *Greek-English Lexicon of the New Testament: Based on Semantic Domains* (2nd ed.; New York: United Bible Societies, 1996), 2:108, 2:6; H.R. Balz and G. Schneider, *Exegetical Dictionary of the New Testament* (Grand Rapids: Eerdmans, 1990), 1:39, 2:79.

[87] Resseguie, *Narrative Criticism of the New Testament*, 58; Mallen, *The Reading and Transformation of Isaiah*, 79; Parsons, *The Departure of Jesus in Luke-Acts*, 72-77. Rowe focuses on Luke's use of κύριος in Luke 1 and Luke 24 (*Early Narrative Christology*, 39).

[88] J.B. Chance, *Jerusalem, the Temple, and the New Age in Luke-Acts* (Macon: Mercer University Press, 1988), 63.

In the framing narratives, the joy of Mary and her faithful response stands in contrast to Zechariah. It is likely that Jesus functions in this vein: he is not only a priest but a faithful Israelite. Jesus constitutes the restoration of Israel as the perfection of what it means to fulfill a priestly role. He likely appears here as a priest who blesses the restored people of God. The people of God respond with worship and 'great joy'. Their own faithfulness exhibits that they are now fulfilling what is now required: worship and praise to Jesus. Such a depiction bids the reader to ask if they are participating in this temple-like worship of Jesus.

Joy and Intertexture

There are few interpreters who are willing to make strong conclusions about any intertextual echoes in Luke 24:50-53. There may be two intertextual echoes. The first may be an echo of Leviticus 9:22 in Jesus' blessing and the second may be a reference to the heavenly departure of figures throughout the Old Testament (Genesis 17:22; 35:13; Judges 6:21; 13:20; 2 Kings 2, etc.).[89] Any connection to the New Exodus motif comes from the suggestion that Jesus' ascension may parallel the ascension of Moses when he entered the cloud and ascended the mountain into God's presence for 'forty days' (Exod 24:15-18).[90] The presence of the joy theme provides persuasive evidence that the restoration of the people of God has begun.

One example of innertextual analysis finds that the conclusion of the Gospel of Luke 'recalls its beginning, especially the settings in the Temple and the expectations of salvation'.[91] If there are intertextual considerations at the beginning of Luke where the theme was established and if that theme appears elsewhere then it is reasonable to conclude that Luke had intertextual connections between both. The use of the Old Testament is intimately related to narrative considerations as Luke intentionally creates literary relationships within his Gospel. One must be careful not to find an intertextual relationship behind every nook and cranny. Yet one must not dismiss major themes and repetition of keywords that produce rhetorical effects such as amplification.[92] This is why it is important to examine the innertexture and establish the presence of a theme before examining the intertexture. This can be justified by the text itself. Luke's use of prophecy and fulfillment is well known. Although some have disputed how prophecy and fulfillment are related to intertextuality, the very use of fulfillment language (Lk 24:44) directs the reader to consider the narratives analeptically and proleptically (making connections throughout

---

[89] Pao and Schnabel, 'Luke', *CNTUOT*, 402.

[90] Evans and Sanders, *Luke and Scripture*, 82.

[91] Kurz, *Reading Luke-Acts*, 28.

[92] For an example of following a *Leitwort* through the whole of Luke's Gospel and bringing together narrative considerations see the comments by Rowe, *Early Narrative Christology*, 198-99.

the whole).

The theme of joy in the temple appears in both Luke 1 and Luke 24 for good reason. The joy of the people in the temple arguably fulfills a whole trajectory of Zion theology in the Old Testament wherein Jerusalem is longing for comfort and restoration. The reversal of the sorrow of the destruction of the first temple in 586 B.C. as found in Lamentations finds its 'definitive answer' in Isaiah 40:1 – the keystone text for the Isaianic New Exodus.[93] It is significant to observe that the Isaianic New Exodus is first addressed to Jerusalem (Isa 40:2).

In the third chapter of this study it was argued that the New Exodus intertextual framework established by explicit appropriation of Isaiah 40:3-5 in Luke 3:4-6 provides a hermeneutical key that can be read retroactively into the themes beforehand. This was supported by the connection between the joy theme as a response to the birth narratives and the restoration of Israel in Luke 1 and Isaiah 40-55. In the case of Luke 1, the joy of Zechariah was never totally fulfilled because his response was mixed with unbelief. The temple could have been the site of joy at the inauguration of the New Exodus. That which was initially frustrated by sin is now overturned and the temple is filled with joyous disciples because of the vindication of Jesus in Luke 24. The joy of the disciples is humble yet victorious.

Amplification or repetition also points to potential parallels between the joy in the Temple in Jerusalem and two similar passages in LXX Isaiah 35:10 and 51:11.[94] The vocabulary stresses the joy theme of the restoration of Zion and his comfort. The poetic vocabulary in Isaiah 51:11 stresses the emotion of joy:

> For by the Lord they shall be returned and come to Sion with joy (εὐφροσύνη) and everlasting gladness (ἀγαλλίαμα); for gladness (ἀγαλλίασις) and praise (αἴνεσις) shall be upon their heads and joy (εὐφροσύνη) shall take hold of them; pain and sorrow and sighing have fled away.[95] (LXX Isaiah 51:11)

The text of Isaiah 35:10 LXX is very similar to this and is strongly reminiscent of the way in which Luke uses repetition of emotional words for joy. If one reads through Luke's gospel and follows the narrative threads, it is not hard to understand how these Isaianic texts could lie behind the brief description of the joyful disciples in the temple in Luke 24:50-53.

The combination of repetition and the recitation and re-contextualization of texts (based on the LXX) produces the rhetorical feature of narrative amplification.[96] The use of joy as it relates to the intertexture of Luke 24:50-53 is persuasive evidence that Isaiah's promise of 'comfort' for Jerusalem has

---

[93] B. Webb, *Five Festal Garments: Christian Reflections on The Song of Songs, Ruth, Lamentations, Ecclesiastes and Esther* (Downers Grove: IVP, 2000), 63.

[94] Thanks to H. Morrison for directing me to these passages.

[95] *NETS*, Book of Esaias, 864.

[96] Robbins, *Exploring the Texture of Texts*, 51.

begun.[97]

Joy and Sacred Texture

The sacred texture of Luke 24:50-53 is critical for understanding the rhetorical development of Luke's Gospel. The sacred texture is composed of those things that focus on divine-human interaction. Before the arrival of Jesus, the temple in Jerusalem provided a focus point for Israel's interaction with YHWH. Here in Luke 24:52, Jesus himself receives the same worship (προσκυνέω) that is due to YHWH alone. The tight connection between Jerusalem and the temple means that one may conclude that what characterizes one will characterize the other (peace, war, joy, etc.).[98] The presence of joy in the temple in Jerusalem makes the sacred texture an important yet neglected feature. The presence of joy in the temple provides a vantage point for understanding an inaugurated eschatology or an inaugurated view of the restoration of the Davidic kingdom through Jesus.

It is evident from the shouts of the disciples in the Triumphal Entry that the 'peace' was not on earth or in Jerusalem but in 'heaven' (Lk 19:38). This stands in stark contrast to the joyful shouts of the shepherds who shouted for 'peace on earth' (Lk 2:14). The lack of peace in Jerusalem at the point of the Triumphal Entry is important for the developing 'Way' that proceeds to the cross. However, the lack of peace must not lead one to conclude that the restoration of the Davidic kingdom has absolutely no impact on earth.[99] The spiritual nature of the kingdom must not be triumphalistic. The joy in the final ascension pericope unites the former locus of YHWH's presence in the temple with the locus of the ever-present risen Jesus who reigns in heaven. The heavenly kingdom will influence the emotions of its members even now. Thus, peace comes to the temple but only in a qualified way, that reflects an inaugurated eschatology.

The joy in the temple/Jerusalem provides partial (incomplete) but important evidence that the Davidic monarchy has been inaugurated and that the reader may now participate in it. Because Jesus ascended into heaven, he may be worshipped as YHWH from any place. This completes a trajectory begun in infancy narratives.[100] There are many clues to direct the reader who is already

---

[97] What is being suggested here is that the burdensome Deuteronomistic theology and triumphalistic Zion theology are joined together in Isaiah's New Exodus (Isaiah 40). The conclusions about the centrality of Isaiah do not undermine the importance of Deuteronomy 12-26 in the travel narrative (*Lord of the Banquet*, 284-85).

[98] Hahn, 'Kingdom and Church in Luke-Acts', 304.

[99] Borgman states 'in Jerusalem, at least, there is no true peace'. This statement must be qualified by the fact that the cross and resurrection provide a temporary or inaugurated *shalom* in Jerusalem (*The Way According to Luke*, 93).

[100] 'Let us remember that the shepherds returned to the field on the day of Jesus' birth, not by singing to the baby, but praise and glory to God'. ['Erinnern wir uns, dass die

familiar with the concept of a Davidic monarchy. These clues would have aided the reader to answer the question: 'does the shape of Jesus' kingship as portrayed by Luke resemble that of David?'[101] By recalling Luke's interest in the affections (of the heart; καρδία) in Luke 24:25-27 as noted previously in this study, an additional characteristic must be added to the list: the Davidic monarchy will be inaugurated with joy. This joy of the disciples provides both objective evidence and a reality into which the reader can enter. Thus, the sacred texture of the temple and Jerusalem intersects with Luke's rhetorical purpose to impact the intellect and emotions of the reader.

Joy and Ideological Texture

The way that Luke shapes this last pericope is suggestive that he wants the reader to respond to Jesus' ascension with joy. However, Luke shapes the narrative so that the joy of the disciples is connected to both the Ascension and Jerusalem. This is achieved by the word order of the sentence which separates the action of worship from the action of having joy (Lk 24:52). Thus, the reader is led to associate Jerusalem with joy.[102]

In continuity with Luke 2, we find that Luke positions the text so that it challenges the Temple in Jerusalem. The joyful songs communicates that 'the new Israel has begun'.[103] Jerusalem provides an element of continuity between Jesus and the Church.[104] We may agree that Jerusalem provides discontinuity between Jews and Gentiles because it is in the City of David that YHWH fulfilled his promises, although his salvation now will go into all the world.[105]

The fact that Luke creates an intimate and lasting impression of the disciples worshipping Jesus joyfully in the temple in Jerusalem has significant ideological implications. The worshipping and joyful disciples present a snapshot of what characterizes God's people who are faithful to the Law of Moses. Luke has Jesus explain on the Road to Emmaus that Jesus fulfills what 'all of the prophets have spoken' (Lk 24:25). Those who want to remain faithful to the Law must now engage in acts of worship to Jesus in joyful celebration. To reject this is to reject the prophets. The geographical location of the Temple in conjunction with the joy theme support a new approach to temple worship: it must be centred on the ever-present Jesus.

The joy in Luke 24:50-53 as well as in the Triumphant Entry (Lk 24:36-49)

Hirten am Tag von Jesu Geburt auf das Feld zurückgekehrt sind, indem sie nicht dem Neugeborenen, sondern Gott Lob und Preis sangen (2:20)'.] F. Bovon, *Das Evangelium nach Lukas* (4 Vol.; EKK; Zurich: Benziger, 1989), 4:619.

[101] Hahn, 'Kingdom and Church in Luke-Acts', 303.

[102] Morrice, *We Joy in God*, 27.

[103] Bernadicou, *Joy in the Gospel of Luke*, 29; for a similar conclusion see Chance, *Jerusalem, the Temple, and the New Age*, 83.

[104] Conzelmann, *Theology of St. Luke*, 133.

[105] Pao, *Acts and the Isaianic New Exodus*, 90-91.

stands in contrast with the mocking and jeering at the cross. Jesus is mocked by the leaders (Lk 23:35), the soldiers (Lk 23:37) and one of the criminals crucified beside him (Lk 23:39).[106] This mockery attacks Jesus' messianic identity.[107] This begs the question: will Jesus be vindicated? The resurrection appearance of Jesus offers the definite answer: God has vindicated him. The joy of the worshippers functions as a contrast to the mockery at the cross and continues this ideological challenge to the mockery. The joy of the worshippers only adds to the vindication of Jesus as a confirmatory witness. Conceptually this joy functions as an attack upon the parody that was made of the cross.

Joy is at the center of parallelism between the temple scenes in the opening (Luke 1) and closing of Luke's Gospel (Luke 24). The key element of discontinuity in the closing is that 'worship has been transformed by the resurrection and ascension of Christ'.[108] *The presence of the worshippers in the temple directly replaces of Old Covenant worship with New Covenant Jesus worship.*

Conclusion

The joy theme in the Gospel of Luke runs like a thread from the introduction to the final sections. The presence of joy in the final sections of Luke's Gospel is used for rhetorical and pastoral ends.[109] The joy theme also connects with the theme of God's plan. Divine necessity is an important means by which 'persons are confronted with the invitation to align themselves with God's purposes.'[110] Joy functions in a similar way. The portrayal of the joyful response to the fulfillment of God's promises provides an emotional component of the message that sinners are welcome to participate in God's joyful redemptive programme.

James Resseguie asks the question, 'If the narrator writes to persuade the reader to view the world differently, how can we know what the narrator wants us to "see"?'[111] Luke's presentation of the Triumphal Entry bids us to have eyes to see Jesus as the king who is inaugurating his heavenly kingdom on his path to the cross in Jerusalem. When Jesus appears to the disciples in Luke 24:36-49, Luke is keen to explain that they were in a mixed state of joy and misunderstanding. Luke wants the readers to be in a disposition that is ready to accept Jesus joyfully, even if they do not fully understand. We must see through the eyes of faith and feel the emotion of joy. This is not only faith seeking understanding, it is *joyful* faith seeking understanding.

The presence of the joyful disciples in the temple responding to the

---

[106] Brawley, *Text to Text Pours Forth Speech*, 43.

[107] Brawley, *Text to Text Pours Forth Speech*, 43.

[108] Morrice, *We Joy in God*, 46.

[109] Bernadicou, *Joy in the Gospel of Luke*, 27; Kuhn, *Heart of Biblical Narrative*, 35.

[110] Green, *Theology of the Gospel of Luke*, 35.

[111] Resseguie, *Narrative Criticism of the New Testament*, 21.

resurrected Lord Jesus provides a victorious yet non-triumphalistic signal.[112] God has truly begun to provide 'comfort' for Jerusalem as he promised in Isaiah 40:1. The disciples are pictured as praising God without hindrance but the picture is brief enough to avoid a sense of finality. The conclusion of Luke's gospel achieves two key functions: (1) it highlights the central message of salvation in terms of forgiveness of sins, and (2) it builds a bridge to the second volume of Acts.[113] The role that the joy theme plays in the book of Acts is examined in the next chapter.

---

[112] Kuhn's comments are general but his observation applies here: 'the tragedy of Jesus' rejection, while painful (cf. Lk 19:41-44), does not ultimately undermine or overcome the joyful proclamation of the salvation God will accomplish in Jesus (*Heart of Biblical Narrative*, 130).

[113] Kim, *Christ and Caesar*, 137.

Chapter 7

Joy in the Journey of the Word from Jerusalem

William Morrice declares, 'The same note of joy [as found in Luke] is visible in the Acts of the Apostles'.[1] In fact, the joy theme in Acts is so strong that it is has been labeled 'The Sequel to the Gospel of Joy'.[2] Jesus' death and resurrection has turned the world upside-down. The New Age has dawned and the good news is *joyfully* going out to the ends of the earth.

Introduction

Central to the purpose of Acts is to persuade the reader about the nature of the kingdom that Jesus inaugurated. This kingdom is characterized by reversal; it is essentially the 'turning the world upside down' (Acts 17:6). In the second volume of Luke's corpus, the narrative is partially oriented around journeying and Jerusalem. With respect to Jerusalem, the Gospel of Luke is centripetal and Acts is centrifugal. Whereas Jesus moves toward Jerusalem in the Gospel of Luke, the Word moves out from Jerusalem in the book of Acts.[3]

David Moessner summarizes Luke's plot in Acts as 'stories of the journeying of the people of God whose leaders imitate their Prophet Messiah in proclaiming the glad tidings of the Kingdom of God'.[4] Ben Witherington's consideration of Acts leads him to conclude that Luke 'conceptualizes his whole historical project in rhetorical ways'.[5] Whether one uses terms such as

---

[1] W. Morrice, *Joy in the New Testament* (Exeter: Paternoster, 1984), 96.

[2] Morrice, *Joy in the New Testament*, 96; also 99.

[3] De Long provides a helpful list of parallel usages between 'the word of the Lord' and 'the word of God' (*Surprised by God*, 258 n20).

[4] Moessner, *Lord of the Banquet*, 296.

[5] Witherington, *New Testament Rhetoric*, 44. His analysis of rhetoric in Acts focuses primarily on speeches and not on the narrative as a whole. Nor does Witherington consider the role of emotion or pathos as an important element of persuasion. A significant problem with Witherington's approach is apparent in his lack of attention to the relationship between intertextuality and rhetoric in Acts. It is undisputed that rhetoric shapes the very 'character, structure [and] order of the speech summaries and accounts' (*New Testament Rhetoric*, 93). However, this rhetorical character of the speeches *and* the narrative as a whole must account for the importance that Luke continues to give to intertextual sources such as Isaiah. The Old Testament must be accounted for in one's analysis of Luke's rhetoric in Acts, whether on a macro or micro-level scale.

'rhetoric' or 'apologetic' to describe Acts, the concept of persuasion is present.[6] It is important to state that the apologetic interests are not exclusive of ecclesiological interests: the Book of Acts seeks to shape identity. Integral to the persuasive task(s) is not only logic (*logos*) but also emotion (*pathos*). The socio-rhetorical method used in this study intersects well with Luke's own desire to persuade the reader of the ongoing work of Jesus post-resurrection, the church's continuity with Israel, and the legitimacy of the inclusion of the Gentiles.[7]

The previous chapters have sought to demonstrate how the emotion of joy added emotional power to the rhetoric of reversal. Here we will only be able to examine three of the major occurrences of the joy theme in Acts. The joy theme in the Book of Acts remains an open area for further scholarship. There are threads of continuity between Luke and Acts. Themes in Acts have their seed in Luke.[8] The joy theme is one thread that ties the beginning of Acts with the end of Luke's Gospel. For example, the believers who returned to Jerusalem with great joy (Lk 24:52-53), worshipping in the temple are the same believers who are with Jesus at the beginning of Acts (1:1-11).[9] In spite of some discontinuities, the central thesis remains viable for Luke and Acts: *the emotion of joy empowers the rhetoric of reversal.*[10]

The socio-rhetorical study employed in my study is intentionally interdisciplinary.[11] It will be helpful to briefly review the nature of this approach. It includes four distinct but progressively overlapping questions.

The first question asks: how does joy function as *inner texture*? This is concerned with the text itself. The second question asks: how does joy function as related to *intertexture*? This is concerned with the rewriting of texts.[12] The third question asks: how does joy function as part of *sacred texture*? This question focuses on the intersection of human life and the divine. The fourth

---

[6] For Acts as 'apologetic' see J. Jervell, *The Theology of the Acts of the Apostles* (Cambridge: Cambridge University Press, 1996), iv; Mallen, *Reading and Transformation of Isaiah*, 5.

[7] Mallen, *Reading and Transformation of Isaiah*, 163-4. Here I follow Mallen's helpful suggestion that ecclesiology, eschatology, and Christology all fall under Luke's broad vision of God's plan and 'what has been fulfilled among us' (Lk 1:1).

[8] Puskas, *Conclusion of Luke-Acts*, 108.

[9] O'Toole, *Unity of Luke's Theology*, 196.

[10] Our study of joy in Acts is limited to the three occurrences that follow the pathway highlighted in Acts 1:8. The thesis is not a universal claim about every instance of joy or reversal in Acts. Rather, the thesis focuses on prominent or foregrounded patterns.

[11] For succinct summary of the socio-rhetorical methodology of V.K. Robbins see Shillington, *Introduction to the Study of Luke-Acts*, 53-54.

[12] Some of these questions will overlap as they progressively inform each other. For example, Mallen argues that Luke uses Isaiah as 'subversive intertextuality' (*Reading and Transformation of Isaiah*, 67). According to my approach, this links intertextuality with ideological texture.

question is: how does joy function with respect to *ideological texture*? This question evaluates the emotion of joy as part of ideological conflict.

This interdisciplinary approach can be justified by the text itself for Acts is a mix of genres.[13] The power of emotion in persuasion would have been recognizable with Greco-Roman readers familiar with the loci of *logos-ethos-pathos* and with Jewish readers regarding the fulfillment of YHWH's promises in the Hebrew Scriptures. As demonstrated in the second chapter of my study, the emotion of joy was present in reversal of fortunes in both Greco-Roman and Hebrew literature that would have been recognizable to Luke's readers.[14]

One of the secondary conclusions of the study of joy in the Gospel of Luke is that the Septuagint version of Isaiah was a major source point of intertextuality. In Luke, the Book of Isaiah serves as a source for providing proof from prophecy (promise-fulfillment), explanation, narrative framework, and as a rhetorical source of legitimization.[15] The Gospel of Luke's use of joy and reversal likely derives from the relationship that Isaiah itself provides between joy and reversal. The Book of Acts is similar in that Isaiah provides a narrative backbone, often referred to as the Isaianic New Exodus (Isa 40:1-11). Luke specifically uses Isaiah in the preface of Acts 1:16, 20, providing evidence that a focus on the intertextual relationship with Isaiah is justified.[16] Furthermore, granting that Luke-Acts is a two-volume work, we must take into account the prominence that Isaiah plays in shaping the framing narratives and synagogue scene in Nazareth (Lk 4:16-30). Central to Luke's ecclesiastical focus is persuading the reader that the New Covenant community is the legitimate heir of the promises to the people of God. The emotion of joy is an integral part of persuading the reader that the church's identity is in continuity with and derives from God's programme for Israel.[17]

---

[13] Spencer, *Rhetorical Texture and Narrative Trajectories*, 26; Mallen, *Reading and Transformation of Isaiah*, 26.

[14] A discussion about methodology must intersect with the question of audience. Jervell's conclusion that Acts was written for 'Christian Jews' who were returning back to their synagogues may be a bit over-stated. Jervell is correct to conclude that Acts assumes the reader to be familiar with the Septuagint. However, the interest in the Gentile mission (Acts 1:8) is also reflected in Luke's interest in (re-)defining the people of God. Gentiles are also part of the implied readers as indicated by Lk 1:4 (Jervell, *Theology of Acts*, 16-17).

[15] Mallen's survey of recent literature on the use of Isaiah in Luke-Acts does not make any connection between rhetoric and the concept of 'legitimization' (*Reading and Transformation of Isaiah*, 4-9). But using Scripture ecclesiologically to redefine the people of God according to the New Covenant community is inherently a persuasive task.

[16] Mallen notes that Luke includes 'more extended quotations from Isaiah than any other scriptural book' (*Reading and Transformation of Isaiah*, 2).

[17] Pao, *Acts and the Isaianic New Exodus*, 69.

In the study of Luke, we examined the programmatic quotations from Isaiah in the early sections of the Gospel and used them as hermeneutical keys that framed the discourse or narrative. With respect to Acts, we begin with David Pao's exegesis of Acts 1:8. He focuses his study of intertextuality on Isaiah because of the way that Isaiah provides Luke a 'programmatic' ground plan for the narrative as found in Acts 1:8.[18] This use of Isaiah functions similarly to the programmatic placement of the quotation of Isaiah by Jesus in Luke 1:4. Pao argues that the phrase 'until the ends of the earth' is a reference to Isaiah 49:6 and the promise of the Holy Spirit recalls Isaiah 32:15.[19] The allusion to Isaiah 32:15 suggests the end of exile and the inauguration of the new age – the 'dawn of the Isaianic New Exodus'.[20] Lastly, Pao argues that the statement 'you will be my witnesses' in Acts 1:8 'signifies the presence of a reversal'.[21]

Deafness and blindness are part of the covenantal curses upon Israel in Isaiah 6:9-10 as well as Isaiah 42:18-25. The reference to Isaiah 32:15 indicates that Luke understands the New Exodus to inaugurate the reversal that Isaiah envisions. This is significant because it locates Luke's reversal concept in Isaiah and provides a programmatic statement for reading Acts: the fulfillment of God's promises amongst the people of God will bring about reversals. This is largely the same relationship between reversal and fulfillment that was found in the Gospel of Luke. The categories of the New Exodus that Acts 1:8 inaugurates include: (1) the dawn of salvation in Jerusalem, (2) reconstitution and reunification of Israel, and (3) inclusion of the Gentiles in the people of God.[22] Each of these three items can be considered 'reversals' because the new age overturns the 'previous oracles of doom' such as exile, exclusion, and covenant judgments.[23]

The emotion of joy is used to persuade the reader that the Isaianic reversals have taken place in the people of God that stands in continuity with Israel. Our study of the joy theme in Acts will begin with an examination of joy as it appears early in the text and is used to establish the joy theme and its importance for Luke's rhetoric of reversal. The conversion narratives in Acts 8-16 constitute a large textual unit because they are linked together by Luke's use

---

[18] For the view that Acts 1:8 is 'programmatic' see Mallen, *Reading and Transformation of Isaiah*, 79.

[19] Pao, *Acts and the Isaianic New Exodus*, 92.

[20] Pao, *Acts and the Isaianic New Exodus*, 93.

[21] Pao, *Acts and the Isaianic New Exodus*, 93.

[22] Pao, *Acts and the Isaianic New Exodus*, 95. Although the title 'Israel' is not applied to the Church by the narrator of Acts, it is evident that there is an *element* of continuity between the righteous remnant of Israel and the Jewish followers of Jesus. On distinctions between Israel and the Church see Shillington, *Introduction to the Study of Luke-Acts*, 130.

[23] Pao, *Acts and the Isaianic New Exodus*, 107.

of the Isaianic New Exodus motif of the 'Way'.[24] The church is the people of God that fulfills the promises of YHWH. Joy provides a source of *objective* evidence that God has brought about his promises. And the emotion of joy provides a narrative experience that persuades the reader to identify *subjectively* with the people of God through personal engagement.[25] Throughout this 'Way', Luke uses the emotion of joy in his rhetorical programme as he seeks to persuade the reader of the reversals established by Jesus in light of the Isaianic New Exodus.

The label of 'the Way' is not only useful for describing the followers of Jesus (Acts 19:23, 22:4, 24:22); it captures the concept of movement that reflects the centrifugal path of the word of the Lord out from Jerusalem. Following David Pao's analysis of Acts 1:8 the three categories will be examined: (1) Jerusalem, (2) Judea-Samaria, and (3) the ends of the earth. Pao explains:

> Taken together, then, the three categories correspond to the three stages of the Isaianic New Exodus that signifies the arrival of the new era: (1) the dawn of salvation upon Jerusalem; (2) the reconstitution and reunification of Israel; and finally (3) the inclusion of the Gentiles within the people of God.[26]

The reality that these categories are also geographical locations cannot be ignored.[27] Perhaps it would be better to call these *theo-geo-political* terms. As the word of the Lord travels out from Jerusalem, the geographical locations of the word become critical points of fulfillment. Each of these fulfillments along this 'way' can be described as reversal because of the dramatic nature in which the new age overturns previous conditions. Following the pattern established in Luke's Gospel, the emotion of joy is integral to these events. The presence of joy provides emotional force to the narrative. Objectively, joy is one of the indicators of God's fulfillment of his promises. Subjectively, the emotion of joy affects the reader so that he or she is individually drawn into the narrative. The next sections of this chapter examine the three theo-geo-political realms outlined in Acts 1:8.

The Reversal of Jerusalem: Joy in Acts 2:42-47

One of the strongest pieces of evidence for the importance of the joy theme for

---

[24] M.C. Parsons, *Luke: Storyteller, Interpreter, Evangelist* (Peabody: Hendrickson, 2007), 156.

[25] On one level, the Book of Acts is to be read as 'a play in which we are invited to become actors ourselves'. N.T. Wright, *Acts for Everyone: Part One* (Louisville /London: SPCK, 2008), 3.

[26] Pao, *Acts and the Isaianic New Exodus*, 95.

[27] Talbert also views 'the ends of the earth' as a geographical statement (*Reading Acts*, 74).

Luke's two volume corpus is the fact that the joy theme appears early in both Luke and Acts and is used to frame the discourse or narratives that follow.[28] The joy (ἀγαλλίασις) in Acts 2:46 establishes the 'primitive life of the new community' and frames the narratives to follow by establishing joy as the dominant emotion that characterizes the community of disciples.[29] The rhetorical quality of the speech in Acts 2 is widely recognized but it is not immediately clear how or why the summary of this episode is filled with emotion.[30] Through the use of parallels between Acts and the previous narrative of Luke's Gospel, the reader can feel what it means to be a follower of Jesus. Specific parallels include being full of the Holy Spirit, possessed of power, grace, and joy.[31] The theme of reversal has been established by the miraculous ability of the Jews from every nation to understand the Apostles in their own language (Acts 2:5-13). This likely overturns or reverses the curse of Babel.[32] The rhetoric of reversal in Acts 2:42-47 also utilizes the motif of reversal with respect to Jerusalem. For Luke, the followers of Jesus were part of the righteous remnant of Israel and as representatives of Israel, they reflect the inauguration of Israel's new age.[33] Joy provides a key emotion that empowers and characterizes the inauguration of the restoration of Israel in Jerusalem.

Joy and Inner Texture

The analysis of the inner texture of the joy in Acts 2 must account for the use of

---

[28] Kurz comments on this framing action: 'Acts 2-3 functions as integral to the introduction to Acts, as Luke 1-4 function as introduction to Luke. They provide the implied readers with the biblical context of God's saving plan within which to understand the rest of the events in the narrative'. Kurz, *Reading Luke-Acts*, 80. Navone, *Themes of St. Luke*, 86.

[29] Bernadicou stresses that joy in Acts is always communitarian (*Joy in the Gospel of Luke*, 30). However, this likely reflects Luke's interest in identity and ecclesiology.

[30] Shillington, *Introduction to the Study of Luke-Acts*, 138. Witherington finds formal Greco-Roman rhetorical qualities in Acts 2:14-42 that reflect Hellenistic historians such as Thucydides or Dionysius of Halicarnassus (*New Testament Rhetoric*, 48-49). But it is not clear how Luke can create a rhetorical narrative that is both 'Septuaginalizing' in form and 'deliberative in form'. Perhaps more work needs to be done on identifying 'form' as it relates to formal rhetoric. Mallen also doubts that Lukan rhetoric can be considered 'formal' according to Greco-Roman standards (*Reading and Transformation of Isaiah* (161, also 173).

[31] O'Toole, *Unity of Luke's Theology*, 79.

[32] Wright, *Acts for Everyone: Part One*, 28-29. Witherington disputes this claim because the differences in languages remain (*Acts of the Apostles*, 131). But given Luke's inaugurated eschatology wherein events of the present are microcosms of the future, this cannot be ruled out. After all, the event of Pentecost was only the first-fruits of the fullness yet to come.

[33] Witherington, *Acts of the Apostles*, 163.

semantic parallels for joy between Luke and Acts.[34] First, those who attended the temple to praise God and share bread are described as having 'glad (ἀγαλλίασις) and generous hearts' (Acts 2:46). This use of the word ἀγαλλίασις parallels the joy theme in Luke 1:14, 44 and the verb form ἀγαλλιάω in Luke 1:47, 10:21. Second, the 'praising' (αἰνέω) in Acts 2:47 parallels the words for praising in Luke 2:13, 20; 19:37, and 24:53. The presentation of the apostles having 'fellowship' (Acts 2:42) and 'attending the temple' (Acts 2:46) stands in continuity with the end of Luke's Gospel.

In the previous chapter of my study, I examined the role of joy in Luke 24:50-53. I concluded that the temple is inextricably linked to the entire city of Jerusalem.[35] Luke wants to present Jerusalem or the temple's status as reversed (even if temporarily): it is the place where true worship is taking place by the true people of God. The presence of joy in the temple indicates the inauguration of the fulfillment of the restoration of Israel. The joy is part of a matrix of objective signs that the God of Israel was and is at work. Subjectively, the joyful worshippers of Jesus in the temple present a direct ideological challenge to the mockery once experienced by Jesus at the cross. In a very real way, Jesus and his followers have the last laugh. Although Stephen's speech in Acts 7 presents a negative appraisal of the temple or of false ideas about the temple, this portrait in Luke 24 and Acts 2 is totally positive.[36] The trend away from the positive portrait of worship in the Temple may reflect the growth in opposition to followers of the Way and their need to worship separately from the various flavours of traditional Judaic worship.

As a textual unit, Acts 2:42-47 presents the first major summary of the progress in the narrative. As a summary statement, it is a Lukan composition as opposed to a redaction of a text drawn from another source.[37] In addition, the joy theme appears within Peter's Pentecost speech itself in Acts 2:26-7 as a quote from Psalm 16:8-11: 'my heart was glad (εὐφραίνω) and my tongue rejoiced (ἀγαλλιάω); moreover, my flesh will dwell in hope'.[38] What is striking

---

[34] It is Talbert's conjecture that Acts 2:41-47 forms an ABCBA chiasm. If this is true then the appearance of joy in vv.46-47 parallels the description of the community in v.42. This pattern creates a chiasm that is largely out of balance. C.H. Talbert, *Reading Acts: A Literary and Theological Commentary* (Rev. ed.; Macon: Smyth and Helwys, 2005), 31. For critical comments on chiasm in this pericope as it relates to textual critical issues see R.I. Pervo, *Acts* (Hermeneia; Minneapolis: 2009), 93.

[35] The following OT passages also strongly connect Jerusalem with the Temple: 1 Kings 2:27; Ezra 5:15; Isa 44:28; Dan 5:3. Wright comments that Jerusalem was 'more like a temple with a city around it' in *New Testament and the People of God*, 225.

[36] Stephen's issue with the temple is not the temple cult per se, but the false notion that human temples can confine God. See Witherington, *New Testament Rhetoric*, 61.

[37] For notes on the summary as a Lukan composition see J.A. Fitzmyer, *The Acts of the Apostles* (AB 31; NY/London: Doubleday, 1998), 268; O'Toole, *Unity of Luke's Theology*, 238.

[38] O'Toole, *Unity of Luke's Theology*, 238.

is that the joy theme occurs not only in the speech itself but also in the summary. These facts strengthen the case that Luke has intentionally brought the joy theme to the forefront through repetition.

Joy and Intertexture

Marshall's assessment of the intertextual dimensions of Acts 2:42-47 is that relationships with the Old Testament are 'confined to echoes'.[39] Of these echoes, those that point to Joel 2 receive the most attention. The description of the 'wonders and signs' performed by the apostles implies the fulfillment of prophecy of Joel 2 as quoted by Peter.[40] The use of criteria to discern the role of echoes in Acts 2 is especially important as echoes 'swirl deep into the other'.[41] Here is where the inner texture intersects intertexture. We have just established in the inner texture analysis that the joy theme is present based on repetition. The evidence of repetition and amplification of the joy theme provides another avenue of intertextual echoes. If Luke has intentionally created parallelisms between the emotion of joy in the temple in Luke 24 and Acts 2, there is warrant to consider Isaiah as a possible source of these echoes. Although it is simply conjecture, Isaiah 66 may provide an intersection of two key items. First, Isaiah 66 calls for Israel to consider the true nature of God's 'house' (Isa 66:1). The 'house' of God cannot be built by hands because he inhabits the whole earth. Yet the text goes on to remain committed to the geographical centre of Israel in Jerusalem. The Hebrew text uses the qal imperative and the LXX uses the imperative to call for joy in Isaiah 66:10:

> *Rejoice* with Jerusalem, and *be glad* for her,
> all you who love her;
> *rejoice* with her in *joy*,
> all you who mourn over her;

If the 'wonders and signs' is an intentional signal that the new age of Joel 2 has arrived, the joyful Christian community may be an intentional signal that the new age has come to both Jerusalem and the temple (Isa 66:6). The strength of the case for an intertextual echo in Acts 2:46-47 rests upon the repetition of words within the Lukan joy theme. This is particularly strong if one views Luke-Acts as a two volume corpus written by the same author. The text of Isaiah 66 presents a plausible source for the joy theme in this narrative summary in Acts 2.

---

[39] Marshall, 'Acts', *CNTUOT* 543.

[40] The echo of Joel 2 in Acts 2:43 indicates that the 'wonders and signs' are signals of the dawn of the new age. Marshall, 'Acts', *CNTUOT* 544; F.F. Bruce, *The Book of Acts, Revised* (NICNT; Grand Rapids: Eerdmans, 1988), 73.

[41] Brawley, *Text to Text Pours Forth Speech*, 87.

Joy and Sacred Texture

The direct object of the 'praising' disciples in Acts 2:47 is God (θεός). After this statement, Luke identifies the divine cause behind the swelling ranks of the Way as the κύριος (Acts 2:47b). The sacred texture of this summary presents a certain ambiguity about the referent of these titles. The use of divine titles provides elements of continuity and discontinuity between the Way and the nation of Israel. The use of the word θεός within the summary provides evidence that the believers were standing in communion with the God of Israel. The emotion of joy toward God is ideological and rhetorical because it is an implicit claim upon the exclusive traditions of Israel. With respect to the reversal of Jerusalem, this establishes the church as the people of God who are able to present acceptable worship to the God of Israel in the City of David.[42]

The ambiguity of the referent of κύριος is one of the distinctives of the Lukan corpus. Recent scholarship by Kavin Rowe on Luke's Christology has established that the use of the title 'Lord' or κύριος in the Gospel of Luke can refer to either God or Jesus.[43] Contextually, the use of 'the Lord our God' (κύριος ὁ θεὸς ἡμῶν) in Acts 2:39 refers to the one who gave the 'promise'. Those who hear Peter are like the crooked generation who have rejected Jesus who is the Lord our God. A conceptual parallel relationship is established between 'the Lord our God' and YHWH for the 'crooked generation' of the Exodus (Deut 32:5) and the generation contemporaneous to Peter's speech.[44] This is all prefaced by the argument that Jesus is the heir and Lord of David as evidenced in Acts 2:34-5 and the parallel in Psalm 110:1. The point of the argument is summarized in Acts 2:36 – Jesus has been made 'both Lord and Christ'.[45] Thus, the use of κύριος in Acts 2:47 is ambiguous and can refer to

---

[42] Luke's use of λαός in Acts 2:47 may not be 'hyperbole' as Fitzmyer suggests (*Acts of the Apostles*, 272). This may be Luke's way of associating the worshipping disciples with Israel. If this is the case, it would have supported Luke's agenda to portray the followers of the Way as standing in continuity with Israel as a people that God himself had formed. Compare with Exo 11:3 'And the LORD gave the people favour in the sight of the Egyptians'. Jervell also concludes that λαός is reserved for Israel (*Theology of Acts*, 23).

[43] Rowe concludes: 'This ambiguity in the referent of κύριος is permanent in each case: to ask after the identity of the κύριος is to answer θεός and Ἰησοῦς' (*Early Narrative Christology*, 200).

[44] For comments on the relationship between the Tetragrammaton and the use of the title κύριος for Jesus see R.B. Hays, 'The Liberation of Israel of Luke-Acts' in *Reading the Bible Intertextually* (eds. R.B. Hays, S. Alkier, and L.A. Huizenga; Waco: Baylor University Press, 2009), 110.

[45] For an excursus on 'Kyrios, Identity, and Acts 2:36' see Rowe, *Early Narrative Christology*, 189-196. Rowe reads Acts 2:36 in light of the Lukan corpus and concludes that the resurrection of Jesus proves who Jesus always was with respect to his divine identity: 'there was not when Jesus was not κύριος' (*Early Narrative Christology*, 195).

Jesus who is both the Christ and YHWH. The joy theme is rhetorically provocative because of the object(s) of the emotion are Jesus and God.

Joy and Ideological Texture

The notion that Jerusalem is full of joy due to the presence of followers of Jesus who claim to be the true Israel would have been highly divisive.[46] Those familiar with the Gospel of Luke would know that the 'temple represents the place par excellence where the most recalcitrant enemies of Christ operated'.[47] The ideological function of joy in Acts 2:42-47 is similar to the ideological function of joy in Luke 24. Luke is indeed interested in portraying the 'primitive life of the saints' in the sense that he is interested in describing the life and emotions of the saints.[48] One of the objective pieces of evidence that the believers in Jesus are the true people of God and heirs of the temple is their joy.

The temple was the place where the crowds would be found and where they were to bear witness but he does not set this alongside the fact that these would have possibly been *some* of the same crowds who put Jesus to death (Acts 2:36).[49] The Jewish authorities in Jerusalem had 'power to arrest and detain the apostles'.[50] The joy of the disciples in the temple represents something almost incomprehensible just prior to Peter's preaching and the repentance/belief that followed (Acts 2:38).

The nation of Israel is divided and is in conflict over the Messiah Jesus.[51] Yet the portrayal of the disciples in the temple in Acts 2:42-47 does not present them offering sacrifices according to the Levitical system. This is suggestive of some discontinuity alongside the continuity of the disciples representing a reconstituted Israel worshipping God in the temple. Rather than offering animals, they simply offer praise to God.[52] Many commentators observe that Luke is portraying community life as something that is an ideal. This

---

[46] Chance comments on the temple being the site of Israel's confrontation with the message of salvation: 'Jerusalem was believed to be the place where the salvation of God would be manifested to Israel. Jerusalem would be the place of the restored people of God who would return to the city from all corners of the earth (Isa 35:8-10; 2 Esdr 13:12-13, 39-40; Bar 5:5-9; Ps. Sol. 11:5-7; 4QpPs 37, III:10-11; Pes. De Rab Kah. 20:7; b. B. Bat 75b)' (*Jerusalem, the Temple, and the New Age*, 82).

[47] Padilla, *Speeches of Outsiders in Acts*, 108.

[48] W.H. Willimon, *Interpretation: A Bible Commentary for Teaching and Preaching: Acts* (Atlanta: John Knox Press, 1988), 42.

[49] J.B. Polhill, *Acts* (NAC 26; Nashville: Broadman, 1992), 121.

[50] Chance, *Jerusalem, the Temple, and the New Age*, 84.

[51] Jervell, *Theology of Acts*, 36.

[52] Fitzmyer argues that the disciples were 'exemplary Jews' but this may not take some aspects of discontinuity into account (*Acts of the Apostles*, 272). Even though they may have been offering animal sacrifices Luke does not take note of it. At the very least they may have worshipped YHWH as worship to Jesus.

community is described in a way that Luke 'would desire to be characteristic of all Christians'.[53] One of Luke's ideological goals is to shape the readers of Acts. The joyful followers in the temple are evidence of who is the rightful heir of Israel because their unhindered worship suggests their presence is unchallenged in the temple.[54]

In a great reversal, Israel has been restored in Jerusalem and the joy theme provides emotion that moves the reader to embrace this truth. The joy theme is objective evidence of the identity of the Way and also provides an emotional force to the narrative that shapes the emotion of the reader.

The Reversal of Judea and Samaria: Joy in Acts 8:4-40

The second movement of the word of the Lord out from Jerusalem is among those who were considered outside of Israel but retained some historical connection to the nation. The Isaianic vision of the New Exodus includes the 'reunification of the divided kingdom'.[55] The emphasis on the Twelve as the rulers and judges of the Twelve Tribes of Israel in Acts 1:12-26 has established expectations regarding the restoration or reconstitution of the nation of Israel.[56] The theo-geo-political realm of 'Judea and Samaria' was established in Acts 1:8 as the second stage of the New Exodus. The joy theme appears in two related pericopae in Acts 8.[57] The textual unit of Acts 8:4-40 is held together by the character Philip who takes the Word of God outside of Jerusalem.[58] The joy theme appears specifically in Acts 8:8 and 8:39. First, in spite of the challenge of Simon the Magician in Acts 8:9-25, it is clear that the word of the Lord has arrived in Samaria in Acts 8:4-8.[59] Second, the status of Samaritans as outcasts with respect to Israel is paralleled by the inclusion of Ethiopian eunuch in Acts 8:26-40. Many have recognized the presence of the joy theme in Acts 8.[60] What has not been sufficiently explored is how the emotion of joy contributes to Luke's rhetorical purposes. The emotion of joy is critical to Luke's desire to communicate that the identity of those who were outcasts is now reversed.

---

[53] Fitzmyer, *Acts of the Apostles*, 269.

[54] Chance, *Jerusalem, the Temple, and the New Age*, 84.

[55] Pao, *Acts and the Isaianic New Exodus*, 127.

[56] Pao, *Acts and the Isaianic New Exodus*, 126-27.

[57] As recognized by Bernadicou, *Joy in the Gospel of Luke*, 30; Morrice, *Joy in the New Testament*, 97.

[58] Talbert, *Reading Acts*, 68; Fitzmyer, *Acts of the Apostles*, 400; Kurz, *Reading Luke-Acts*, 84.

[59] Barrett has a helpful discussion about whether Samaria should be considered a city or region. Barrett suggests that Luke was not interested in that level of precision (*Acts 1-14*, 402-3). How one understands the geographic location of Samaria will not impact the conclusions of my study.

[60] Morrice, *Joy in the New Testament*, 74; O'Toole, *Unity of Luke's Theology*, 81; Fitzmyer, *Acts of the Apostles*, 415.

Joy and Inner Texture

The great joy (πολλὴ χαρὰ) in Acts 8:8 is a direct response to the signs (σημεῖον; Lk 8:6) that accompanied the ministry of Philip. The word for joy (χαίρω) in Acts 8:39 is used to describe the state of the eunuch as he departed after his baptism by Philip. The repetition of joy within this larger textual unit provides strong evidence of narrative amplification. The joy theme occurs at key points in the narrative. The first reference to joy (Acts 8:8) is a definitive and concluding comment about the state of the city or region of Samaria. In the second reference to joy, another definitive and concluding statement is made about the emotional state of the eunuch. The joy theme receives emphasis by its placement and position in the narrative. It is the concluding thought of the small textual units. It is as though Luke intended for them to function as a finale. This fact supports the conclusion that the joy theme adds an emotional dynamic to points of reversal within the larger narrative.

A few other points about the inner texture of Acts 8 are noteworthy. The emotion of joy in the region (or city) of Samaria is directly attributed to the effect of the preached word. Luke is keen to connect the signs with the verbal message of Philip in Acts 8:4. Thus, while some attribute the emotion of joy only to the 'cure of the sick and possessed', this is only partially accurate.[61] The way that Luke summarizes the ministry of Philip and other evangelists in Acts 8:4 is significant: 'now those who were scattered went about preaching the word (λόγος)'. This summary sentence encourages a reading of the emotion of joy as a response to the whole ministry of Philip that encompasses both the ministry of the λόγος and σημεῖον.[62] Thus, one can conclude that the χαρά in Acts 8:8 is partially a response to the spread of the λόγος. In both Acts 8:8 and 39 the subjects who have the emotion of joy received drastic changes in their state of being. In the former, they moved from being paralyzed, lame, and under demonic oppression to receiving the word of Christ. In the later, an unclean outcast was received by the Holy Spirit, baptized as a follower of the Way, and given eyes to see so as to understand the Scriptures.

Joy and Intertexture

The intertextual dimensions of the spread of the gospel to Samaria in Acts 8:4-8 are based completely on echoes. Because this textual unit represents Luke's own summary of the historical account it is not the subject of much intertextual analysis. An exclusive focus on the presence of the joy theme may point to Luke using a theme to evoke scripture. If one accepts the presence of the joy theme in the larger textual unit related to Philip, then it is best to understand Acts 8:8 as anticipating the joy theme in Acts 8:26-40. Such a relationship

---

[61] C.K. Barrett, *Acts 1-14* (London: T&T Clark, 1994), 404.
[62] Moessner notes that this link between joy and signs is also reflected in Lk 10:17-20. Moessner, *Lord of the Banquet*, 241 n207.

would suggest that Acts 8:8 is possibly an echo of the Isaianic vision found in texts such as Isaiah 56:7. In order to understand this thematic intertextual relationship it is necessary to examine Acts 8:26-40.

The intertextual dimensions of the pericope of the Ethiopian eunuch in Acts 8:26-40 is challenging because the significance of Isaiah can be found on two levels. First, the eunuch is reading a scroll of Isaiah 53 that requires Christocentric interpretation in order to be understood. Second, when reading the narrative of Acts 8, the repetition of the description 'eunuch' comes to the foreground. This is best understood as using the narrative itself to evoke scripture, particularly the Isaianic vision of Isaiah 56:3-5. One does not have to choose between Isaiah 53 and Isaiah 56.[63] Rather, Luke's intertextual references to Isaiah are present in both his explicit quotations and in his narrative.

The presence of the joy theme in Acts 8:39 supports the conclusion that Isaiah 56 lies behind Luke's depiction of the eunuch. David Pao's examination of Isaiah 56 focuses only on verses 3-5. However, the promise for foreigners continues in LXX Isaiah 56:7:

> these I will bring to my holy mountain, and make them joyful (εὐφραίνω) in my house of prayer; their burnt offerings and their sacrifices will be accepted on my altar; for my house shall be called a house of prayer for all peoples.

If Pao's thesis that Isaiah 56 lies behind Luke's narrative of the eunuch is correct, it also provides an explanation for Luke's interest in describing the joy of the eunuch after his baptism. Furthermore, an interpretation of Isaiah 56:7 that was applied to eunuchs, foreigners, and outcasts would have stood in contrast to the Maccabean vision of the Jerusalem Temple that excluded foreigners (1 Maccabees 7:37 calls the temple a 'house of prayer... for *your* people').[64] The Isaianic vision reverses the concepts of clean and unclean with respect to membership in the people of God and who may stand in the presence of God's Spirit. The presence of the joy theme functions as an objective indicator that God's promise has been fulfilled. The result is a dialogical relationship: the text of Isaiah 56 explains the joy of the eunuch and the joy of the eunuch explains what God is doing.

---

[63] The eunuch is not described as a proselyte. The repetition of the description of being a eunuch points to his status as someone who was unclean according to Deut 32:2 and 21:17-21. However, the presence of the Spirit of the Lord with Philip provides evidence that he has been accepted. This acceptance of the unclean along with his description as a 'eunuch' points to the importance of Isa 56:3-4. Fitzmyer, *Acts of the Apostles*, 410; Marshall, 'Acts', *CNTUOT* 573.

[64] For a discussion of OT antecedent theology for the inclusion of the nations in temple worship see G.K. Beale, *The Temple and the Church's Mission: A Biblical Theology of the Dwelling Place of God* (NSBT 17; Downers Grove: IVP, 2004), 179, 239, 398.

Joy and Sacred Texture

By locating the sacred texture after the study of inner texture and intertexture, it is easier to understand how the text achieves its effects in the real world. This could be described as avoiding 'disembodiment' of the text.[65]

Here, the central issue of Isaiah 56 is the reversal of the status of the foreigner in the people of God. But the reversal of status is not without a purpose. The purpose is explained in Isaiah 56:7: the worship of the foreigner will be accepted. Those who were once unclean and not able to approach YHWH will be able to offer acceptable worship in the 'house' of God. The Isaianic vision of the new age provides access and proximity to God that would have previously resulted in death.

The sacred appears throughout Acts 8:4-40 but is particularly important for understanding the role of the joy theme in Acts 8:39. The Holy Spirit's actions immediately after the baptism of the eunuch communicate not only divine approval but establish the proximity of the eunuch to God's presence. The eunuch's baptism is related first to his understanding of the 'Scripture' of Israel (Acts 8:35) and then to the 'good news about Jesus'. The sense of movement is sudden in Acts 8:39: 'and when they came up out of the water...'. The Holy Spirit carries Philip away immediately and the eunuch goes on his way rejoicing.

The Holy Spirit's actions fulfill the promise of acceptance and proximity as communicated by Isaiah 56. The presence of the sacred (as the Holy Spirit) is significant because God's presence is working in a powerful way in the midst of those who were previously excluded. If Isaiah 53 provides Christology, then Isaiah 56 provides ecclesiology in the sense of confirming the identity of those who can approach YHWH's presence. The Holy Spirit is, after all, the Spirit of Holiness![66] The foreigner and the eunuch can now 'join himself to the LORD' (Isa 56:3).

Joy and Ideological Texture

Talbert locates the conflict in Acts 8 between Simon and Peter in the 'power-oriented society' of Samaria.[67] The joy in Samaria arrives after the preaching of the word conquers the opposing evil spirits. The result of the preaching of the word leaves those who hear free from spiritually caused impairments such as paralysis (Acts 8:7). There is joy in Samaria because of its benefits. In the larger scheme of Luke's narrative, the reader is aware that this summary statement in Acts 8:8 indicates that God's word has been fulfilled. The presence of the Holy Spirit in Samaria fulfills the path described in Acts 1:8. It is not only unclean spirits that are overcome but the entire history of enmity between

---

[65] Robbins, *Exploring the Texture of Texts*, 130.
[66] Thanks to Mike Bird for pointing this out.
[67] Talbert, *Reading Acts*, 71.

the people of God and Samaria. Israel has begun to be restored in this moment that overturns or reverses much of her history.

The joy theme also provides ideological texture to the conflict that follows the reference in Acts 8:8. The conflict with Simon the Magician in Acts 8:9-25 appears between the two pericopae that contain the joy theme. The appearance of the conflict between Peter and Simon depicts a struggle between a magical view of the gospel and the Word of God (Acts 8:14).[68] Simon's challenge to the gospel is particularly important because of the attention that he received (Acts 8:10-11).[69] What is significant about this power encounter is how Luke uses the emotion of joy to frame the conflict. Before the conflict begins, Luke simply describes the state of Samaria after receiving the 'word' as having 'great joy' (πολλὴ χαρά) in Acts 8:8. In the larger narrative, the struggle between Peter and Simon is also a struggle of evil in the midst of a city that has joyfully embraced the gospel.

Luke is certainly interested in more than the emotional state of those who receive the word of the Lord. Simon is an example of someone who believed but in a defective way. Yet the place of the emotion of joy plays a prominent role once again in how Luke summarizes the state of the eunuch who was baptized by Philip. In this case, the repetition of the description of the eunuch in Acts 8:27, 34, 38, and 39 places an emphasis on his identity as one who would have been formerly unclean amongst the people of God.[70] Whereas the ideological conflict for Simon revolved around power, Luke's portrayal of the eunuch provides a challenge or reversal of what is considered unclean in the community of the Way. The Ethiopian eunuch is indeed a foreigner but more importantly in the narrative, he is located within Judea.[71] The word of the Lord has arrived in Judea-Samaria and in spite of conflicts; it has conquered and resulted in the fulfillment of the pathway established in Acts 1:8. The joy theme works in conjunction with Luke's ideology of the people of God as inclusive of all disciples of Jesus as the circle of inclusion widens.[72]

---

[68] Talbert, *Readings Acts*, 69; Fitzmyer, *Acts of the Apostles*, 401.

[69] Simon's failure to humble himself by seeking self-exaltation is likely an instance of the form of bi-polar reversal established in the Gospel of Luke. York's analysis of this rhetoric of reversal doesn't locate Simon in relationship to the eunuch who is a positive example of reversal (*Last Shall Be First*, 172).

[70] Pao argues convincingly that repeated use of the title 'eunuch' in Acts 8:27, 34, 36, 38, 39 takes the emphasis off of his ethnic identity and onto his status as an outcast (*Acts and the Isaianic New Exodus*, 141). Even if Fitzmyer's conclusion that the eunuch is a Jew or a proselyte, he is still defined primarily in terms of categories that would have made him unclean and an outcast according to Deut 23:2 (*Acts of the Apostles*, 410).

[71] Talbert, *Reading Acts*, 74.

[72] Robbins uses Acts 8:26-40 to create a 'study guide' to facilitate questions about 'ideological texture' as it relates to social identity and race (*Exploring the Texture of Texts*, 115-16).

The Reversal of the Ends of the Earth: Joy in Acts 13:48-52

Thus far, Luke has taken care to mention that joy is now present in the theo-geo-political realms of Jerusalem and Judea-Samaria. As the word of the Lord moves forward from Jerusalem, God's promises are being fulfilled. The third stage of the broad plan as articulated in Acts 1:8 is the 'ends of the earth'. In this third stage, the reversal is focused on the inclusion of the Gentiles in the people of God. The first 'sustained effort' to take the gospel outside of the land of Israel is found in Acts 13-14.[73] As the movement of the word of the Lord spreads to the Gentiles at the ends of the earth, the episode at Pisidian Antioch is recognized as the 'climax' or chiastic centre of Acts 13-14.[74] The pericope that contains the references to the joy theme (Acts 13:48-52) occurs within this larger Pisidian Antioch episode and the exegesis will draw from that larger scope. Here, the identity of the people of God is established as inclusive of the Gentiles. The rhetoric of reversal is present here as Paul and Barnabas 'turn' (Acts 13:46) to the Gentiles after the rejection of the gospel by the Jews.[75] The ends of the earth are now the locus of God's salvation and the reversal is empowered by the presence of joy.

Joy and Inner Texture

The pericope of Acts 13:48-52 provides a summary of Paul's speech. The joy theme appears in Acts 13:48: 'And when the Gentiles heard this, they began rejoicing (χαίρω) and glorifying the "word of the Lord"'. The joy theme also appears in the last statement of the pericope (Acts 13:52): 'And the disciples were filled with joy (χαρά) and with the Holy Spirit'.[76] This echoes the summary statement made of those who were worshipping in the Temple (Lk 24:52), those who received the gospel after Peter's preaching in Jerusalem (Acts 2:46-7), and the description of the eunuch (Acts 8:8, 39).[77] The location of the joy theme at the end of this section is striking due to the repetition and its place as the bookend of the Pisidian Antioch episode.

---

[73] Pao, *Acts and the Isaianic New Exodus*, 98.

[74] Pao, *Acts and the Isaianic New Exodus*, 99. G.H. Twelftree also argues that the 'problem and solution of how Gentiles could be included in the group of followers of Jesus' is specifically taken up in the section of Acts 12:25-16:5 in *People of the Spirit: Exploring Luke's View of the Church* (London: SPCK, 2009), 40.

[75] Witherington views Acts 13:13-52 as deliberative rhetoric that can be divided up according to (1) an *exordium*, (2) a *narratio*, (3) a *propositio*, (4) a *probatio* and 5) a *peroratio*. I am in agreement that this is a Diaspora Jewish audience but it is not clear how Witherington can argue that Paul's speech in Acts 13 reflects such finely tuned Greco-Roman patterns and 'Jewish patterns of argumentation' concurrently (*New Testament Rhetoric*, 62).

[76] Navone recognizes the joy theme in Acts 13:52 (*Themes of St. Luke*, 86).

[77] O'Toole argues that the joy theme creates a relationship between the episode at Pisidian Antioch and Pentecost (*Unity of Luke's Theology*, 242).

The subjects who produce the emotion of joy are also noteworthy. Those following the narrative learn that the spread of the word of the Lord (Acts 13:49) was facing opposition in the form of persecution. Yet it seems that while this opposition was serious enough to be included in the narrative, it was not powerful enough to change the disposition or emotional state of the 'disciples'. The referents of the 'disciples' are surely not limited to Paul and Barnabas.[78] The joyful disciples are the Gentiles who were rejoicing at receiving the word of the Lord in Acts 13:48.

At each turn in the narrative, the word of the Lord arrives and conquers in spite of all types of opposition. The victory of the word of the Lord and the fulfillment of the path established in Acts 1:8 (Jerusalem, Judea-Samaria, the Ends of the Earth) is evident in the emotions of those who receive it. In Acts, each major reversal of the New Exodus is accompanied by joy. A pattern has been established and the turn to the Gentiles in Acts 13 follows it. In Acts 2, the word of the Lord brought joy and established who the heirs of the temple were. In Acts 8, the word of the Lord brought joy and provided evidence of the reconstitution of Israel as outcasts became joyful. Now, in Acts 13, the turn to the Gentiles is accompanied by joy.

Joy and Intertexture

The movement of the inclusion of the Gentiles into the people of God has been foreshadowed by Simeon but is also rooted in Isaiah.[79] Evidence of Luke's interest in developing the Isaianic vision is found in the reference to Isaiah 49:6 in Acts 13:47. This quotation is directly related to the third movement to 'the ends of the earth' as articulated in Acts 1:8. The reference is more of a transformation or application than a direct quotation.[80] Regardless of the source, the use of Isaiah 49:6 provides 'legitimization' to Paul's turn to the Gentiles.[81] What has not been developed is how the joy (rejoicing) of the Gentiles in Acts 13:38 relates to this Isaianic vision of universal mission.

Some commentators have recognized that the joy of the disciples is part of the fulfillment of the Isaianic promise.[82] What has gone relatively unnoticed is that Isaiah 49 promises a restoration of Israel that will be characterized by joy

---

[78] As Fitzmyer suggests in *Acts of the Apostles*, 522.

[79] De Long makes a similar conclusion about the nature of the inclusion of the Gentiles in the Pisidian Antioch episode as it relates to Isaiah, but her comments are cursory (*Surprised by God*, 259).

[80] For a comparison between Acts, the LXX, and the MT see Marshall, 'Acts,' *CNTUOT* 587-8. Fitzmyer prefers to see this quotation as corresponding to the MT (*Acts of the Apostles*, 521).

[81] Marshall, 'Acts', *CNTUOT* 588.

[82] 'So God's intention is realized and his plan of salvation is seen to be implemented in the case, not of Jews in Antioch, but of some Gentiles'. Fitzmyer, *Acts of the Apostles*, 521.

when the people of God will be re-gathered. They will come even from the diaspora Jewish settlement in Egypt (the land of Syene, Isa 49:12). The result of God's restoring action is described thus:

> Rejoice (εὐφραίνω), O heavens, and let the earth be glad (ἀγαλλιάω); let the mountains break forth with joy (εὐφροσύνη), and the hills with righteousness, because God has had mercy on his people and he has comforted the humble of his people.[83] (LXX Isaiah 49:13)

The fact that the Gentiles are rejoicing provides a sense of fulfillment within Luke's appropriation of Isaiah that incorporates the nations into the promises given to Israel. The joy of the Gentiles functions as objective evidence that Isaiah's promise has been fulfilled regardless of the Jewish rejection of the Gospel. This relationship between the joy theme and the Isaianic vision parallels the use of the joy theme in Luke 2:32.[84] There is some discrepancy between the words for joy in Acts and Isaiah. However, two things must be considered. First, Luke's use of the joy theme appropriates a wide lexical range. Even within LXX Isaiah 49:13, the use of various words for joy is poetic and not technical. Second, the weight of the argument rests on conceptual parallels rather than on word choice. The use of joy here is primarily objective in nature: it is evidence that God has fulfilled part of his promise. That the Gentiles are rejoicing is fulfillment of the intertextual framework that Luke develops through his short quotation of Isaiah 49:6.

Joy and Sacred Texture

The goal of separating the sacred texture as an individual thread of interpretation is to ensure that the interpretation of the text is sufficiently 'thick'.[85] The Holy Spirit in Acts does not appear as a sanctifier per se, rather he guides and empowers and is also associated with the emotion of joy.[86] O'Toole suggests that Acts 13:52 is a hendiadys that could be understood as 'they were filled with the joy of the Holy Spirit'.[87] The Holy Spirit gave a 'sense of joy' but it is not clear how this occurs.[88] Here, the *object* of emotion is important.[89] In Acts 13:48, the joy of the disciples is connected with the attending circumstance of glorifying 'the word of the Lord' (τὸν λόγον τοῦ

---

[83] *NETS*, Book of Esaias, 862.

[84] Marshall, 'Acts', *CNTUOT* 588.

[85] Robbins, *Exploring the Texture of Texts*, 130.

[86] Marshall, *New Testament Theology*, 479.

[87] O'Toole, *Unity of Luke's Theology*, 243. Hendiadys is broadly defined as the substitution of one part of speech for another. Often two words connected by a conjunction are used to express a single idea.

[88] Marshall, *New Testament Theology*, 177.

[89] Elliott, *Faithful Feelings*, 91.

κυρίου). The 'word of the Lord' appears in Acts 13:49 and is described as 'spreading throughout the whole region'. The joy theme and the 'word of the Lord' are two prominent features of the summary of Acts 13:48-52.

The joy theme and the rhetoric of reversal in Acts 13:48-52 is directly related to the sacred in two distinct ways. First, the joy of the Gentiles in Acts 13:48 is a direct response to the command of the Lord. Paul and Barnabas explain that the reversal or turn to the Gentiles is what the 'Lord has commanded' (Acts 13:47). Second, the rejoicing is connected to glorifying the Lord (Acts 13:48): 'And when the Gentiles heard this, they began rejoicing and glorifying the word of the Lord, and as many as were appointed to eternal life believed.' This passage is unique and significant because the object of glorification is the 'word of the Lord'. This glorifies 'word' or λόγος takes on many of the characteristics highlighted by David Pao: (1) the λόγος of God is part of the Isaianic New Exodus, (2) it takes on the characteristics of a person or character, (3) it is the powerful force that conquers, and (4) the word's journey is linear.[90]

Another intriguing aspect of Pao's thesis is that 'the word of God should not be examined apart from the other theological emphases of Acts'.[91] This is significant in light of the intentional word-play used with respect to the title κύριος. This 'word of the Lord' is not only the fulfillment of the Isaianic New Exodus, it is directly related to Jesus' state as the resurrected Lord who has demonstrated that he is and always has been YHWH.[92] In some sense, the object of their joy is the word of Jesus. The nature of the 'word of the Lord' is such that when Gentiles are rejoicing and glorifying it, it serves to further Luke's purpose in establishing the identity of the Gentiles.

Joy and Ideological Texture

The text containing the joy theme (Acts 13:48-52) appears after a Pauline speech that is clearly meant to be persuasive toward Diaspora Jews in a synagogue context.[93] The possession of joy in the midst of persecution provides the reader with a sense of victory in the midst of conflict. The spread of God's word cannot be stopped.[94] The joy theme is used in two summary statements about two characters that reflect major points along the 'Way' out of Jerusalem. The joy theme empowers the turn to the Gentiles. The use of emotion is subversive and rhetorical. Their joy is one objective indicator that YHWH has received them as part of the people of God. The word that conquers is both the word of YHWH and the word of Jesus. Only those who are truly God's people

---

[90] Pao, *Acts and the Isaianic New Exodus*, 147-79.

[91] Pao, *Acts and the Isaianic New Exodus*, 149.

[92] Rowe, *Early Narrative Christology*, 117.

[93] Witherington, *New Testament Rhetoric*, 62.

[94] Kurz, *Reading Luke-Acts*, 92.

can claim this, and they are Gentiles to boot. Subjectively, the narrative portrays an emotional group of disciples that is inviting to the reader. It provides an emotional power that beckons the reader to also become a disciple of Jesus.

Conclusion

This chapter has sought to relate the joy theme in Acts to the wider Lukan narrative by demonstrating that it provides an emotional force to Luke's rhetorical goals. Specifically, the book of Acts provides some framework for the reader in Acts 1:8. Whereas the Gospel of Luke moved toward Jerusalem, the movement of Acts is outward from Jerusalem, to Judea-Samaria, and to the ends of the Earth. Each of these three items was defined as a theo-geo-political realm. The journey of the word of the Lord to each of these three realms is definitely marked by the joy theme. Each step along this path marks a reversal of conditions in Luke's inaugurated view of the kingdom. First, Jerusalem and the temple are reinvigorated as Israel is re-established through the Twelve. Second, the outcasts are gathered together in the outlying areas of Judea-Samaria. Third, when the Jews reject the good news about Jesus, the Gentiles become the recipients. Whereas Tannehill concluded that the 'Lukan narrative is reticent about expressing characters' emotions', we must conclude that Luke was careful to include the joy theme at each major stage in the book of Acts.[95]

Here we have sought to understand Luke's 'conspicuous' joy theme and his rhetorical intentions. If Talbert's conclusion that there is no 'clear-cut' pattern to the operations of the Holy Spirit in Luke-Acts is correct then it is all the more striking that Luke ensures that the emotion of joy is present at each narrative turn as it progresses along the Way out of Jerusalem to the ends of the earth.[96] In one sense, C.K. Barrett was correct in pointing out that the joy of the Christians was 'of a harmless kind'.[97] But in another sense, the emotion of joy is part of Luke's ideological and rhetorical matrix that challenged the very Jewish authorities who put Jesus to death. The claim that one was rejoicing in YHWH was staking a claim about one's identity and who was the recipient of the fulfillment of YHWH's promises. The rejoicing Christians in the temple are portrayed as victorious. This portrayal would have persuaded some and perhaps caused others to respond negatively. If Luke has any rhetorical aspirations, they are certainly not void of emotion. The joy theme provides objective indicators of the fulfillment of God's promises as reversals characterize those who receive the word of God. It also provides an explanation of how God is at work in those who are followers of the Way of Jesus. Subjectively, the emotion of joy works

---

[95] Tannehill, *Shape of Luke's Story*, 275.

[96] Talbert, *Reading Acts*, 31.

[97] Barrett, *Acts 1-14*, 171.

rhetorically upon the reader and draws him or her into a narrative that challenges their beliefs through emotional engagement.[98]

---

[98] Kuhn explains, 'emotions are a measure of what we really believe, what really moves us' (*Heart of Biblical Narrative*, 26).

Chapter 8

The Broader Joy Theme in Acts

Thus far, it has been successfully demonstrated that the joy theme is an integral part of the narrative sub-structure of the book of Acts. Joy occurs at the reversal of each major juncture outlined in Acts 1:8 (Jerusalem, Judea-Samaria, and the ends of the Earth).[1] In this chapter we will consider other instances of the joy theme in Acts.

Table: Joy in Acts vs. the Gospels [2]

	Mt	Mk	Lk	Jn	Acts
ἀγαλλιάω	1	0	2	2	2
ἀγαλλίασις	0	0	2	0	1
εὐφραίνω	0	0	6	0	2
σκιρτάω	0	0	3	0	0
χαίρω	6	2	12	9	5
συγχαίρω	0	0	3	0	0
χαρά	6	1	8	9	4
αἰνέω	0	0	4	0	3

---

[1] Mallen follows a well-established thesis that Acts 1:8 summarizes 'the plot outline for Acts and is therefore programmatic in nature' (*Reading and Transformation of Isaiah*, 79).

[2] This is a modified version of the table in the article by Painter, 'Joy', *Dictionary of Jesus and the Gospels*, 394. Painter's table does not include Acts.

Introduction

As noted in the introductory and previous chapter, the joy theme in Acts is strong enough to warrant particular attention.[3] This is supported by the table above. The vocabulary that is central to the joy theme in Luke is also prominent in Acts.[4] This is especially evident when compared to Mark and Matthew.

If we look at word-count alone, the joy theme in Acts is weaker than in Luke. However, this must not be over-exaggerated. When we consider the role and function of joy, we see that it plays a strong role in the narrative sub-structure and in persuasive narratives.[5] The joy theme is also present in significant vignettes such as the delivery of Jerusalem Council's conclusion in Acts 15.

In this chapter, we will attempt to encapsulate the joy theme in Acts by examining the patterns and instances of joy as they are woven through the four-fold textures as laid out in our methodology. This chapter will attempt to summarize the broader joy theme in Acts and provide test cases for the thesis that *the book of Acts uses joy to empower the rhetoric of reversal.*

Joy and Inner Texture in Acts

The inner texture of Acts reflects the fact that the joy theme occurs at critical narrative junctures and in introductory textual units that provide narrative framework. The theme is spread throughout the Lukan corpus with the balance tipped toward the Gospel of Luke. The vocabulary of joy in Acts generally reflects the non-technical usage of the joy vocabulary that appears in Luke's Gospel. There is considerable overlap between words that have an emotional component that can only be characterized as joy. For example, Kindalee P. De Long agrees that there is a distinction between praising God and having joy in God, but this distinction is not very strong.[6]

Redaction and comparison studies between Luke and the other gospels have repeatedly demonstrated that the joy theme reflects Luke's unique style without

---

[3] B. Barton provides a chart of the joy theme in Acts in his popular-level commentary entitled *Acts: Life Application Bible Commentary* (Wheaton: Tyndale House, 1999), 40. Marshall remarks: 'in Acts the Christian life is characterized by expressions of joy and praise made in prayer to God' in *Luke: Historian and Theologian*, 204. Strauss, *Davidic Messiah in Luke-Acts*, 78.

[4] Navone aligns with many other Lukan scholars in understanding the joy theme to cover a wide semantic range (*Themes of St. Luke*, 71-73).

[5] Again, we cite Spencer as a recent foil of this thesis who states that 'pathos is the least relevant for Luke-Acts' (*Rhetorical Texture and Narrative Trajectories,* 52).

[6] De Long, *Surprised by God*, 8.

examining how this interest in joy is related to other matters such as rhetoric.[7] Of particular importance is the strong element of joy in the 'major summary' textual unit of Acts 2:42-47 (and 2:26).[8] The repetition of the joy theme at this early point in the narrative provides the same framing that we see in the Gospel of Luke: the introductory material creates expectations for the whole. In addition, the obvious influence of Luke as a writer to insert the joy theme into a summary section demonstrates his interest in the joy theme.

The leper cured by Peter and John in Acts 3 is a good example of how the emotion of joy empowers the rhetoric of reversal. Here, the leper is described as 'walking and leaping and praising God' (Acts 3:8) and then 'walking and praising God' (Acts 3:9) after he is healed. It is clear that Luke wants to draw attention to his emotional response to the miracle through word repetition that is related to joy (αἰνέω).

If we exclude the three narrative turning points examined in this study (e.g. Acts, 2, 8, 13), then we still have the joy theme occurring in eight other instances: Acts 3:8-9; 5:41; 11:23; 12:14; 14:17; 15:3; 15:31; 16:34. This brings the total number of textual units that contain the joy theme to eleven. If we include the μακάριος language of 'blessing' due to its emotional component, then the total increases to thirteen (Acts 20:35; 26:2).[9] Based on word-count alone, joy vocabulary occurs seventeen times in Acts but only three times in Mark. Of course, this comparison is one of apples and oranges but we must also remember the narratival, theological, and authorial unity of Luke-Acts. This unity provides some warrant for comparing the book of Acts to works such as Mark and Matthew. Even if one disagrees about the unity of Luke-Acts, the joy theme stands firm in Acts based on narrative structure relationships as well as word-count.[10]

The joy theme occurs not only at the three critical narrative posts as identified by Acts 1:8, it also occurs at the equally important textual unit based on the Jerusalem Council in Acts 15. The occurrence of the joy theme immediately before and after the Jerusalem Council lends credence to the thesis that joy does indeed play an important role in Acts.

---

[7] For notes on Luke's addition of the joy theme in Acts see Barrett, *Acts 1-14*, 185, 552. For a discussion about Luke's uses of rhetoric and word choice see Witherington, *What's in the Word*, 128.

[8] Major summaries include Acts 2:42-47; 4:32-35; 5:12-16. Fitzmyer, *Acts of the Apostles*, 97. For an in-depth account of Lukan summaries or 'narrative asides' see S.M. Sheeley, *Narrative Asides in Luke-Acts* (JSNTSup 72; Sheffield: JSOT Press, 1992), passim.

[9] Morrice, *Joy in the New Testament*, 98. For a discussion on *makarios* as an emotion see Elliott, *Faithful Feelings*, 165.

[10] For a discussion of repetition and amplification see Witherington, *New Testament Rhetoric*, 52.

Because our investigation considers the narrative dimensions of the whole of Acts, it is pertinent to ask what type of characters express joy.[11] The instance of joy in Acts 2:25-28 is the only instance of joy that is a part of direct citation of the Septuagint rather than integrated into the narrative flow. This quotation from Psalm 16:8-11 puts joy on the lips of Jesus as Luke identifies it as a prophecy from David that foresaw Christ (Acts 2:31). In Acts 2:46-47, the fellowship of the believers is filled with gladness and praise to God. In Acts 3:8-9 the lame beggar who is healed is filled with joy and praises God. In Acts 5:41, Peter and the rest of the apostles rejoice in being counted worthy to suffer for the gospel's sake. The joy in the city of Samaria in Acts 8:8 is the most broad representation of joy but it is clearly a direct response to the miracles and preaching of the word (Acts 8:4).[12] The eunuch who went on his way rejoicing (Acts 8:39) does so after being baptized by Philip.

In Acts 11:23, Barnabas expresses joy (χαίρω) when he arrives at the church of Antioch from Jerusalem to see the great number of conversions. Barnabas is described as identifying with and ministering to the church of Antioch through exhortation (Acts 11:24). Barnabas' own joy is confirmed as a positive expression in the description of him as 'a good man, full of the Holy Spirit and of faith' (Acts 11:24). Rhoda the servant girl who finds Peter at the gate is described as joyful (Acts 12:14). The Gentiles who receive the word of the Lord are joyful (Acts 13:48, 52). Paul and Barnabas brought great joy to 'all the brothers' as they passed through Phoenicia and Samaria in Acts 15:3. The church 'rejoiced' when they read the letter from the Jerusalem Council in Acts 15:31. Lastly, the Philippian jailer and his whole household rejoiced when he believed in the Lord Jesus in Acts 16:34.

In most instances in the book of Acts, joy is expressed by those who follow the Way. The only exception to this is the appeal to the 'common grace' of joy (εὐφροσύνη) that Paul refers to in his speech in Lystra (Acts 14:17). Despite the fact that Jesus warned of receiving his word with joy and then falling away in the Parable of the Soils (Luke 8:4-15), we see no instance of this. But there is good reason not to equate this ubiquity with an emotional triumphalism. The primary reason for this is that it ignores the role of the 'word of the Lord' as a central character. If the characters listed above have any power at all, it is because Luke already made clear that they have received 'power' from the Holy Spirit to be 'witnesses' (Acts 1:8).[13] Because God is conquering through the preaching of his word, there is no sense that the characters in Acts are self-reliant. Rather, it reinforces David Pao's thesis that the Isaianic New Exodus

---

[11] Padilla explains: 'in order to correctly grasp the meaning of the biblical text we must pay close attention to the function of its characters' (*Speeches of Outsiders in Acts*, 109).

[12] Barrett also suggests that the joy in Samaria is a response to the healings as well as subsequent conversions (*Acts 1-14*, 404).

[13] Pao notes that this promise of the Spirit from on high recalls the phraseology from Isa 32:15, *Acts and the Isaianic New Exodus*, 92.

creates a prominent hermeneutical sub-structure for the book of Acts. This point is nuanced: the Isaianic New Exodus is prominent and foregrounded without being the exclusive controlling motif.[14]

What we may note about the joy theme in Acts is that it also occurs throughout the whole book. This is a significant fact because it reinforces the thesis that the joy theme truly is a theme or a motif and not simply an isolated narrative feature. Many studies have observed the joy theme in Luke and some have even noted its presence in Acts. In addition, it is widely recognized that both Luke and Acts heavily reference Isaiah in the introductory textual units that frame the discourse. Peter Mallen observes that Lukan studies often fail to consider 'how Luke might use Isaiah from a rhetorical perspective in order to gain a desired response from his audience'.[15] As we turn to the intertextual dimension we will seek to answer the question that Mallen comes so close to asking: *did Luke use Isaiah from a rhetorical perspective in order to elicit a joyful faith from his audience?*

Joy and Intertexture in Acts

Recent studies have supported the thesis that the Jewish or Hebrew Scriptures provide support for the narrative and theology of Acts. Kenneth Litwak argues that 'the Scriptures of Israel pervade Luke-Acts from its beginning until its end, and not just when being quoted'.[16] Likewise, David Moessner states, 'I am still convinced that the Jewish Scriptures were emblematic for Luke's way of rewriting the events of Jesus'.[17] To be more specific requires great nuance and careful attention. It is easy to overstate one's case about the importance of any given intertextual relationship. For example, Peter Mallen argues that 'the New Exodus story supports key themes in Luke's narrative rather than being the controlling element'.[18] While the Isaianic New Exodus is not totalizing it does bear the weight of the narrative substructure according to Acts 1:8.

For our purposes, it is important to observe that joy provides a source of *objective* evidence that God has brought about his promises. Joy also provides a narrative experience that persuades the reader to identify *subjectively* with the people of God through personal engagement and experiential belief.[19] We may now develop the following question: if there is a joy theme in Acts, how does Isaiah support this key theme? In the previous chapter, we have defended the position that Isaiah provides a foregrounded source of joy in the three

---

[14] Mallen, *Reading and Transformation of Isaiah*, 15.

[15] Mallen, *Reading and Transformation of Isaiah*, 19.

[16] Litwak, *Echoes of Scriptures in Luke-Acts*, 1.

[17] Moessner, *Lord of the Banquet*, xvii.

[18] Mallen, *Reading and Transformation of Isaiah*, 19.

[19] On one level, the Book of Acts is to be read as 'a play in which we are invited to become actors ourselves'. Wright, *Acts for Everyone: Part One*, 3.

movements that frame the entire book of Acts. In this chapter, I will attempt to utilize broad perspectives and detailed exegetical evidence to argue that *Isaiah stands in the foreground as the mostly likely source for the joy theme in Acts.*

The first step in understanding intertextuality in Acts is to allow the text itself to provide introductory texts that frame the narrative or discourse by establishing relationships. In the last chapter, we clearly established how the introduction functions. The introduction (Acts 1:8) provides a broad narrative structure: the word of the Lord will be carried by witnesses from Jerusalem to Judea-Samaria to the Ends of the Earth. This path will turn the world upside-down with dramatic reversals.

To be clear, we are not arguing in this chapter that Isaiah is the only source of intertextuality in Acts. This is clear on the face of the text as references and quotes are derived from Joel and the Psalms in Acts 1-2. With respect to the joy theme in Acts, we are simply trying to ascertain how this theme is related to the Septuagint (or the Scriptures of Israel). Even when trying to understand the relationship between the joy theme and Isaiah, it is not always possible to isolate one particular text in favor of another. The writer of Acts (Luke) draws from various Isaianic passages at once. This is often called 'conflation'.[20] In the programmatic text of Acts 1:8, Luke likely draws from Isaiah 32:15 (until the Spirit is poured out from on high) and Isaiah 49:6 (I will make you as a light for the nations).[21] In the case of Acts 1:8, it is sufficient to state that Isaiah stands in the foreground for his source of intertextuality.

Some imprecision is 'unavoidable' when dealing with the lines between different intertextual relationships.[22] Yet we find that Luke begins his second volume with a clear reference to his own first book (the Gospel of Luke) in Acts 1:1. This reference to the Gospel of Luke sets up some measure of expectation because of the way that Isaiah 40:3-5 was cited in Luke 3:4-6 and Isaiah 61:1-2 was cited in Luke 4:18-19. Having found Isaiah on the lips of Jesus in Luke, the reader expects to find continuity in Acts, which is the narrative of the ever-present resurrected Jesus in the church.

We find that the key framing text (Acts 1:8) is based on echoes from Isaiah. The categories of the New Exodus that Acts 1:8 inaugurates include: (1) the dawn of salvation in Jerusalem, (2) reconstitution and reunification of Israel, and (3) inclusion of the Gentiles in the people of God.[23] In both Luke and Acts we find that the introductory texts that frame the narrative rely on Isaiah to provide the reader with relationships that provide anticipation and a hermeneutical lens for the whole.

We cannot separate intertextuality from the narrative. Thematic relationships create literary relationships that endure through the narrative. When the joy

---

[20] Hays, 'The Liberation of Israel in Luke-Acts', 107.

[21] Litwak, *Echoes of Scriptures in Luke-Acts*, 153.

[22] Litwak, *Echoes of Scripture in Luke-Acts*, 52.

[23] Pao, *Acts and the Isaianic New Exodus*, 95.

theme occurs, it is likely that it is part of a thread that connects to patterns and sources established in the introductory material. Intertextual studies are often atomistic and do not interact with narrative and literary concerns. On the other hand, this must be used with caution lest studies become bogged down in parallelomania.

At the beginning of this chapter, we established that the joy theme occurs in the Gospel of Luke and in Acts. In Acts, the joy theme occurs at every key narrative point laid out by the programmatic text of Acts 1:8. There is also enough repetition of joy vocabulary throughout the narrative to establish it as a theme in its own right. Once we established that the individual texts that constitute the joy theme cannot be isolated from each other, we may suggest how intertextual relationships exist based on the framing texts and on the context.

Establishing proximity means that some sources or relationships are stronger than others. Those that are stronger are foregrounded as opposed to weaker relationships that are in the background. Luke's use of the Hebrew Scriptures often conjoins various texts into a new transformed text.

Let us consider the matter of proximity with respect to the presence of the joy theme in the reversal of the leper in Acts 3:8-9. In this text, the joy theme intersects with the praise of God and physical expressions of joy in the form of leaping. Witherington finds that the scenario of the leper in Acts 3 testifies to the inaugurated eschatology of Isaiah's vision wherein the lame are leaping like deer (cf. LXX Isaiah 35:6).[24] Isaiah 35 contains images of lame being healed as well as images of God's people rejoicing. Attention is drawn to the emotion at the very point of reversal from weak to strong or unclean to clean. This happens on the basis of the powerful name of Jesus that Peter proclaims. Witherington goes on to say this about the rhetorical use of joy in this instance:

> Rhetoricians stress that for a communication to be persuasive it must not only appeal to the intellect but tug at the heartstrings as well, including an appeal to the deeper and more powerful emotions, and Luke knows how to accomplish this rhetorical aim.[25]

In the quote above, Witherington independently concludes that the joy theme is significant for Luke's persuasive task. The use of joy in Acts 3:9 parallels much of the findings of the joy theme in the Gospel of Luke.

The joy theme in passages such as Acts 11:23; 12:14; 14:17; 15:3, 31 and 16:34 cannot be related to any intertextual source as *echoes* if they are isolated and understood individually. However, if one concludes that they are all connected from a literary perspective, then one must ask these natural questions: why and where? Luke is interested in using emotion (*pathos*) in

---

[24] Witherington, *Acts of the Apostles*, 176; Fitzmyer, *Acts of the Apostles*, 279.
[25] Witherington, *Acts of the Apostles*, 176.

order to provide a persuasive account that will shape the reader and lead him or her into belief that God has visited his people in Jesus. Litwak has demonstrated the importance of programmatic texts or framing texts that establish expectations for the whole narrative. Because the text of Acts has created key relationships with Isaiah in Acts 1:8, the book of Isaiah becomes the first source that provides understanding. Kenneth Litwak explains: 'the Scriptures of Israel pervade Luke-Acts from its beginning until its end'.[26] This links the literary theme of joy with the intertextuality established by Luke himself.

Although one does not have to choose between promise-fulfillment and coherence, the echo of Isaiah here in Acts 3:8-9 is more about coherence and hermeneutics. The emphasis on the emotion of joy provides a lens through which the reader can participate. In doing so, the reader becomes the implied reader of faith who is growing in knowledge of the ministry of the risen Jesus according to Acts 1:1-3. This confirms and expands the thesis that 'Luke reads Isaiah as providing models for perception'.[27] Our study provides a more detailed analysis so that we may conclude that: Luke reads Isaiah as providing models for emotional response to YHWH's visitation in Jesus. Specifically, Isaiah provides Luke with a model of joyful response which in turn helps the reader by contributing to a robust hermeneutical lens of the actions of the Apostles and early disciples of the risen Jesus. The emotion of joy is intimately connected with Septuagintal texts at the beginning of Acts. As the joy theme continues, these echoes grow faint but the connection is maintained through consistent and constant repetition. The occurrence of joy in the historical record vindicates the followers of the Way because the scriptures are being fulfilled. The presence of joy works upon the reader in a subjective way and works in tandem with other aspects of the text to provide an integrative lens of understanding.

The presence of the clear citation of Psalm 16:8-11 in Peter's sermon (Acts 2:25-28) requires that we qualify this thesis as stated above. This citation occurs in the introductory texts that frame the narrative and as such it creates expectations for what follows. In addition, the citation of the Septuagintal text includes references to the Davidic shepherd-king experiencing joy as he saw the Lord. This emotional experience of the 'heart' and 'tongue' rejoicing provides a promise-fulfillment paradigm. Jesus is the one who fulfilled the words of David by having a glad (εὐφραίνω) heart and joyful (ἀγαλλιάω) speech. This picture of the joyful servant Jesus from Psalm 16 offers a reversal of the negative Isaianic model of the blind and deaf servant (Isaiah 6:9-10).[28] This use of Psalm 16 does not undermine the broader thesis about Isaiah because we have all along contended that Luke often writes with multiple

---

[26] Litwak, *Echoes of Scripture in Luke-Acts*, 1.

[27] Mallen, *Reading and Transformation of Isaiah*, 206.

[28] Mallen, *Reading and Transformation of Isaiah*, 206.

scriptural influences in view. What is clear is that the joy theme is related to both promise-fulfillment and coherence in Acts.

In sum, we conclude that the joy theme can be understood as an entire literary theme that consists of echoes and citations that are all related to the Hebrew Scriptures of which Isaiah stands in the foreground. Objectively, the presence of joy provides an insight into the power of the preaching of the word of the Lord. Subjectively, only a little imagination is required to enter into the joy that this lame man must have experienced as he received full and immediate healing. These two aspects provide a richer explanation of how 'intertextual narration' is used as a 'countercultural practice' that shapes identity and belief.[29] With respect to proximity, the presence of the joy theme in conjunction with images of lame being healed provides evidence for seeing Isaiah 35 not far behind the text of Acts 3.

Joy and Sacred Texture in Acts

Past studies of the Lukan joy theme have observed that it is often associated in some manner with God. It is easily demonstrated by lists of references that joy is associated with the Holy Spirit.[30] Previous studies have summarized the way in which joy is associated with the divine in Acts by listing the connections with the Holy Spirit. Here, we want to move beyond a surface level association by probing why emotion is so important. This will help us later as we move forward to the ideological dimensions of the text. Once again, this brief overview of Acts will make sweeping statements and provide specific examples. When studying emotion, it is the *object* of emotion that is important.[31] The cognitive response of joy to the mighty deeds of the God of Israel who has visited his people in Jesus provides persuasive power to the narrative. The emotion of joy is an important component in the texts that portray the God of Israel as present in the people of the Way. Here we will provide three examples of this phenomenon from Acts 3:6; 15:3; and 16:34.

In our first example from Acts 3:6, the 'name' of Jesus Christ of Nazareth is the power that mediates healing to the leper at the gate of the temple. If the Isaianic reference (LXX Isaiah 35:6) is truly behind this man's healing, this would create an even stronger connection between the risen Jesus and YHWH. Whereas the name of Jesus heals the man, the man clearly praises God (θεός; Acts 3:8, 9). In Acts 2:36, the shift between the language of Jesus and the language of God 'does not alter Jesus' identity itself; indeed it confirms this identity'.[32] This type of language is part of 'God's *reversal* of the human

---

[29] Hays, 'The Liberation of Israel in Luke-Acts', 108.

[30] Johnson, *Religious Experience in Earliest Christianity*, 9n31; Morrice, *Joy in the New Testament*, 96-99.

[31] Elliott, *Faithful Feelings*, 91.

[32] Rowe, *Early Narrative Christology*, 194.

rejection of Jesus'.[33] The language of joy is provocative because it is the response of a man who finds healing in God and in Jesus. The reader is naturally faced with the question: who healed this man? This rhetorical ambiguity reflects Luke's interest in the narrative of identity of Jesus who is the κύριος.

In our second example from Acts 15:3, Paul and Barnabas are responding to the conflict with some men from Judea who were teaching that 'unless you are circumcised according to the custom of Moses, you cannot be saved' (Acts 15:1). This challenge brings together ecclesiological and soteriological interests. This teaching challenged Paul and Barnabas' message that the status of the Gentiles has been reversed: they are no longer unclean if they believe in Jesus. Paul and Barnabas, having been sent by the Antioch church, then experience the 'conversion of the Gentiles' as they passed through Phoenicia and Samaria. This is significant because Gentiles are identified as the people of God (ecclesiology) and receive salvation apart from the so-called boundary marker of circumcision (soteriology).[34] Paul and Barnabas report these conversions with the following result (Acts 15:3): 'and brought great joy (χαρά) to all the brothers'. The 'great joy' is at the center of persuasion. For our purposes, it is significant that in the next sentence this is described as the work of 'all that God had done with them' (Acts 15:4). God is the one who saved the Gentiles and God is the one who brought them into the people of God. God is on the side of Paul and Barnabas and this may be demonstrated (in part) by the converts in Phoenicia and Samaria.[35] The very 'turning-point' of Acts demonstrates that the proper response to the work of the God of Israel in including the Gentiles is great joy.[36]

In our third example from Acts 16:34, another explicit parallelism lies at the center of the joyful response of believing in Jesus and believing in God. When the Philippian jailer hears the 'word of the Lord' (Acts 16:32), the content of which is 'believe in the Lord Jesus, and you will be saved' (Acts 16:31), he and his household are saved and baptized. The summary statement of this episode parallels believing in Jesus with believing in God: 'And he rejoiced with his entire household that he had believed in God' (Acts 16:34). Again, the referent of belief is nebulous and reflects Luke's intentional provocative depiction of Jesus as the one who embodies the God of Israel. Following Rowe, this is part

---

[33] Rowe, *Early Narrative Christology*, 195. Emphasis mine.

[34] Witherington suggests that the joyful response divides soteriology from ecclesiology because it is only a response to the conversion of the Gentiles. But contra Witherington, the conversion of the Gentiles is only possible if the gospel is truly a Law-free or circumcision-free offer of salvation (*Acts of the Apostles*, 452).

[35] The inclusion of Samaria is arguably part of the restoration of Israel as those who were once on the boundaries are now fully included and allowed full participation. This also develops the pathway of the word of the Lord according to the pattern in Acts 1:8.

[36] For a discussion on the 'watershed' nature of the Jerusalem Council see D.G. Peterson, *The Acts of the Apostles* (Grand Rapids: Eerdmans, 2009), 417.

of the reversal or vindication of the resurrected Jesus who is now present in the people of God. The joy also reflects the reversal of the jailer who is both a Gentile and a direct member of Caesar's benefaction pyramid.

The joy theme is an important element in the provocative proto-trinitarianism that pervades the book of Acts. The book of Acts follows the Gospel of Luke in that it intentionally blurs distinctions between divine persons.[37] In the first example, the relationship between Jesus and God is difficult to explain without accepting that the risen Jesus is Yahweh. In the second example from Acts 15:3, joy is used to persuade the reader that the Gentiles who believe in Jesus are truly saved and are truly members in the people of God. Jesus is the one who saves and Jesus is the one who establishes identity in the people of God. The use of joy in the critical narrative of the Jerusalem Council sets up the reader to accept the inclusion of the Gentiles into the people of God. This inclusion of the Gentiles is also an important element in the Isaianic New Exodus. We may now modify Rowe's conclusion: *the emotion of joy is an important element in persuading the reader that Jesus is the presence of the God of Israel acting.*[38]

Joy and Ideological Texture in Acts

The ideological texture focuses on persuasion amidst conflict. This texture is progressively complex and takes into account innertexture, intertexture, and sacred texture. It is also where the text meets the implied reader of the first century. Luke was most likely a God-fearer who was familiar with the patterns of Jewish argumentation present in synagogues.[39] Furthermore, the persuasive or rhetorical content of Acts must not be limited to the speeches. While the speeches in Acts record a range of speeches, some of which have strong Greco-Roman elements, we must also consider the narrative as a whole that has been framed in terms of Jewish elements. In this section we will argue that *the stance or positioning of the text of Acts utilizes the emotion of joy in narratives that stand against prevailing cultural norms and values in the first-century Mediterranean society.*

As noted earlier in our study, we do not have to identify one particular people group to locate Luke-Acts in the first-century Mediterranean. To do so, would in fact, violate the broad intentions of the text itself. Patrick Spencer has provided a rigorous account of the 'elusive' nature of the 'authorial audience'

---

[37] Hays notes that this blurring 'would not be so striking if it were not entirely distinctive in Luke in contrast to the other Gospels' ('The Liberation of Israel in Luke-Acts', 111). Following Hays, we can also add that the book of Acts is distinctive in the same way.

[38] Rowe's thesis in *Early Narrative Christology* (p. 201) is a development of Hans Frei's work.

[39] Witherington, *What's in the Word*, 53.

of Luke-Acts.[40] Others have provided some broad contours that have guided much of our discussion thus far. There are three relationships that provide the context for reversal in Acts.[41] First, there are patron-client relationships that create group dynamics within one's social network. Second, there are relationships and public cultural expectations that are based on honour and shame. Third, there are boundary markers (such as table fellowship and circumcision) that define purity and pollution.

The cross in Luke's Gospel clarifies the world stage and the nature of the conflict. The cross is turning the whole world upside-down (Acts 17:6).[42] The book of Acts is seeking to primarily shape the identity of the implied reader in the first century. There is likely an apologetic element to Acts that absolves the followers of the Way from charges of political insurrection. However, Acts places the emphasis on identity formation and salvation (ecclesiology and soteriology). In the last chapter, we noted that Acts seeks to persuade the reader of the ongoing work of Jesus post-resurrection, the church's continuity with Israel, and the legitimacy of the inclusion of the Gentiles. The church has a mission to take the word of the Lord to the world even as they struggle to be faithful members of the Way.

The resurrection of Jesus provides the context for a worshipping and joyful community who are identifying themselves as the true worshippers of YHWH. The textual unit in Acts 2:46-47 portrays a joyful community and provides essential framework for the whole discourse of Acts. By joyfully eating together, the church is staking a claim about who the community is (and who is not in the community). It has been suggested that 'the breaking of bread' is exclusive to the Lord's Supper which is a transformation of the Passover.[43] It is unlikely that this would have been repeated with such repetition. It is likely that this reference to eating is broad and encompasses close family-like fellowship as well as participation in specific cultic worship acts toward Jesus.

What is important is that those outside of the worshippers of Jesus are outside of the community that truly worships YHWH. The presence and gifts of the Holy Spirit (including joy) are part of the evidence that this is the 'reconstituted Israel'.[44] Those who reject Jesus are perhaps like those who did

---

[40] Spencer, *Rhetorical Texture and Narrative Trajectories*, 30.

[41] I rely heavily on F.S. Spencer, *Journeying through Acts: A Literary-Cultural Reading* (Peabody: Hendrickson, 2004), 23; J.H. Neyrey (ed.), *The Social World of Luke-Acts: Models for Interpretation* (Peabody: Hendrickson, 2004), passim.

[42] Jervell notes: 'In his attempt to express in a summary form what Scripture says, Luke does not mean to extract an ideology from the Scriptures while ignoring other statements of the text' (*Theology of Acts*, 62). This comment by Jervell is judicious and reflects the fact that Luke was simply operating in a world in which Jesus was both killed and resurrected. The conflict that culminated in the cross was indicative of what was going on in the whole world.

[43] Marshall, *Luke: Historian and Theologian*, 205.

[44] Talbert, *Reading Acts*, 32.

not put any blood on their doorpost in the Exodus from Egypt! This follows the pattern of double or bi-polar reversal in which those who are outsiders become insiders and those who are insiders become outsiders.[45] This is quite a reversal for what was originally a small group of fishermen. In some sense, this household-based community was competing with temple.[46] The conflict with the Jews (and Gentiles and Satan) is real but Jerusalem remains the center from which blessings are being sent out at this point in the Lukan narrative. Perhaps it is best to identify Jerusalem as a tension-filled place of both blessings and cursing.

Joy empowers the rhetoric of reversal in the midst of different scenarios of conflict. In Acts 2, with the exception of the citation of Psalms 16:8-11, the first occurrence of joy is in the Lukan summary section from Acts 2:42-47. This summary section that describes the community of the Way is set in the context of the 'temple' (v.46) and their 'homes' (v.46). The reference to the temple cannot be separated from Jerusalem where Jesus was 'crucified and killed by the hands of lawless men' (v.23). Another sociologically and theologically significant reversal occurs when Peter heals the lame beggar (Acts 3:1-10). The Way is not only accepting of those who were outcasts and lowly, it is a source of healing in the name of Jesus. Other joyful scenes of conflict reversal include the Sanhedrin,[47] the city of Samaria,[48] the inclusion of a eunuch,[49] persecution in Jerusalem,[50] the release of Peter from prison,[51] jealousy from Jews in Jerusalem,[52] the pagan crowd at Lystra,[53] the tensions surrounding the Jerusalem Council,[54] and the conversion of the jailer of Paul and Silas.[55] Wherever the joy theme occurs, conflict is not far away. This is because joy provides the emotional component (*pathos*) to Luke's rhetoric of reversal. Each instance of the joy theme is an instance of reversal.

Looking closer at some of these scenes of conflict will demonstrate the strength of the case. From an ideological perspective, the healing of the lame beggar in Acts 3 provides a strong connection between Jesus' name (Acts 3:6) and God. The narrative of the joyful man is based on an implicit claim that the

---

[45] York explains, 'In Acts, bi-polar reversal as a theme gives way to a community in which the divine principles have been enacted' (*The Last Shall Be First*, 172).

[46] Pervo, *Acts*, 94.

[47] Acts 5:41

[48] Acts 8:8

[49] Acts 8:39

[50] The joyful reception of the gospel in Antioch is a direct result of those displaced by persecution in Jerusalem over the stoning of Stephen (Acts 11:19-23).

[51] Acts 12:14

[52] Acts 13:44-52

[53] Acts 14:17

[54] Acts 15:3 and 15:31

[55] Acts 16:34

risen Jesus is somehow the same subject who receives praise (God).[56] The man's emotional response powerfully draws the reader into the world in which Jesus is the Lord who heals even as God is the Lord who heals.

In Acts 15, the joy theme occurs in the description of the letter (ἐπιστολή) that contained the results and instructions from the Jerusalem Council. Here, the joy theme is not far away from conflict.[57] The power of the Holy Spirit not only brought together the council and provided unity, but resolves the disputes in Antioch. When Judas (Barsabbas) and Silas read the letter, the church at Antioch 'rejoiced' (χαίρω). The emotion of joy provides objective evidence of the power of the Holy Spirit who is at work amongst the people of God. Luke takes care to demonstrate that unity (Acts 15:25) in the Holy Spirit and subjection to the teachings of the Council produced the emotion of joy.

The emotion of joy plays an important role in internal conflict as well as external conflict. The presence of the joy alongside disbelief in vignette wherein Peter is rescued from Herod's prison echoes the reaction of disbelief, joy, and astonishment when Jesus appears after the resurrection (Luke 24:41). In the narrative of Peter's rescue, the disciples do not believe the report of the joyful servant girl Rhoda who forgets to open the door for Peter in her astonishment (Acts 12:14). Rhoda's own mixed reaction is still superior to those who would have dismissed the matter altogether if it were not for her insistence. It is only after Peter continues to knock that 'they say him and were amazed' (Acts 12:16). Rhoda is filled with joy whereas the disciples are missing out on the joy because of their unbelief in the power of God.

Our conclusion from Luke 24 remains true here in Acts: one of the neglected obstacles that must be overcome is the lack of joy (*pathos*) that is present with lack of understanding (*logos*) and lack of faith in who Jesus is (*ethos*). The emotion of joy provides emotional power to a text that challenges the 'symbolic universe' that is defined by Greco-Roman and Jewish norms that must be overturned by the message of the cross. Jesus is the risen Lord who is able to overcome any obstacle that gets in the way of proclaiming the word of the Lord.

Conclusion

The joy theme in Acts is distinct and works in tandem with the divine principle elucidated by Jesus in his 'Sermon on the Plain' (Luke 6): the first shall be last and the last shall be first. The divine visitation of YHWH in Jesus has turned

---

[56] Willimon comes to a similar conclusion: 'The healing power is unleashed "in the name of Jesus Christ of Nazareth" (3:6), as the name of Jesus is the direct link between the living and active Lord in heaven and his community on earth' (*Acts*, 45).

[57] Shillington's analysis based on a socio-rhetorical method finds that 'opposition' is a distinguishing feature of the Jerusalem Council narrative (*Introduction to the Study of Luke-Acts*, 60).

the world upside-down.[58] The emotion of joy provides emotional and rhetorical power (*pathos*).[59] Like the use of joy in Luke's Gospel, joy in the book of Acts is not an ecstatic outburst without warrant. In fact, joy is an emotion that is based on a cognitive understanding of what the God of Israel has accomplished in Jesus for his people. In other words, in each occurrence of joy there is a reason for it: a dramatic reversal has occurred. The joy theme is part of a matrix that is rooted in *objective* historical events. These occurrences of joy develop Luke's interest in promise-fulfillment as well as Luke's interest in utilizing the Septuagint (Isaiah) to provide a narrative sub-structure (Isaianic New Exodus).[60] Joy is hermeneutically important because it identifies God's activities through promise-fulfillment and it evokes emotion within the reader.[61] In addition, the emotion of joy functions as a tool of persuasion amidst conflict. The Book of Acts is a document that forms and shapes the reader. We might say that the joy theme is 'apocalyptic' because it is used to indicate that the Hebrew Scriptures are being fulfilled.[62] The joy theme is an integral part of this ecclesiological function because it *subjectively* draws the reader into the world that been turned upside-down.

---

[58] York states, 'there is almost no end to reversal in Luke-Acts!' (*The Last Shall Be First*, 173).

[59] The book of Acts, like the Gospel of Luke, is essentially aimed at persuasion. The Lukan corpus aims at *both* didactic instruction and rhetorical persuasion. Contra Bovon who seems to focus exclusively on persuasion (*Luke 1: Gospel of Luke 1:1-9:50*, 5).

[60] Hays concludes that the 'overall design' of Luke-Acts may be characterized as 'God's purpose in fulfilling the promise of redemption for his people Israel ('The Liberation of Israel in Luke-Acts', 103).

[61] De Long develops the way in which praise to God provides interpretation of divine visitation in *Surprised by God*, 152-53.

[62] I.H. Marshall explains that 'apocalyptic language' in Luke is 'in reality nothing more than material drawn from the Old Testament and is used to indicate that a particular event is to be seen as fulfilling the Old Testament prophecy or fitting the pattern of some typology'. See 'Political and Eschatological Language in Luke', in *Reading Luke: Interpretation, Reflection, Formation* (eds. C.G. Bartholomew, J.B. Green, and A.C. Thiselton; Carlisle: Paternoster, 2006; Grand Rapids: Zondervan, 2005), 165.

Chapter 9

Conclusion: The Rhetorical Power of Joy and the Textures of Luke-Acts

Introduction

There are few thorough investigations of the joy theme in Luke-Acts, and even less that seek to understand Luke's use of emotion from a socio-rhetorical standpoint. Within Lukan studies a paradox has remained. The joy theme has been widely acknowledged while Luke's interest in *pathos* or emotion has been denied or mostly ignored.[1] This study demonstrates, however, the thesis that the use of the emotion of joy is rhetorically significant. Specifically, the joy theme empowers Luke's use of reversal of expectations.

Analysis of the joy theme in Luke-Acts reveals that it is likely derived from Isaiah's own use of emotion. The conclusions of my study should come as no surprise to those who are familiar with the claims that Luke's Gospel is the 'gospel of joy' and that Isaiah is the 'fifth gospel'.[2] Luke's use of Isaiah is manifold but often refers to the New Exodus motif and the joyful reversals of the new age that Isaiah envisions.

The appearance of emotion at points of reversal would have been understandable to Greco-Roman and Jewish audiences who would have come from a spectrum of Hellenistic influences and backgrounds.

This chapter will review the broader findings of the analysis of the joy theme in Luke-Acts, summarize the findings that emerged from the prior analysis, and lastly will examine potential implications and areas for further exploration.

The Rhetoric of Joy and Reversal

The socio-rhetorical methodology used to analyze the joy theme was tied to Luke's own statements that prefaced his Gospel and Acts. This was done so that the methodology did not drown out the voice of the text. Attention was given to the prefaces and introductory matter of Luke-Acts because of the way that they frame the discourse or narrative that follows. Our study focused on the

---

[1] Patrick Spencer first states that *pathos* is 'least relevant' but then argues that it is 'central' to Luke's rhetorical strategy. Whatever the case is, Spencer does not analyze emotion in the text or its impact upon the reader in *Rhetorical Texture and Narrative Trajectories*, 52, 186.

[2] Mallen, *Reading and Transformation of Isaiah*, 1.

rhetorical technique of reversal of expectation and related techniques such as repetition/amplification and intertextuality rather than formal Greco-Roman categories of rhetoric.

Peter Mallen laments that all of the studies he reviewed lacked an investigation into how Luke used Isaiah from a rhetorical perspective in order to achieve a response from his audience.[3] This study contributes to the filling of this lacuna by proving that Isaiah provided a framework of reversal for Luke and a source for adding emotional force to his task of persuasion. Mallen also concludes that a 'rhetoric of perception pervades the entire narrative of Luke-Acts'.[4] This can now be sharpened to include the rhetoric of emotion. Joy is one of the positive emotions that Luke seeks to elicit from his readers. This is one of the ways that the joy theme works subjectively to draw the readers into the narrative.

The development of the joy theme rests upon the conclusion that the emotion of joy is simply an *emotion*.[5] This contrasts with many New Testament exegetes who read theological content into references to emotion. This is significant for our purposes because it is important to let the range of references to joy simply be references to joyful emotion. What makes emotion theologically important is the *object*. Yet this raises the question: why was Luke so interested in joy in particular? The answer lies in Luke's interest in using the Hebrew Scriptures and Isaiah in particular to develop a pattern of promise and fulfillment and to provide a narrative framework.

The rhetorical nature of Luke's use of emotion can be understood in terms of what it provides objectively for the narrative and for the promise-fulfillment motif. The emotion of joy as found on the lips of disciples is often part of a matrix of events that reflects the inauguration of the new age. This conclusion provides confirmation and development the thesis that 'the writings of Isaiah lend strong credibility to Luke's narrative since their predictions match how events actually turned out in practice'.[6] In other words, the record of events is persuasive because it depicts the fulfillment of events in the Scriptures that connect the emotion of joy to God's mighty deeds. Luke seeks to persuade the reader by communicating that the joyful events in his διήγησις are structured according to motifs in Isaiah such as the New Exodus.

The joy theme can also be understood in terms of what it provides subjectively for the reader. In other words, 'the rhetorical effect of a work on an audience is now considered important to the understanding of a text'.[7] The joy theme provides an emotional force that bridges the narrative world to the world of the reader. As the joy theme is enacted within the narrative world it connects

---

[3] Mallen, *Reading and Transformation of Isaiah*, 19.

[4] Mallen, *Reading and Transformation of Isaiah*, 196.

[5] Elliott, *Faithful Feelings*, 165-78.

[6] Mallen, *Reading and Transformation of Isaiah*, 201.

[7] Resseguie, *Introducing Narrative Criticism*, 30.

positive cultural codes with a message that was not readily accepted. The emotion of joy works together with other elements to force the question: is there warrant for the reader to engage in joy even as the characters in the text are engaging in joy at the mighty acts of YHWH? Joy works subjectively upon the reader by providing an accessible emotional gateway into the narrative world that Luke wants the reader to accept as corresponding to the experiential world.

The subjective and objective sides of rhetoric work together in a narrative that is also continually presenting reversals of expectation. The emotion of joy propels the reversal forward within the narrative as well as confronting the reader with the ideological claims therein. The emotional component of the divine principle of reversal is joy.[8]

Summary of the Joy Theme in Luke-Acts

The analysis of each textual unit was broken down into four overlapping and progressively integrated foci. The methodology employed in this study is essentially interdisciplinary.[9] It includes four distinct but progressively overlapping questions. The first question asks: how does joy function as *inner texture*? This is concerned with the text itself. The second question asks: how does joy function as related to *intertexture*? This is concerned with the rewriting of texts.[10] The third question asks: how does joy function as part of *sacred texture*? This is focused on the intersection of human life and the divine. The fourth question is: how does joy function with respect to *ideological texture*? This question evaluates the emotion of joy as part of conflict.

In chapter 1, we established the thesis that joy provides emotional force to the rhetoric of reversal throughout Luke-Acts. The literature review of the joy theme in Luke-Acts revealed that it is both widely recognized and underdeveloped. Prior studies on the joy theme provided redaction information that demonstrated Luke's unique interest in joy but did not engage with rhetorical concerns.

Chapter 2 examined the joy theme at the inauguration of the new age in Luke 1. With Luke 1, the joy theme occurs at the reversal of Zechariah and Elizabeth (Lk 1:5-25). This text frames the narratives and discourses that follow it and establishes certain expectations regarding the joy theme: the God of Israel is at work and the reader should expect to respond with the same joy

---

[8] York, *The Last Shall Be First*, 183.

[9] For succinct summary of the socio-rhetorical methodology see Shillington, *Introduction to the Study of Luke-Acts*, 53-54.

[10] Some of these questions will overlap as they progressively inform each other. For example, Mallen argues that Luke uses Isaiah as 'subversive intertextuality' (*Reading and Transformation of Isaiah*, 67). According to my approach, this links intertextuality with ideological texture.

that accompanies a baby born to a previously barren woman. If the reference to Isaiah 40:3-5 in the speech of John the Baptist is understood as a hermeneutical key that can be read retroactively into the narrative, then Isaiah's depiction of the reversal of Israel is likely in view (Isa 49:9-16; 54:1-5). Luke is often drawing from themes and concepts in the Isaianic texts that relate the appearance of joy to the restoration of Israel, anti-idol polemic, the power of the word of God, and a universal concern for the salvation of the nations. The emotional response of joy depicts how one must respond to the surprising work of YHWH who makes the barren fruitful. The joy theme immediately takes on rhetorical and ideological force as the young maiden Mary is contrasted with the priest Zechariah. The joy theme works together with other textual and narrative features to empower a reversal of expectations that would have both signaled the inauguration of the new age and forced the reader to come to terms with their own response to God's mighty deeds, particularly the arrival of Jesus.

Chapter 3 was an extension of the study of joy at the inauguration of the new age in Luke 1-2. This chapter sought to tie together the joy theme in the series of three vignettes in Luke 1-2. These are significant because the volume of the joy theme is so great that it prepares the reader for further development. The joy theme clearly is part of Luke's rhetorical matrix that empowers his use of reversal to persuade the reader about the inauguration of the new age (or New Exodus) and the identity of Jesus. The first two vignettes of Mary's pregnancy and the birth of John the Baptist are woven together (Luke 1:26-66). The reversal from barrenness to pregnancy reflects the Isaianic New Exodus themes of reversal of barrenness in Isaiah 40-55. Mary's own song indicates that this reversal is not for her alone, it is an event with corporate ramifications for all of Israel. A new age has dawned with the arrival of the infant messiah and the prophet who prepares the way for him. John's work as a prophet begins before he is even born. He jumps for joy at the presence of Jesus while still in the womb (Luke 1:41). What the reader learns is that hearing and speaking *and feeling* are crucial for responding properly to the mighty deeds of YHWH. The third vignette explores the joy theme as the poles of honour and dishonour are turned upside down in this new age. Instead of nobility, lowly shepherds are the first to visit the infant king of Israel.

Chapter 4 examines three textual units that are related to the joy theme. The salvific message of Jesus can be appropriately summarized as 'reversal'. This chapter contributed to our study by establishing a relationship between joy and reversal. The use of reversal would simply be powerless without emotion. There is also a tension in this chapter between the restoration of Israel and messianic blessings that Jesus proclaims to all of Israel and are only received by those who are the least expected to be important. This chapter of the study makes an important contribution by demonstrating that Isaiah continues to play a large role in forming Luke's integration of the joy theme across his Gospel. The emotion of joy works together with the subversive appropriation of Isaiah's new age that belongs to the outsiders and the excluded. The ideological challenge of appropriating the emotion of joy in the narrative is apparent in the clear way that reversal works to place the rich and powerful on the lower level of honour in the kingdom (Luke 7:18-23). The expectation that the emotion of joy will be an objective marker of reversal of status in the kingdom of God is so clear that Jesus must teach against absolutizing the emotion of joy in his Parable of the Sower (Luke 8:9-15). The presence of joy is so powerful that it can deceive those who participate: it must be mixed with hearing and obeying the word of the Lord.

Chapter 5 continues to follow Jesus' journey to Jerusalem. There are still lessons to be taught before the cross. Specifically, the lessons that relate to the emotion of joy focus on the problem of triumphalism. This chapter qualifies the joy theme and prevents this important emotional dimension from becoming a barrier to participation in the kingdom. First, the seventy-two disciples return victorious from spiritual battles only to learn that the object of their joy is misplaced (Luke 10:17-24). Rejoicing in the submission of demonic powers must be replaced by joy in the divine action of election; their names having been written in heaven. Luke 15 provides three parables (the Lost Sheep, the Lost Coin, and the Lost Son) that are related thematically through the use of 'lostness' and 'joy' at the recovery of what was lost. The last and longest parable places the emphasis on the joy of the father in receiving the lost son in contrast to the older son who does not receive the sinner with joy. The presence of emotion provides a contrast between those who identify with and accept repentant sinners and those who oppose Jesus and his kingdom. The possession of the emotion of joy is an identity marker and an ideological tool. The emotion of joy provides the force that moves honour to shame and shame to honour as repentant sinners are embraced. The reversals that characterize the kingdom are powerful because they are emotionally charged. The joy theme is integral to the reversals as it creates dissonances that will challenge the world-view of the reader. The journey to Jerusalem anticipates the cross by turning the world – its values, and the object of one's joy – upside down.

Chapter 6 follows the joy theme through Jesus' persecution and vindication. The last chapter provided the information about joy that prevented it from becoming triumphalism and a barrier to the cruciform vision of the kingdom. The first reversal examined in this chapter is the overturning of what kingship means as Jesus rides into Jerusalem on a donkey (Luke 19:28-40). The emotion of joy of those in the city empowers the vision of the servant-king entering Jerusalem – the City of David. Jesus' entry is triumphal and is immediately followed by conflict with some Pharisees over the joyful people who receive him. The narrative forces the question as the reader is drawn into the narrative world; which group do you identify with? The presence of joy functions to provide objective evidence of fulfillment of covenantal promises as found in texts such as Isaiah 55:12. The second reversal involves the change that Luke develops in the characterizations of the disciples. Luke wants to provide a

rhetorically powerful picture of how doubt turns into faith as Jesus interacts
with the disciples after his resurrection (Luke 24:36-49). This movement
requires changes in the minds, hearts, and emotions as the disciples interpret
the resurrection in light of the 'Scriptures' (Luke 24:45). In spite of joy being
the first and immediate reaction to Jesus' resurrection (Luke 24:41), they did
not really understand what had happened. Thus, the ideal state of a disciple is
one who is filled with both joy and understanding. The third and final reversal
in chapter 7 is also the final reversal of the Gospel of Luke. The joy in
Jerusalem at the Triumphal Entry seemed to have dissipated entirely with the
crucifixion.[11] The conclusion of Luke's Gospel completes the reversal that
began with Jesus' resurrection by relating it to Jerusalem and the temple (Luke
24:52-53). The promises in Isaiah of the restoration of Israel through a New
Exodus have clearly been inaugurated as Jerusalem and the temple are filled
with joy. Jesus' vindication overturns his death sentence and fills the disciples
with emotion. The resurrection has transformed the personal lives of his
disciples as well as the corporate life of Israel as represented by the temple in
Jerusalem. Ideologically, this joy directly challenges the mockery and powers
that only recently put Jesus to death. The sense of victory at the end of Luke's
Gospel anticipates the conquering word of God that goes forth to the ends of
the earth.

Chapter 7 examines the book of Acts in order to develop an understanding of
the joy theme across the entirety of Luke's corpus. Despite elements of
discontinuity between Luke and Acts, such as fewer instances of the joy theme,
there are important elements of continuity. The joy theme occurs at critical
junctures along the path of the 'Way' established in Acts 1:8. Specifically, the
joy theme occurs at each major turn as the word of the Lord moves from
Jerusalem to Judea-Samaria to the ends of the earth.[12] This builds on Pao's
argument that Jesus' quotation of Isaiah 61 is part of the hermeneutical
framework for both Luke and Acts.[13] In Acts the emphasis is placed upon
persuading the reader about the on-going work of Jesus as he reigns from
heaven and the identity of those who claim to be the people of God. In the
broadest sense, Luke-Acts provides an account of the plan and purposes of God
to bring about salvation in Jesus.[14] The changes brought about by this
establishment of the kingdom are so radical that they can be understood
conceptually as reversals. This chapter demonstrates that the emotion of joy is

---

[11] The joy theme also provides emotional power behind reversals that end in tragedy.
The Triumphal Entry suggests that Jerusalem will respond positively to Jesus. De Long
explains that Luke 'immediately reverses this expectation' (*Surprised by God*, 231).
[12] The central or main theme of Luke-Acts is arguably salvation to the ends of the earth.
Spencer, *Rhetorical Texture and Narrative Trajectories*, 35.
[13] Pao, *Acts and the Isaianic New Exodus*, 70-80, esp. 80.
[14] Mallen, *Reading and Transformation of Isaiah*, 60; J.T. Squires, *The Plan of God in Luke-Acts* (SNTSMS 76; Cambridge: Cambridge University Press, 1993).

used to empower this plan that unfolds along the three critical turns outlined in Acts 1:8. The characteristics of the inaugurated new age unfold as the word of the Lord goes forth from Jerusalem and conquers everywhere it goes. The result is that there is joy at the dawn of salvation in Jerusalem, joy at the constitution of Israel, and joy at the inclusion of the Gentiles in the people of God.

Chapter 8 examines the broader joy theme in Acts. Due to space constraints, this chapter seeks to draw together the large pattern of the joy theme in Acts while carefully examining particular instances. When compared to the Gospel of Luke, the joy theme in Acts is not as strong. However, the joy theme plays an important role because it occurs at important narrative joints and throughout the narrative. The joy theme in Acts stands on its own and is worthy of further examination and development. This chapter argued that the joy theme reflects Luke's use of intertextual references to Isaiah (and other sources such as the Psalms) to further his interest in promise-fulfillment and hermeneutical coherence. The joy theme provides evidence that God is fulfilling and his fulfilled his covenantal promises. The joy theme also provides emotional power to the provocative proto-trinitarian picture of Jesus. Jesus praises God even as his very name evokes the healing power of divinity. Jesus is the Lord *and* God the Father is the Lord (Acts 2:36). The resurrection reversed the human rejection of Jesus and confirmed that he is the κύριος even as God is the κύριος. Furthermore, the emotion of joy is used to further the ecclesiological interest in forming identity. At the crucial point of contention over the laws of Moses at the Jerusalem Council (Acts 15), the emotion of joy places a key role in providing evidence of the Holy Spirit and unity. Luke portrays Christian identity and unity as a confluence of spiritual, intellectual, and emotional factors. The emotion of joy is part of a matrix of requirements for the implied reader to enter into the upside-down world that Acts portrays.

Implications

In this study we have demonstrated how the joy theme provides emotion for Luke's rhetoric of reversal. The socio-rhetorical analysis used has approached the exegesis of the text from four interdisciplinary viewpoints. The results of this study have demonstrated the value of the four-fold socio-rhetorical method.[15]

1. The *inner texture* of the text is concerned with the text itself. This is the aspect of the Lukan joy theme that has received the most scholarly attention. It has been well established that the Lukan corpus and his Gospel in particular devotes a disproportionate amount of attention to joy. But the tendency of many

---

[15] For example, De Long views 'praise to God' as having objective value (my term) because it 'fulfills prophetic promises' and having subjective value (my term) because it aids the reader in 'interpreting' the visitation by God in Jesus (*Surprised by God*, 152-53). However, she does not explain how emotion relates to ideology.

studies of the joy theme in Luke-Acts has been to overlook the basic emotional content and how this emotion empowers Luke's rhetorical purposes. Some have discussed the Lukan joy theme in terms of eschatology but this terminology likely obscures the fact that the joy theme extends across the whole corpus and involves a wide range of speech acts. The sematic range of words that covers the joy theme is quite extensive and Luke appears to be significantly interested in the object of one's emotions as much as in the emotion itself. The entirety of one's conversion can be summarized in the word 'joy'. But this is not without qualification. The hearing of faith and feeling of joy must be mixed with the 'doing' of obedience (Luke 8:9). Because the joy theme is widely acknowledged in Luke-Acts it provides a good test case for studying repetition, volume, or amplification.[16] This study has demonstrated that an atomistic methodology is required to understand how this repetition works together with other features or textures.

2. The *intertexture* of the text is concerned with the rewriting of other texts. Due to the prominence of Isaiah, this study has focused largely on Luke's use of Isaianic quotations in the first four chapters of Luke's Gospel that frame the narrative and provide the reader with hermeneutical keys for what follows.[17] This study has attempted to draw connections between the separate conclusions that (1) Luke's corpus is dominated by joy, (2) Luke's corpus is filled with reversals, and (3) the plotline and rhetoric of Luke's corpus is often related to Isaiah. These three elements were related by demonstrating that joy provides emotional power for the rhetoric of reversal that is the expression of the New Exodus or new age that Isaiah envisions. The rhetorical use of Isaiah involves Luke's implicit and explicit claims that God has inaugurated the fulfillment of drastic reversals of expectations that characterize the new age. Among these is the Isaianic motif of reversing barrenness into pregnancy or fruitfulness. The study of the rhetorical use of the Old Testament in the New Testament is a growing area. This study makes two conclusions that may be helpful for future studies. First, the rhetorical use of the Old Testament must include a study of how the citations add emotional power. Studies of rhetoric in Hellenistic-Jewish literature must examine the logic (*logos*) and the credentials (*ethos*) as well as emotion (*pathos*). Second, the study of the use of the Old Testament in the New Testament needs to draw upon narrative approaches that are sensitive to themes and motifs such as the Lukan joy theme. Once one understands that the Lukan joy theme runs like a thread through his whole tapestry, one will also understand the significance of intertextual import for the theme. Methodologically, the relationship between themes and intertextuality can be demonstrated by examining repetition or volume on a macro-scale. The nature of narrative themes to intertextuality in Luke's Gospel was demonstrated by the

---

[16] Witherington, *New Testament Rhetoric*, 52.
[17] A path for further exploration includes the study of the relationship between the joy theme and the Psalms.

way that the introductory narratives frame the whole corpus by creating relationships that shape expectations. Isaiah also plays a role in the plotline of the Book of Acts as evidenced by David Pao's study on the relationship between the New Exodus of Isaiah 40:1-11 and the programme of the 'Way' according to Acts 1:8. This study demonstrated that the relationship between Luke's corpus and Isaiah's New Exodus is more extensive than previously documented. Luke's appropriation of the New Exodus motif is not exclusive of other Isaianic motifs. Nevertheless, its presence is significant. This study demonstrated that the source of Luke's joy theme is likely the Isaianic joy theme that describes the emotional reversals that will come about in the age to come.

3. The *sacred texture* of the text is concerned with the intersection of human life and the divine. Luke's narrative world is not a closed system but a system that is open to surprising and mighty acts of God that achieve what was previously thought impossible. In the social and religious matrix of first century Judaism one could argue that 'joy in God is at the centre'.[18] This study supports the conclusion that Luke's understanding of the role of emotion amongst those who followed 'the Way' was largely in continuity with many contemporaries who adhered to the collective religion of Israel. The joy theme places the whole narrative of Luke-Acts within the common traditions of Jewish culture and writings. This overlaps with the ideological function of the joy theme. To claim to rejoice in the mighty deeds of YHWH is to assume or claim a certain identity because such actions can only be done by the people of God. Joy takes on an inherently subversive dimension when the referent of the κύριος includes Jesus and YHWH.[19] The narrative filled with joy in YHWH-Jesus will draw the reader into a narrative world that is difficult to resist. Future studies of narrative Christology and theology-proper must seek to integrate Luke's use of joy to persuade the reader about the divine identity of Jesus and mighty deeds of YHWH on behalf of both Jews and Gentiles.

4. The *ideological texture* of the text is concerned with the way that the text calls for a new value system, world-view, or pattern of thinking. The terms 'rhetoric' and 'ideology' are terms that overlap in the conceptual realm of persuasion. The notion of rhetoric deals specifically with persuasion but it cannot be separated from the social and cultural conflicts that take place during this process. The text of Luke has rhetorical and ideological goals that seek to reverse the world of the reader.[20] Most studies of the Lukan joy theme have largely left the relationship between joy and rhetoric untouched. Whereas Spencer concludes that 'pathos is the least relevant for Luke-Acts', this

---

[18] Elliott, *Faithful Feelings*, 91.

[19] Rowe, *Early Narrative Christology*, 231.

[20] For example, Kuhn describes the rhetoric of reversal in Luke 1-2 as 'world reversing' (*Heart of Biblical Narrative*, 117).

conclusion must be significantly qualified.[21] Furthermore, studying Luke's rhetorical strategy must not be limited to an atomistic study of the speeches. The rhetoric of the speeches in Luke-Acts must be studied concurrently with the narrative as a whole. The rhetoric of reversal is empowered by joy in an objective sense and a subjective sense. The objective nature of joy intersects with intertextuality.

The prologue of Luke's Gospel states his intention to provide 'certainty' about that which has been fulfilled (Luke 1:1-4). The joy theme provides objective evidence that the fulfillment of God's promises have begun to be fulfilled. Part of Luke's rhetorical power lies in portraying the mighty deeds of God in a holistic way that includes *logos*, *ethos*, and *pathos*. The subjective side of Luke's rhetoric of reversal is apparent by the way in which the emotion of joy is used to create narrative scenes such as the joyful mother Mary (Luke 1) or the joyful temple (Luke 24, Acts 1). The emotion of joy draws the reader into Luke's narrative world that is based on certain presuppositions and conclusions. As the reader engages the narrative world, the emotion of joy presents them with an attractive world of beliefs and facts that one must accept or reject. This explains how the joy theme functions in a narrative that allows Luke to persuade the reader about the ongoing work of Jesus after the resurrection, the church's continuity with Israel, and the legitimacy of the inclusion of the Gentiles.

Further inquiries and research need to be made into the way that *logos*, *ethos*, and *pathos* are related and work together in Luke's rhetorical strategy. This should interact with Luke's use of Isaiah as well as the Psalms. The study of Luke's rhetoric needs to consider not only the speeches but his entire narrative. The Lukan corpus points to an interest in these three areas as broad qualities of a persuasive text in the Hellenistic-Jewish history tradition. The persuasiveness of the text is most likely not based on technical Greco-Roman rhetorical structures. A specific example of further inquiry might develop the rhetorical implications of the qualities of the characters in the introductions of Luke and Acts. These qualities point toward an interest in establishing character or reputation (*ethos*). This could then be related to Luke's use of joy (*pathos*) and reasoning (*logos*) that sought to provide Theophilus (and others) with certainty (Luke 1:4).

Concluding Summary

Given Luke's Hellenistic world where appeals to reason, character, and emotion were significant for both Jews and Greek, it is easy to imagine how powerful Luke's corpus would have been. This study of joy has been narrow and focused but it also attests to the importance of interdisciplinary methodologies that are able to examine the various textures within the text. The

---

[21] Spencer, *Rhetorical Texture and Narrative Trajectories*, 52.

joy theme provides an important element of emotion or *pathos* to Luke's rhetorical agenda(s) in both Luke and Acts. When the readers of Luke's corpus encountered the joy theme it provided evidence of the work of YHWH that could not be ignored. The narrative world in which Jesus is the risen Lord of Israel is a compelling and joyful world. Yet it is a world turned upside down by the crucified and risen Jesus. The upside-down nature of the new age or New Exodus is so extreme that reversals characterize the whole corpus. More than one scholar has concluded that Isaiah 40-66 is the Old Testament 'gospel of joy'.[22] Thus, it should not surprise us to find that when Luke borrows and develops Isaianic motifs his gospel is labelled the New Testament 'gospel of joy'. Those who appropriate this narrative through faith are characterized by joy along with hearing and doing the word of God. *Those who embrace the risen Lord Jesus by faith must: listen, do, and feel.*[23]

---

[22] Laniak, *Shepherds After My Own Heart*, 125; Westermann, *Isaiah 40 – 66*, 12.

[23] Mallen, *Reading and Transformation of Isaiah*, 159.

Bibliography

Primary Sources

Aland, B., K. Aland, J. Karavidopoulos, C.M. Martini and B.M. Metzger (eds). *Novum Testamentum Graece*. 27th ed. Stuttgart: Deutsche Biblelgesellschaft, 1993.

Biblia Hebraica Stuttgartensia: With Westminster Hebrew Morphology. Electronic edition. Stuttgart. Glenside: German Bible Society; Westminster Seminary, 1996.

The Holy Bible: English Standard Version. Wheaton: Crossway, 2001.

Secondary Sources

Amador, J.D.H., *Academic Constraints in Rhetorical Criticism of the New Testament: An Introduction to a Rhetoric of Power*. JSNTSup 174. Sheffield: Sheffield Academic Press, 1999.

Alexander, L. *The Preface to Luke's Gospel: Literary Convention and Social Context in Luke 1.1-4 and Acts 1.1*. SNTSMS 78. Cambridge: Cambridge University Press, 1993.

— 'Formal Elements and Genre'. Pages 9-26 in *Jesus and the Heritage of Israel: Luke's Narrative Claim upon Israel's Legacy*. Edited by D. Moessner. Harrisburg: Trinity Press International, 1999.

Bailey, K.E. *The Cross and the Prodigal: Luke 15 Through the Eyes of Middle Eastern Peasants*. Downers Grove: InterVarsity, 2005.

Balz, H.R. and G. Schneider. *Exegetical Dictionary of the New Testament*. Grand Rapids: Eerdmans, 1990.

Barrett, C.K. *Acts 1-14*. London: T&T Clark, 1994.

Barton, B. *Acts: Life Application Bible Commentary*. Wheaton: Tyndale House, 1999.

Bauckham, R. 'The Restoration of Israel in Luke-Acts'. Pages 435-488 in *Restoration: Old Testament, Jewish, and Christian Perspectives*. Vol. 72 in JSJSup. Edited by J.M. Scott. Leiden: Brill, 2001.

— *God Crucified: Monotheism and Christology in the New Testament*. Grand Rapids, MI: Eerdmans, 1998.

Bauer, W. *A Greek-English Lexicon of the New Testament and Other Early Christian Literature*. Edited by F.W. Danker. 3rd ed. Chicago: University of Chicago Press, 2000.

Beale, G.K. *Handbook on the New Testament Use of the Old Testament*. Grand Rapids: Baker, 2012.

— *The Temple and the Church's Mission: A Biblical Theology of the Dwelling Place of God*. NSBT 17. Downers Grove: InterVarsity, 2004.

— *We Become What We Worship: A Biblical Theology of Idolatry*. Downers Grove: InterVarsity, 2008.

Berlin, A. 'Interpreting Torah Traditions in Psalm 105'. Pages 20-36 in *Jewish Biblical Interpretation and Cultural Exchange: Comparative Exegesis in Context*. Edited by N.B. Dohrmann and D. Stern. Philadelphia: University of Pennsylvania Press, 2008.

Bernadicou, P. *Joy in the Gospel of Luke*. Rome: Gregorian Pontifical University, 1970.

Bird, M.F. *Are You the One Who is to Come?: The Historical Jesus and the Messianic Question*. Grand Rapids: Baker, 2009.

— 'The Unity of Luke-Acts in Recent Discussion'. *JSNT* 29:4 (2007): 425-47.

Black, C.C. *The Rhetoric of the Gospel: Theological Artistry in the Gospels and Acts*. St. Louis: Chalice, 2001.

Bock. D. *A Theology of Luke-Acts*. Grand Rapids: Zondervan, 2012.

— *Luke 1:1-9:50*. BECNT. Grand Rapids: Baker, 1994.

— *Luke 9:51-24:53*. BECNT. Grand Rapids: Baker, 1996.

— 'Luke'. Pages 349-72 in *The Face of New Testament Studies: A Survey of Recent Research*. Edited by S. McKnight and G. Osborne. Grand Rapids: Baker/ Apollos, 2004.

Borgman, P.C. *The Way According to Luke: Hearing the Whole Story of Luke-Acts*. Grand Rapids: Eerdmans, 2006.

Bovon, F. *Das Evangelium nach Lukas*. 4 Volumes. EKK. Zurich: Benziger, 1989.

— *Luke 1: A Commentary on the Gospel of Luke 1:1-9:50*. Translated by C.M. Thomas. Hermeneia. Minneapolis: Fortress Press, 2002.

— *Luke the Theologian: Fifty-Five Years of Research (1950-2005)*. Waco: Baylor University Press, 2006.

Braun, W. *Feasting and Social Rhetoric in Luke 14*. SNTSMS 85. Cambridge: Cambridge University Press, 1995.

Brawley, R.L. *Centering on God: Method and Message in Luke-Acts*. Louisville: WJKP, 1990.

— *Text to Text Pours Forth Speech: Voices of Scripture in Luke-Acts*. ISBL. Bloomington/Indianapolis: Indiana University Press, 1995.

Bruce, F.F. *The Book of Acts, Revised*. NICNT. Grand Rapids: Eerdmans, 1988.

Campbell, C.R. *Basics of Verbal Aspect in Biblical Greek*. Grand Rapids: Zondervan, 2008.

Carey, G. 'Review of Academic Constraints in Rhetorical Criticism of the New Testament by J.D.H. Amador'. in *Review of Biblical Literature* [http://www.bookreviews.org] (2000).

Chance, J.B. *Jerusalem, the Temple, and the New Age in Luke-Acts*. Macon: Mercer University Press, 1988.

Conver, C.C. *The Portrayal of Joy in the Gospel of Luke*. Ph.D Dissertation. The Southern Baptist Theological Seminary, 1985.

Conzelmann, H. *The Theology of St. Luke*. Translated by G. Buswell. Philadelphia: Fortress, 1961.

Craddock, F. *Luke*. Louisville: WJKP, 1990.

De Long, K.P. *Surprised by God: Praise Responses in the Narrative of Luke-Acts*. BZNW 166. Berlin: Walter de Gruyter, 2009.

Doble, P. 'The Psalms in Luke-Acts.' Pages 83-118 in *Psalms in the New Testament*. Edited by S. Moyise and M.J.J. Menken. London: T&T Clark, 2004.

Downing, F.G. 'Theophilus's First Reading of Luke-Acts'. Pages 91 to 109 in *Luke's Literary Achievement: Collected Essays*. Edited by C.M. Tuckett. JSNTSup 116. Sheffield: Sheffield Academic Press, 1995.

Du Toit, A.B. *Der Aspekt der Freude im urchristlichen Abendmahl*. Winterthur: P.G. Keller, 1965.

Ekblad, E.R. *Isaiah's Servant Poems According to the Septuagint: An Exegetical and Theological Study*. Louvain: Peeters, 1999.

Elliott, M.A. *Faithful Feelings: Rethinking Emotion in the New Testament*. Grand Rapids: Kregel, 2006.

Eslinger, L. 'Inner-Biblical Exegesis and Inner-Biblical Allusion: The Question of Category'. *VT* 42 (1992): 47-58.

Evans, C.A. 'Jesus and the Spirit: On the Origin and Ministry of the Second Son of God'. Pages 26-45 in *Luke and Scripture: The Function of Sacred Tradition in Luke-Acts*. Edited by C.A. Evans and J.A. Sanders. Minneapolis: Fortress Press, 1993.

— 'Prophecy and Polemic: Jews in Luke's Scriptural Apologetic'. Pages 171-211 in *Luke and Scripture: The Function of Sacred Tradition in Luke-Acts*. Edited by C.A. Evans and J.A. Sanders. Minneapolis: Fortress Press, 1993.

Farris, S. *The Hymns of Luke's Infancy Narratives: Their Origin, Meaning, and Significance*. JSNTSup 9. Sheffield: JSOT Press, 1985.

Fishbane, M. *Biblical Interpretation in Ancient Israel*. Oxford: Oxford University Press, 1988.

Fitzmyer, J.A. *The Acts of the Apostles*. AB 31. London: Doubleday, 1998.

France, R.T. *The Gospel of Matthew*. Grand Rapids: Eerdmans, 2007.

Friesen, I.D. *Isaiah*. Scottdale: Herald Press, 2009.

Geldenhuys, N. *Commentary on the Gospel of Luke*. Grand Rapids: Eerdmans, 1977.

Goheen, M. 'A Critical Examination of David Bosch's Missional Reading of Luke'. Pages 229-264 in *Reading Luke: Interpretation, Reflection, Formation*. Edited by C.G. Bartholomew, J.B. Green, and A.C. Thiselton. Carlisle: Paternoster, 2006. Grand Rapids: Zondervan, 2005.

Grams, R. 'The Temple Conflict Scene'. Pages 41-65 in *Persuasive Artistry: Studies in New Testament Rhetoric in Honor of George A. Kennedy*. Edited by D.F. Watson. JSNTSup 50. Sheffield: Academic Press, 1991.

Green, J.B. *The Theology of the Gospel of Luke*. Cambridge: Cambridge University Press, 1995.

— *The Gospel of Luke*. NICNT. Grand Rapids: Eerdmans, 1997.

Gulin, E.G. *Die Freude im Neuen Testament. I.* Helsinki: Druckerei-A.G. der Finnischen Literatur-Gesellschaft, 1932-1936.

Hahn, S.W. 'Kingdom and Church in Luke-Acts: From Davidic Christology to Kingdom Ecclesiology'. Pages 294-321 in *Reading Luke: Interpretation, Reflection, Formation*. Edited by C.G. Bartholomew, J.B. Green, and A.C. Thiselton. Carlisle: Paternoster, 2006. Grand Rapids: Zondervan, 2005.

Harrison, T. *Divinity and History: The Religion of Herodotus*. Oxford: Oxford University Press, 2000.

Hays, R.B. *Echoes of Scripture in the Letters of Paul*. New Haven: Yale University Press, 1989.

— *The Conversion of the Imagination: Paul as the Interpreter of Israel's Scripture*. Grand Rapids: Eerdmans 2005.

— 'The Liberation of Israel of Luke-Acts'. Pages 101-17 in *Reading the Bible Intertextually*. Edited by R.B. Hays, S.Alkier, and L.A. Huizenga. Waco: Baylor University Press, 2009.

Humphrey, E. *And I turned to See the Voice: The Rhetoric of Vision in the New Testament*. Studies in Theological Interpretation Series. Grand Rapids: Baker, 2007.

Inselmann, A. *Die Freude im Lukasevangelium: Ein Beitrag zur Psychologischen Exegese*. WUNT 322. Tübingen: Mohr Siebeck, 2012.

Jeremias, J. *The Parables of Jesus*. NY: Charles Scribner's Sons, 1963.

Jervell, J. *The Theology of the Acts of the Apostles*. New Testament Theology Series. Cambridge: Cambridge University Press, 1996.

Jobes, K.H., and M. Silva. *Invitation to the Septuagint*. Grand Rapids: Baker, 2000.

Johnson, L.T. *Religious Experience in Earliest Christianity: A Missing Dimension in New Testament Studies*. Minneapolis: Fortress, 1998.

— *The Gospel of Luke*. Collegeville: Liturgical Press, 1991.

Jung, C-W. *The Original Language of the Lukan Infancy Narrative*. JSNTSup 267. London: T&T Clark, 2004.

Karris, R.J. *Luke: Artist and Theologian: Luke's Passion Account as Literature*. Mahwah: Paulist, 1985.

Kennedy, G.A. *New Testament Interpretation Through Rhetorical-Criticism*. Chapel Hill: North Carolina Press, 1984.

Kim, S. *Christ and Caesar: The Gospel and the Roman Empire in the Writings of Paul and Luke*. Grand Rapids: Eerdmans, 2008.

Kimball, C.A. *Jesus' Exposition of the Old Testament in Luke's Gospel*. JSNTSup 94. Sheffield: JSOT Press, 1994.

Kittel, G. and G. Friedrich, eds. *Theological Dictionary of the New Testament*. Translated by G.W. Bromiley. 10 Vols. Grand Rapids: Eerdmans, 1964–1976.

Knowles, M.P. 'Scripture, History, Messiah'. Pages 59-82 in *Hearing the Old Testament in the New Testament*. Grand Rapids/Cambridge: Eerdmans, 2006.

Koet, B.J. 'Isaiah in Luke-Acts'. Pages 79-100 in *Isaiah in the New Testament*. Edited by S. Moyise and M.J.J. Menken. London: T&T Clark, 2005.

Köstenberger, A. 'Hearing the Old Testament in the New: A Response'. Pages 255-94 in *Hearing the Old Testament in the New Testament*. Edited by S. Porter. Grand Rapids/Cambridge: Eerdmans, 2006.

Kuhn, K.A.. *Luke: The Elite Evangelist*. Collegeville: Liturgical, 2010.

— *The Heart of Biblical Narrative: Rediscovering Biblical Appeal to the Emotions*. Minneapolis: Fortress, 2009.

Kurz, W.S. *Reading Luke-Acts: Dynamics of Biblical Narrative*. Louisville: WJKP, 1993.

Kwong, I.S.C. *The Word Order of the Gospel of Luke: Its Foregrounded Messages*. JSNTSup 298. London: T&T Clark, 2005.

Litwak, K. *Echoes of Scripture in Luke-Acts: Telling the History of God's People Intertextually*. JSNTSup 282. London: T&T Clark, 2005.

Louw, J.P., and E.A. Nida. *Greek-English Lexicon of the New Testament: Based on Semantic Domains*. 2nd Edition. New York: United Bible Societies, 1996.

Mack, B.L. and V.K. Robbins. *Patterns of Persuasion in the Gospels*. Santa Rosa: Polebridge Press, 1989.

Mallen, P. *The Reading and Transformation of Isaiah in Luke-Acts*. LNTS 367. London: T&T Clark, 2008.

Marguerat, D. *The First Christian Historian: Writing the 'Acts of the Apostles'*. SNTSMS 121. Cambridge: Cambridge University Press, 2002.

Marshall, I.H. 'Acts'. Pages 251-414 in *Commentary on the New Testament Use of the Old Testament*. Edited by G.K. Beale and D.A. Carson. Grand Rapids: Baker, 2007.

— *Gospel of Luke*. NIGTC. Cumbria: Paternoster/Eerdmans, 1978.

— *Luke: Historian and Theologian*. Downers Grove: InterVarsity, 1970.

— 'Political and Eschatological Language in Luke'. Pages 157-77 in *Reading Luke: Interpretation, Reflection, Formation*. Edited by C.G. Bartholomew, J.B. Green, and A.C. Thiselton. Carlisle: Paternoster, 2006. Grand Rapids: Zondervan, 2005.

Marten, A. 'Salvation Today'. Pages 100-126 in *Reading the Gospels Today*. Edited by S.E. Porter. Grand Rapids: Eerdmans, 2004.

Maxwell, K. *Hearing Between the Lines: The Audience as Fellow-Worker in Luke-Acts and its Literary Milieu*. LNTS 425. London: T&T Clark, 2010.

Meier, J.P. *Companions and Competitors: A Marginal Jew: Rethinking the Historical Jesus*. Volume 3. NY: Random House, 2001.

Metzger, B. *A Textual Commentary on the Greek New Testament*. 2nd ed. NY/London: United Bible Societies, 1994.

Meynet, R. *Rhetorical Analysis: An Introduction to Biblical Rhetoric*. JSOTSup 256. Sheffield: Academic Press, 1998.

Millar, J.G. *Now Choose Life: Theology and Ethics in Deuteronomy*. NSBT 7. Grand Rapids: Eerdmans, 1998.

Minear, P.S. *To Heal and to Reveal: The Prophetic Vocation According to Luke*. NY: Seabury, 1976.

Morrice, W.G. *Joy in the New Testament*. Exeter: Paternoster, 1984.

— *We Joy in God*. London: SPCK, 1977.

Moessner, D.P. 'Reading Luke's Gospel as Ancient Hellenistic Narrative'. Pages 125-54 in *Reading Luke: Interpretation, Reflection, Formation*. Edited by C.G. Bartholomew, J.B. Green, and A.C. Thiselton. Carlisle: Paternoster, 2006. Grand Rapids: Zondervan, 2005.

— *Lord of the Banquet: The Literary and Theological Significance of the Lukan Travel Narrative*. Harrisburg: Trinity Press International, 1998.

— 'The Appeal and Power of Poetics: Luke 1:1-4.' Pages 84-123 in *Jesus and the Heritage of Israel: Luke's Narrative Claim upon Israel's Legacy*. Edited by D.P. Moessner. Harrisburg: Trinity Press International, 1999.

Navone, J. *Themes of St. Luke*. Rome: Gregorian Press, 1970.

Neyrey, J.H. ed. *The Social World of Luke-Acts: Models for Interpretation*. Peabody: Hendrickson, 2004.

Nolland, J. *Luke 1:1-9:20*. WBC 35A. Dallas: Word, 1989.

— *Luke 9:21-18:34*. WBC 35B. Dallas: Waco, 2002.

— 'The Role of Money and Possessions in the Parable of the Prodigal Son'. Pages 178-209 in *Reading Luke: Interpretation, Reflection, Formation*. Edited by C. Bartholomew, J. Green, and A.C. Thiselton. Carlisle: Paternoster, 2006. Grand Rapids: Zondervan, 2005.

O'Toole, R.F. *The Unity of Luke's Theology: An Analysis of Luke-Acts*. Good News Studies 9. Wilmington: Michael Glazier, 1984.

Padilla, O. *The Speeches of Outsiders in Acts: Poetics, Theology and Historiography*. SNTSMS 144. Cambridge: Cambridge University Press, 2008.

Painter, J. 'Joy'. Pages 394-96 in *Dictionary of Jesus and the Gospels*. Edited by J. Green and S. McKnight. Leicester: InterVarsity, 1992.

Pao, D. *Acts and the Isaianic New Exodus*. Grand Rapids: Baker/Tübingen: J.C.B. Mohr (Paul Siebeck), 2000.

Pao, D. and E.J. Schnabel. 'Luke'. Pages 251-414 in *Commentary on the New Testament Use of the Old Testament*. Edited by G.K. Beale and D.A. Carson. Grand Rapids: Baker, 2007.

Parsons, M. and R.I. Pervo. *Rethinking the Unity of Luke and Acts*. Minneapolis: Fortress, 1993.

Parsons, M. *Body and Character in Luke and Acts: The Subversion of Physiognomy in Early Christianity*. Grand Rapids: Baker, 2006.

— *The Departure of Jesus in Luke-Acts: The Ascension Narratives in Context*. JSNTSup 21. Sheffield: Sheffield Academic Press, 1987.

Patrick, D. *The Rhetoric of Revelation in the Hebrew Bible*. Minneapolis: Fortress, 1999.

Pervo, R.I. *Acts*. Hermeneia. Minneapolis: Fortress, 2009.

Peterson, D.G. *The Acts of the Apostles*. Grand Rapids: Eerdmans, 2009.

Polhill, J.B. *Acts*. NAC 26. Nashville: Broadman, 1992.

Porter, S. 'Scripture Justifies Mission: The Use of the Old Testament in Luke-Acts'. Pages 104-26 in *Hearing the Old Testament in the New Testament*. Edited by S. Porter. Grand Rapids: Eerdmans, 2006.

Powell, M.A. *What Are They Saying About Acts?*. Mahwah: Paulist, 1991.

— *What Are They Saying About Luke?*. Mahwah: Paulist, 1989.

Resseguie, J.L. *Narrative Criticism of the New Testament: An Introduction*. Grand Rapids: Baker, 2005.

Robbins, V.K. 'Beginnings and Developments in Socio-Rhetorical Interpretation'. Unpublished Paper. Emory University, 2004.

— 'Bodies and Politics in Luke 1-2 and Sirach 44-50: Men, Women, and Boys'. *Scriptura* 90 (2005): 724-838.

— *Exploring the Texture of Texts: A Guide to Socio-Rhetorical Interpretation*. Harrisburg: Trinity Press International, 1996.

— 'Socio-Rhetorical Criticism: Mary, Elizabeth and the Magnificat as a Test Case'. Pages 164-209 in *New Literary Criticism and the New Testament*. Edited by E.S. Malbon and E.V. McKnight. JSNTSup 109. Sheffield: Sheffield Academic Press, 1994.

— 'Socio-Rhetorical Interpretation'. Pages 192-219 in *The Blackwell Companion to the New Testament*. Edited by D.E. Aune; Chicester/Malden, MA: Wiley-Blackwell, 2010.

— 'The Claims of the Prologues and Greco-Roman Rhetoric'. Pages 63-83 in *Jesus and the Heritage of Israel: Luke's Narrative Claim upon Israel's Legacy*. Edited by D.P. Moessner. Harrisburg: Trinity Press International, 1999.

— *The Tapestry of Early Christian Discourse: Rhetoric, Society and Ideology*. London: Routledge, 1996.

— 'The Present and Future of Rhetorical Analysis.' Pages 25-52 in *The Rhetorical Analysis of Scripture: Essays from the 1995 London Conference*. Edited by S.E. Porter and T.H. Olbricht. JSNTSup 146. Sheffield: Sheffield Academic Press, 1997.

— 'The Socio-Rhetorical Role of Old Testament Scripture in Luke 4–19'. Pages 81-93 in *Z Noveho Zakona /From the New Testament: Sbornik k narozeninam Prof. ThDr. Zdenka Sazavy*. Edited by H. Tonzarova and P. Melmuk. Praha: Vydala Cirkev ceskoslovenska husitska, 2001.

Romm, J. 'Herodotus and The Natural World'. Pages 143-91 in *The Cambridge Companion to Herodotus*. Edited by C. Dewald and J. Marincola. Cambridge: Cambridge University Press, 2006.

Rothschild, C.K. *Luke-Acts and the Rhetoric of History: An Investigation of Early Christian Historiography*. Tübingen: Mohr Siebeck, 2004.

Rowe, C.K. *Early Narrative Christology: The Lord in the Gospel of Luke*. Grand Rapids: Baker, 2009.

— *World Upside Down: Reading Acts in the Graeco-Roman Age*. Oxford: Oxford University Press, 2009.

Ruddick, C.T., Jr. 'Birth Narratives in Genesis and Luke.' Pages 14-19 in *The Composition of Luke's Gospel: Selected Studies from Novum Testamentum*. Edited by D.E. Orton. Leiden: Brill, 1999.

Sanders, J.A. 'Isaiah in Luke.' Pages 14-25 in *Luke and Scripture: The Function of Sacred Tradition in Luke-Acts*. Edited by C.A. Evans and J.A. Sanders. Minneapolis : Fortress Press, 1993.

— 'Sins, Debts, and Jubilee Release'. Pages 84-92 in *Luke and Scripture: The Function of Sacred Tradition in Luke-Acts*. Edited by C.A. Evans and J.A. Sanders. Minneapolis: Fortress, 1993.

Schnabel, E.J. 'Fads and Common Sense: Reading Acts in the First Century and Reading Acts Today'. *JETS* 54:2 (2011): 251-78.

Sheeley, S.M. *Narrative Asides in Luke-Acts*. JSNTSup 72. Sheffield: JSOT Press, 1992.

Shillington, V.G. *An Introduction to the Study of Luke-Acts*. T&T Clark Approaches to Biblical Studies. London: T&T Clark, 2007.

Snodgrass, K.R. S*tories with Intent: A Comprehensive Guide to the Parables of Jesus*. Grand Rapids: Eerdmans, 2008.

Spencer, F.S. *Journeying Through Acts: A Literary-Cultural Reading*. Peabody: Hendrickson, 2004.

Spencer, P.E. *Rhetorical Texture and Narrative Trajectories of the Lukan Galilean Ministry Speeches: Hermeneutical Appropriation by Authorial Readers of Luke-Acts*. LNTS 341. London: T&T Clark, 2007.

Squires, J.T. *The Plan of God in Luke-Acts*. Cambridge: Cambridge University Press, 1993.

Stamps, D.L. 'The Use of the Old Testament in the New Testament as a Rhetorical Device: A Methodological Proposal'. Pages 9-37 in *Hearing the Old Testament in the New Testament*. Edited by S. Porter. Grand Rapids: Eerdmans, 2006.

Stein, R. *Luke*. NAC 24. Nashville: Broadman & Holman, 1992.

Strauss, M. *The Davidic Messiah in Luke-Acts: The Promise and Its Fulfillment in Lukan Christology*. JSNTSup 110. Sheffield: Sheffield Academic Press, 1995.

Strelhan, R. 'A Note on ἀσφάλεια (Luke 1.4)'. *JSNT* 30:2 (2007): 163-71.

Talbert, C.H. *Literary Patterns, Theological Themes and the Genre of Luke-Acts*. SBLMS 20. Missoula: Scholars Press, 1974.

— *Reading Acts: A Literary and Theological Commentary*. Revised Ed. Macon: Smyth and Helwys, 2005.

— *Reading Luke: A Literary and Theological Commentary on the Third Gospel*. New York: Crossroad, 1982.

Tannehill, R.C. *The Narrative Unity of Luke-Acts: The Acts of the Apostles: A Literary Interpretation*. Minneapolis: Augsburg Fortress, 1994.

— *The Narrative Unity of Luke-Acts: The Gospel According to Luke*. Minneapolis: Augsburg Fortress, 1986.

— *The Shape of Luke's Story: Essays on Luke-Acts*. Eugene: Cascade, 2005.

Tate, W.R. *Biblical Interpretation: An Integrated Approach.* 3rd ed. Peabody: Hendrickson, 2008.

Tuckett, C. 'The Lukan Son of Man'. Pages 198-217 in *Luke's Literary Achievement: Collected Essays.* Edited by C.M. Tuckett. JSNTSup 116. Sheffield: Academic Press, 1995.

—. 'Isaiah in Q'. Pages 51-61 in *Isaiah in the New Testament.* Edited by S. Moyise and M.J.J. Menken. London: T&T Clark, 2005.

Tull, P. 'Rhetorical Criticism and Intertextuality'. Pages 156-80 in *To Each Its Own Meaning: An Introduction to Biblical Criticisms and Their Application, Revised and Expanded.* Edited by S. McKenzie and S. Haynes. Louisville: WJKP, 1999.

Turner, M. *Power from on High: The Spirit in Israel's Restoration and Witness in Luke-Acts.* JPTSup 9. Sheffield: Sheffield Academic Press, 1996.

Twelftree, G.H. *People of the Spirit: Exploring Luke's View of the Church.* London: SPCK, 2009.

Vanhoozer, K.J. *The Drama of Doctrine: A Canonical-Linguistic Approach to Christian Theology.* Louisville: WJKP, 2005.

Vorwhinde, S. *Jesus' Emotions in the Gospels.* London: T&T Clark, 2011.

Walters, P. *The Assumed Authorial Unity of Luke and Acts: A Reassessment of the Evidence.* JSNTSup 145. Cambridge: Cambridge University Press, 2009.

Watts, R.E. *Isaiah's New Exodus in Mark.* Tübingen: J.C.B. Mohr [Paul Siebeck], 1997.

Webb, B. *Five Festal Garments: Christian Reflections on The Song of Songs, Ruth, Lamentations, Ecclesiastes and Esther.* Downers Grove/Leicester: InterVarsity, 2000.

Wenkel, D.H. 'When the Apostles Became Kings: Ruling and Judging the Twelve Tribes of Israel in the Book of Acts'. *BTB* 42:3 (2012): 114-23.

Williamson, H.G.M. *The Book Called Isaiah: Deutero-Isaiah's Role in Composition and Redaction.* Oxford: Oxford University Press, 1994.

Willimon, W.H. *Interpretation: A Bible Commentary for Teaching and Preaching: Acts.* Atlanta: John Knox Press, 1988.

Witherington, B. III. *Jesus the Sage: The Pilgrimage of Wisdom.* Minneapolis: Fortress, 2000.

— *New Testament Rhetoric: An Introductory Guide to the Art of Persuasion in and of the New Testament.* Grand Rapids: Baker, 2009.

— *The Acts of the Apostles: A Socio-Rhetorical Commentary.* Carlisle, Cumbria: Eerdmans/Paternoster, 1998.

— *What's in the Word: Rethinking the Socio-Rhetorical Character of the New Testament.* Waco: Baylor, 2009.

Wright, N.T. *Jesus and the Victory of God.* Minneapolis: Augsburg Fortress, 1997.

— *Acts for Everyone: Part One.* Louisville/London: SPCK, 2008.

— *Luke for Everyone.* London: SPCK, 2004.

— *The New Testament and the People of God.* London: SPCK/Fortress, 1992.

York, J.O. *The Last Shall Be First: The Rhetoric of Reversal in Luke.* JSNTSup 46. Sheffield: JSOT Press, 1991.

Scripture Index

Author Index

ND - #0095 - 270225 - C0 - 229/152/12 - PB - 9781842278192 - Gloss Lamination